The Wisdom of
Andrew Murray Vol. III

The Wisdom of Andrew Murray Vol. III

by Andrew Murray

Absolute Surrender
The Master's Indwelling
The Prayer Life

Absolute Surrender

Table of Contents

Absolute Surrender

"And Benhadad the king of Syria gathered all his host together: and there were thirty and two kings with him, and horses, and chariots: and he went up and besieged Samaria, and warred against it. And he sent messengers to Ahab king of Israel into the city, and said unto him, Thus saith Benhadad, Thy silver and thy gold is mine; thy wives also and thy children, even the goodliest, are mine. And the king of Israel answered and said, My lord, O king, according to thy saying, I am thine and all that I have." (I Kings 20:1-4).

Ahab gave what was asked of him by Benhadad—absolute surrender. I want to use these words: "My lord, O king, according to thy saying, I am thine, and all that I have," as the words of absolute surrender with which every child of God ought to yield himself to his Father. We have heard it before, but we need to hear it very definitely—the condition of God's blessing is absolute surrender of all into His hands. Praise God! If our hearts are willing for that, there is no end to what God will do for us, and to the blessing God will bestow.

Absolute surrender—let me tell you where I got those words. I used them myself often, and you have heard them numerous times. But once, in Scotland, I was in a company where we were talking about the condition of Christ's Church, and what the great need of the Church and of believers is. There was in our company a godly Christian worker who has much to do in training other workers for Christ, and I asked him what he would say was the great need of the Church—the message that ought to be preached. He answered very quietly and simply and determinedly:

"Absolute surrender to God is the one thing."

The words struck me as never before. And that man began to tell how, in the Christian workers with whom he had to deal, he finds that if they are sound on that point, they are willing to be taught and helped, and they always improve. Whereas, others who are not sound there very often go back and leave the work. The condition for obtaining God's full blessing is absolute surrender to Him.

And now, I desire by God's grace to give to you this message—that your God in heaven answers the prayers which you have offered for blessing on yourselves and for blessing on those around you by this one demand: Are you willing to surrender yourselves absolutely into His hands? What is our answer to be? God knows there are hundreds of hearts who have said it, and there are hundreds more who long to say it but hardly dare to do so. And there are hearts who have said it, but who have yet miserably failed, and who feel themselves condemned because they did not find the secret of the power to live that life. May God have a word for all!

Let me say, first of all, that God claims it from us.

God Expects Your Surrender

Yes, it has its foundation in the very nature of God. God cannot do otherwise. Who is God? He is the Fountain of life, the only Source of existence and power and goodness. Throughout the universe there is nothing good but what God works. God has created the sun, the moon, the stars, the flowers, the trees, and the grass. Are they not all absolutely surrendered to God? Do they not allow God to work in them just what He pleases? When God clothes the lily with its beauty, is it not yielded up, surrendered, given over to God as He works in it its beauty? And God's redeemed children, oh, can you think that God can do His work if there is only half or a part of them surrendered? God cannot do it. God is life, love, blessing, power, and infinite beauty, and God delights in communicating Himself to every child who is prepared to receive Him. But ah! this one lack of absolute surrender is just the thing that hinders God. And now He comes, and as God, He claims it.

You know in daily life what absolute surrender is. You know that everything has to be given up to its special, definite object and service. I have a pen in my pocket, and that pen is absolutely surrendered to the one work of writing. That pen must be absolutely surrendered to my hand if I am to write properly with it. If another holds it partly, I cannot write properly. This coat is absolutely given up to me to cover my body. This building is entirely given up to religious services. And now, do you expect that in your immortal being, in the divine nature that you have received by regeneration, God can work His work, every day and every hour, unless you are entirely given up to Him? God cannot. The temple of Solomon was absolutely surrendered to God when it was dedicated to Him. And every one of us is a temple of God, in which God will dwell and work mightily on one condition—absolute surrender to Him. God claims it, God is worthy of it, and without it God cannot work His blessed work in us.

God not only claims it, but God will work it Himself.

God Accomplishes Your Surrender

I am sure there is many a heart that says: "Ah, but that absolute surrender implies so much!" Someone says: "Oh, I have passed through so much trial and suffering, and there is so much of the self-life still remaining. I dare not face entirely giving it up because I know it will cause so much trouble and agony."

Alas! alas! that God's children have such thoughts of Him, such cruel thoughts. I come with a message to those who are fearful and anxious. God does not ask you to give the perfect surrender in your strength, or by the power of your will; God is willing to work it in you. Do we not read: "it is God that worketh in you both to will and to do of his good pleasure" (Philippians 2:13)? And that is what we should seek—to go on our faces before God, until our hearts learn to believe that the everlasting God Himself will come in to turn out what is wrong. He will conquer what is evil, and work what is well pleasing in His blessed sight. God Himself will work it in you.

Look at the men in the Old Testament, like Abraham. Do you think it was by accident that God found that man, the father of the faithful and the friend of God? Do you think that it was Abraham himself, apart from God, who had such faith and such obedience and such devotion? You know it is not so. God raised him up and prepared him as an instrument for His glory.

Did God not say to Pharaoh: "For this cause have I raised thee up, for to show in thee my power" (Exodus 9:16)?

And if God said that of him, will God not say it far more of every child of His?

Oh, I want to encourage you, and I want you to cast away every fear. Come with that feeble desire. If there is the fear which says—"Oh, my desire is not strong enough. I am not willing for everything that maycome , and I do not feel bold enough to say I can conquer everything"—I implore you, learn to know and trust your God now. Say: "My God, I am willing that You should make me willing." If there is anything holding you back, or any sacrifice you are afraid of making, come to God now and prove how gracious your God is. Do not be afraid that He will command from you what He will not bestow.

God comes and offers to work this absolute surrender in you. All these searchings and hungerings and longings that are in your heart, I tell you, they are the drawings of the divine magnet, Christ Jesus. He lived a life of absolute surrender. He has possession of you; He is living in your heart by His Holy Spirit. You have hindered and hindered Him terribly, but He desires to help you to get a hold of Him entirely. And He comes and draws you now by His message and words. Will you not come and trust God to work in you that absolute surrender to Himself Yes, blessed be God! He can do it, and He will do it.

God not only claims it and works it, but God accepts it when we bring it to Him.

God Accepts Your Surrender

God works it in the secret of our heart; God urges us by the hidden power of His Holy Spirit to come and speak it out, and we have to bring and yield to Him that absolute surrender. But remember, when you come and bring God that absolute surrender, it may, as far as your feelings or your consciousness go, be a thing of great imperfection. You may doubt and hesitate and say:

"Is it absolute?"

But, oh, remember there was once a man to whom Christ had said: "If thou canst believe, all things are possible to him that believeth" (Mark 9:23). And his heart was afraid, and he cried out: "Lord, I believe, help thou mine unbelief" (Mark 9:24).

That was a faith that triumphed over Satan, and the evil spirit was cast out. And if you come and say: "Lord, I yield myself in absolute surrender to my God," even though you do so with a trembling heart and with the consciousness: "I do not feel the power. I do not feel the determination. I do not feel the assurance," it will succeed. Do not be afraid, but come—just as you are. Even in the midst of your trembling the power of the Holy Spirit will work.

Have you not yet learned the lesson that the Holy Spirit works with mighty power, while on the human side everything appears feeble? Look at the Lord Jesus Christ in Gethsemane. We read that He, "through the eternal Spirit" (Hebrews 9:14), offered Himself a sacrifice unto God. The Almighty Spirit of God was enabling Him to do it. And yet what agony and fear and exceeding sorrow came over Him, and how He prayed! Externally, you can see no sign of the mighty power of the Spirit, but the Spirit of God was there. And even so, while you are feeble and fighting and trembling, with faith in the hidden work of God's Spirit do not fear, but yield yourself.

And when you do yield yourself in absolute surrender, let it be with the faith that God does now accept it. That is the great point, and that is what we so often miss—that believers should be thus occupied with God in this matter of surrender. Be occupied with God. We want to get help, every one of us, so that in our daily life God will be clearer to us, God will have the right place, and be "all in all." And if we are to have that through life, let us begin now and look away from ourselves and look up to God. Let each believe— I, a poor worm on earth and a trembling child of God, full of failure, sin, and fear, bow here, and no one knows what passes through my heart. I simply say, "Oh God, I accept Your terms. I have pleaded for blessing on myself and others. I have accepted Your terms of absolute surrender." While your heart says that in deep silence, remember there is a God present that takes note of it, and writes it down in His book. There is a God present who at that very moment takes possession of you. You may not feel it, you may not realize it, but God takes possession if you will trust Him. God not only claims it and works it and accepts it when I bring it, but God maintains it.

God Maintains Your Surrender

That is the great difficulty with many. People say: "I have often been stirred at a meeting or at a convention, and I have consecrated myself to God.

But it has passed away. I know it may last for a week or for a month, but it fades away. After a time it is all gone."

But listen! It is because you do not believe what I am now going to tell you and remind you of. When God has begun the work of absolute surrender in you, and when God has accepted your surrender, then God holds Himself bound to care for it and to keep it.

Will you believe that?

In this matter of surrender, there are: God and I—I a worm, God the everlasting and omnipotent Jehovah. Worm, will you be afraid to trust yourself to this mighty God now? God is willing. Do you not believe that He can keep you continually, day by day, and moment by moment?

Moment by moment I'm kept in His love;

Moment by moment I've life from above.

If God allows the sun to shine on you moment by moment, without intermission, will God not let His life shine on you every moment? And why have you not experienced it? Because you have not trusted God for it, and you do not surrender yourself absolutely to God in that trust.

A life of absolute surrender has its difficulties. I do not deny that. Yes, it has something far more than difficulties: it is a life that with men is absolutely impossible. But by the grace of God, by the power of God, by the power of the Holy Spirit dwelling in us, it is a life to which we are destined, and a life that is possible for us, praise God! Let us believe that God will maintain it.

Some of you have read the words of that aged saint who, on his ninetieth birthday, told of all God's goodness to him— I mean George Muller. What did he say he believed to be the secret of his happiness and of all the blessing which God had given him? He said he believed there were two reasons. The one was that he had been enabled by grace to maintain a good conscience before God day by day. The other was that he was a lover of God's Word. Ah, yes, a good conscience is complete obedience to God day by day, and fellowship with God everyday in His Word and prayer—that is a life of absolute surrender.

Such a life has two sides—on one side, absolute surrender to work what God wants you to do; on the other side, to let God work what He wants to do.

First, to do what God wants you to do.

Give yourselves up absolutely to the will of God. You know something of that will; not enough, far from all. But say absolutely to the Lord God: "By Your grace I desire to do Your will in everything, every moment of every day." Say: "Lord God, not a word upon my tongue but for Your glory. Not a movement of my temper but for Your glory. Not an affection of love or hate in my heart but for Your glory, and according to Your blessed will."

Someone says: "Do you think that possible?"

I ask, What has God promised you, and what can God do to fill a vessel absolutely surrendered to Him? Oh, God wants to bless you in a way beyond what you expect. From the beginning, ear has not heard, neither has the eye seen, what God has prepared for them that wait for Him (I Corinthians 2:9). God has prepared unheard-of-things, blessings much more wonderful than you can imagine, more mighty than you can conceive. They are divine blessings. Oh, say now:

"I give myself absolutely to God, to His will, to do only what God wants."

It is God who will enable you to carry out the surrender.

And, on the other side, come and say: "I give myself absolutely to God, to let Him work in me to will and to do of His good pleasure, as He has promised to do."

Yes, the living God wants to work in His children in a way that we cannot understand, but that God's Word has revealed. He wants to work in us every moment of the day. God is willing to maintain our life. Only let our absolute surrender be one of simple, childlike., and unbounded trust.

God Blesses When You Surrender

This absolute surrender to God brings wonderful blessings.

What Ahab said to his enemy, King Benhadad—"My lord, O king, according to thy word I am thine, and all that I have"will we not say to our God and loving Father? If we do say it, God's blessing will come upon us. God wants us to be separate from the world. We are called to come out from the world that hates God. Come out for God, and say: "Lord, anything for You." If you say that with prayer, and speak that into God's ear, He will accept it, and He will teach you what it means.

I say again, God will bless you. You have been praying for blessing. But do remember, there must be absolute surrender. At every tea-table you see it. Why is tea poured into that cup? Because it is empty, and given up for the tea. But put ink or vinegar or wine into it, and will they pour the tea into the vessel? And can God fill you, can God bless you if you are not absolutely surrendered to Him? He cannot. Let us believe God has wonderful blessings for us if we will but stand up for God and say, be it with a trembling will, yet with a believing heart:

"O God, I accept Your demands. I am Yours and all that I have. Absolute surrender is what my soul yields to You by divine grace."

You may not have such strong, clear feelings of surrender as you would like to have, but humble yourselves in His sight, and acknowledge that you have grieved the Holy Spirit by your self-will, self-confidence, and self-effort. Bow humbly before Him in the confession of that, and ask Him to break the heart and to bring you into the dust before Him. Then, as you bow before Him, just accept God's teaching that in your flesh "there dwelleth no good thing" (Romans 7:18), and that nothing will help you except another life which must come in. You must deny self once and for all. Denying self must every moment be the power of your life, and then Christ will come in and take possession of you.

When was Peter delivered? When was the change accomplished? The change began with Peter weeping, and the Holy Spirit came down and filled his heart.

God the Father loves to give us the power of the Spirit. We have the Spirit of God dwelling within us. We come to God confessing that, and praising God for it, and yet confessing how we have grieved the Spirit. And then we bow our knees to the Father to ask that He would strengthen us with all might by the Spirit in the inner man, and that He would fill us with His mighty power. And as the Spirit reveals Christ to us, Christ comes to live in our hearts forever, and the self-life is cast out.

Let us bow before God in humility, and in that humility confess before Him the state of the whole Church. No words can tell the sad state of the Church of Christ on earth. I wish I had words to speak what I sometimes feel about it. Just think of the Christians around you. I do not speak of nominal Christians, or of professing Christians, but I speak of hundreds and thousands of honest, earnest Christians who are not living a life in the power of God or to His glory. So little power, so little devotion or consecration to God, so little perception of the truth that a Christian is a man utterly surrendered to God's will! Oh, we want to confess the sins of God's people around us, and to humble ourselves.

We are members of that sickly body. The sickliness of the body will hinder us and break us down, unless we come to God. We must, in confession, separate ourselves from partnership with worldliness, with coldness toward each other. We must give ourselves up to be entirely and wholly for God.

How much Christian work is being done in the spirit of the flesh and in the power of self! How much work, day by day, in which human energy—our will and our thoughts about the work—is continually manifested, and in which there is little waiting upon God and upon the power of the Holy Spirit! Let us make a confession. But as we confess the state of the Church, and the feebleness and sinfulness of work for God among us, let us come back to ourselves. Who is there who truly longs to be delivered from the power of the self-life, who truly acknowledges that it is the power of self and the flesh, and who is willing to cast all at the feet of Christ? There is deliverance.

I heard of one who had been an earnest Christian, and who spoke about the "cruel" thought of separation and death. But you do not think that, do you? What are we to think of separation and death? This death was the path to glory for Christ. For the joy set before Him He endured the cross. The cross was the birthplace of His everlasting glory. Do you love Christ? Do you long to be in Christ, and yet not like Him? Let death be to you the most desirable thing on earth—death to self, and fellowship with Christ. Separation—do you think it a hard thing to be called to be entirely free from the world, and by that separation to be united to God and His love, by separation to become prepared for living and walking with God every day? Surely one ought to say: "Anything to bring me to separation, to death, for a life of full fellowship with God and Christ."

Come and cast this self-life and flesh-life at the feet of Jesus. Then trust Him. Do not worry yourselves with trying to understand all about it, but come in the living faith that Christ will come into you with the power of His death and the power of His life. Then the Holy Spirit will bring the whole Christ—Christ crucified and risen and living in glory—into your heart.

"The Fruit of the Spirit Is Love"

I want to look at the fact of a life filled with the Holy Spirit more from the practical side. I want to show how this life will reveal itself in our daily walk and conduct.

Under the Old Testament you know the Holy Spirit often came upon men as a divine Spirit of revelation to reveal the mysteries of God, or for power to do the work of God. But He did not dwell in them then. Now, many just want the Old Testament gift of power for work. But, they know very little of the New Testament gift of the indwelling Spirit, animating and renewing the whole life. When God gives the Holy Spirit, His great object is the formation of a holy character. It is a gift of a holy mind and spiritual disposition, and what we need, above everything else, is to say:

"I must have the Holy Spirit sanctifying my whole inner life if I am really to live for God's glory."

You might say that when Christ promised the Spirit to the disciples, He did so that they might have power to be witnesses. True, but then they received the Holy Spirit in such heavenly power and reality that He took possession of their whole being at once and so fitted them as holy men for doing the work with power as they had to do it. Christ spoke of power to the disciples, but it was the Spirit filling their whole being that worked the power.

I wish now to dwell upon the passage found in Galatians 5:22:

"The fruit of the Spirit is love."

We read that "Love is the fulfilling of the law'" (Romans 13: 10), and my desire is to speak on love as a fruit of the Spirit with a twofold object. One is that this word may be a searchlight in our hearts, and give us a test by which to try all our thoughts about the Holy Spirit and all our experience of the holy life. Let us try ourselves by this word. Has this been our daily habit, to seek to be filled with the Holy Spirit as the Spirit of love? "The fruit of the Spirit is love." Has it been our experience that the more we have of the Holy Spirit, the more loving we become? In claiming the Holy Spirit, we should make this the first object of our expectation. The Holy Spirit comes as a Spirit of love.

Oh, if this were true in the Church of Christ, how different her state would be! May God help us to get hold of this simple, heavenly truth that the fruit of the Spirit is a love which appears in the life. Just as the Holy Spirit gets real possession of the life, the heart will be filled with real, divine, universal love.

One of the great causes why God cannot bless His Church is the lack of love. When the body is divided, there cannot be strength. In the time of their great religious wars, when Holland stood out so nobly against Spain, one of their mottoes was: "Unity gives strength." It is only when God's people stand as one body, one before God in the fellowship of love, one toward another in deep affection, one before the world in a love that the world can see—it is only then that they will have power to secure the blessing which they ask of God. Remember that if a vessel that ought to be one whole is cracked into many pieces, it cannot be filled. You can take one part of the vessel and dip out a little water into that, but if you want the vessel full, the vessel must be whole. That is literally true of Christ's Church. And if there is one thing we must pray for still, it is this—Lord, melt us together into one by the power of the Holy Spirit. Let the Holy Spirit, who at Pentecost made them all of one heart and one soul, do His blessed work among us. Praise God, we can love each other in a divine love, for "the fruit of the Spirit is love." Give yourselves up to love, and the Holy Spirit will come; receive the Spirit, and He will teach you to love more.

God Is Love

Now, why is it that the fruit of the Spirit is love? Because God is love (I John 4:8).

And what does that mean?

It is the very nature and being of God to delight in communicating Himself. God has no selfishness; God keeps nothing to Himself. God's nature is to be always giving. You see it, in the sun and the moon and the stars, in every flower, in every bird in the air, in every fish in the sea. God communicates life to His creatures. And the angels around His throne, the seraphim and cherumbim who are flames of fire where does their glory come from? It comes from God because He is love, and He imparts to them part of His brightness and His blessedness. And we, His redeemed children—God delights to pour His love into us. Why? Because, as I said, God keeps nothing for Himself. From eternity God had His only begotten Son, and the Father gave Him all things, and nothing that God had was kept back. "God is love."

One of the old Church fathers said that we cannot better understand the Trinity than as a revelation of divine love the Father, the loving One, the

Fountain of love—the Son, the beloved one, the Reservoir of love, in whom the love was poured out—and the Spirit, the living love that united both and then overflowed into this world. The Spirit of Pentecost, the Spirit of the Father, and the Spirit of the Son is love. And when the Holy Spirit comes to us and to other men, will He be less a Spirit of love than He is in God? It cannot be; He cannot change His nature. The Spirit of God is love, and "the fruit of the Spirit is love."

Mankind Needs Love

Why is that so? That was the one great need of mankind, that was the thing which Christ's redemption came to accomplish: to restore love to this world.

When man sinned, why was it that he sinned? Selfishness triumphed—he sought self instead of God. And just look! Adam at once begins to accuse the woman of having led him astray. Love to God had gone; love to man was lost. Look again: of the first two children of Adam, the one becomes a murderer of his brother.

Does that not teach us that sin had robbed the world of love? Ah! what a proof the history of the world has been of love having been lost! There may have been beautiful examples of love even among the heathen, but only as a little remnant of what was lost. One of the worst things sin did for man was to make him selfish, for selfishness cannot love.

The Lord Jesus Christ came down from heaven as the Son of God's love. "God so loved the world that He gave His only begotten Son" (John 3:16). God's Son came to show what love is , and He lived a life of love here on earth in fellowship with His disciples, in compassion over the poor and miserable, in love even to His enemies. And, He died the death of love. And when He went back to heaven, whom did He send down? The Spirit of love, to come and banish selfishness and envy and pride, and bring the love of God into the hearts of men. "The fruit of the Spirit is love."

And what was the preparation for the promise of the Holy Spirit? You know that promise as found in the fourteenth chapter of John's Gospel. But remember what precedes in the thirteenth chapter. Before Christ promised the Holy Spirit, He gave a new commandment, and about that new commandment He said wonderful things. One thing was: "Even as I have loved you, so love ye one another." To them His dying love was to be the only law of their conduct and fellowship with each other. What a message to those fishermen, to those men full of pride and selfishness! "Learn to love each other," said Christ, "as I have loved you." And by the grace of God they did it. When Pentecost came, they were of one heart and one soul. Christ did it for them.

And now He calls us to live and to walk in love. He demands that though a man hate you, still you love him. True love cannot be conquered by anything in heaven or on earth. The more hatred there is, the more love triumphs through it all and shows its true nature. This is the love that Christ commanded His disciples to exercise.

What more did He say? "By this shall all men know that ye are my disciples, if ye have love one to another" (John 13:35).

You all know what it is to wear a badge. And Christ said to His disciples in effect: "I give you a badge, and that badge is love. That is to be your mark. It is the only thing in heaven or on earth by which men can know me." Do we not begin to fear that love has fled from the earth? That if we were to ask the world: "Have you seen us wear the badge of love?." the world would say: "No, what we have heard of the Church of Christ is that there is not a place where there is no quarreling and separation." Let us ask God with one heart that we may wear the badge of Jesus' love. God is able to give it.

Love Conquers Selfishness

"The fruit of the Spirit is love." Why? Because nothing but love can expel and conquer our selfishness.

Self is the great curse, whether in its relation to God, or to our fellow-men in general, or to fellow Christians, thinking of ourselves and seeking our own. Self is our greatest curse. But, praise God, Christ came to redeem us from self. We sometimes talk about deliverance from the self-life—and thank God for every word that can be said about it to help us, But I am afraid some people think deliverance from the self-life means that now they are no longer going to have any. trouble in serving God. They forget that deliverance from self-life means to be a vessel overflowing with love to everybody all the day.

And there you have the reason why many people pray for the power of the Holy Spirit. They get something, but oh, so little! because they prayed for power for work, and power for blessing, but they have not prayed for power for full deliverance from self. That means not only the righteous self in fellowship with God, but the unloving self in fellowship with men. And there is deliverance. "The fruit of the Spirit is love." I bring you the glorious promise of Christ that He is able to fill our hearts with love.

A great many of us try hard at times to love. We try to force ourselves to love, and I do not say that is wrong; it is better than nothing. But the end of it is always very sad. "I fail continually," many must confess. And what is the reason? The reason is simply this—they have never learned to believe and accept the truth that the Holy Spirit can pour God's love into their heart. That blessed text has often been limited!—"The love of God is shed abroad in our hearts" (Romans 5:5). It has often been understood in this sense: It means the love of God to me. Oh, what a limitation! That is only the beginning. The love of God is always the love of God in its entirety, in its fullness as an indwelling power. It is a love of God to me that leaps back to Him in love, and overflows to my fellow-men in love—God's love to me, and my love to God, and my love to my fellowmen. The three are one; you cannot separate them.

Do believe that the love of God can be shed abroad in your heart and mind so that we can love all the day.

"Ah!" you say, "how little I have understood that!"

Why is a lamb always gentle? Because that is its nature. Does it cost the lamb any trouble to be gentle? No. Why not? It is so beautiful and gentle. Has a lamb to study to be gentle? No. Why does that come so easy? It is its nature. And a wolf—why does it cost a wolf no trouble to be cruel, and to put its fangs into the poor lamb or sheep? Because that is its nature. It does not have to summon up its courage; the wolfnature is. there.

And how can I learn to love? I cannot learn to love until the Spirit of God fills my heart with God's love, and I begin to long for God's love in a very different sense from which I have sought it so selfishly—as a comfort, a joy, a happiness, and a pleasure to myself. I will not learn it until I realize that "God is love," and to claim and receive it as an indwelling power for self-sacrifice. I will not love until I begin to see that my glory, my blessedness, is to be like God and like Christ, in giving up everything in myself for my fellow-men. May God teach us this! Oh, the divine blessedness of the love with which the Holy Spirit can fill our hearts! "The fruit of the Spirit is love."

Love Is God's Gift

Once again I ask, Why must this be so? And my answer is: Without this we cannot live the daily life of love.

How often, when we speak about the consecrated life, we have to speak about temper, and people have sometimes said: "You make too much of temper."

I do not think we can make too much of it. Think for a moment of a clock and of what its hands mean. The hands tell me what is within the clock, and if I see that the hands stand still, or that the hands point wrong, or that the clock is slow or fast, I say that something inside the clock is not working properly. And temper is just like the revelation that the clock gives of what is within. Temper is a proof whether the love of Christ is filling the heart or not. How many there are who find it easier in church, or in prayer meeting, or in work for the Lord—diligent, earnest work—to be holy and happy than in the daily life with wife and children. How many find it easier to be holy and happy outside the home than in it! Where is the love of God? In Christ. God has prepared for us a wonderful redemption in Christ, and He longs to make something supernatural of us. Have we learned to long for it, ask for it, and expect it in its fullness?

Then there is the tongue! We sometimes speak of the tongue when we talk of the better life, and the restful life, but just think what liberty many Christians give to their tongues. They say:

"I have a right to think what I like."

When they speak about each other, when they speak about their neighbors, when they speak about other Christians, how often there are sharp remarks! God keep me from saying anything that would be unloving. God shut my mouth if I am not to speak in tender love. But what I am saying is a fact. How often sharp criticism, sharp judgment, hasty opinion, unloving words, secret contempt of each other, secret condemnation of each other are found among Christians who are banded together in work! Oh, just as a mother's love covers her children and delights in them and has the tenderest compassion with their foibles or failures, so there ought to be in the heart of every believer a motherly love toward every brother and sister in Christ. Have you aimed at that? Have you sought it? Have you ever pleaded for it? Jesus Christ said: "As I have loved you that. ye also love one another" (John 13:34). And He did not put that among the other commandments, but He said in effect:

"That is a new commandment, the one commandment: Love one another as I have loved you" (John 13:34).

It is in our daily life and conduct that the fruit of the Spirit is love. From that comes all the graces and virtues in which love is manifested—joy, peace, long-suffering, gentleness, goodness—no sharpness or hardness in your tone, no unkindness or selfishness, meekness before God and man. You see that all these are the gentler virtues. I have often thought as I read those words in Colossians, "Put on therefore as the elect of God, holy and beloved, bowels of mercies, kindness, humbleness of mind, meekness, longsuffering" (Colossians 3:12), that if we had written this, we should have put in the foreground the strong virtues, such as zeal, courage, and diligence. But we need to see how the gentler, the most tender virtues are especially connected with dependence on the Holy Spirit. These are indeed heavenly graces. They never were found in the heathen world. Christ was needed to come from heaven to teach us. Your blessedness is long-suffering, meekness, kindness; your glory is humility before God. The fruit of the Spirit that He brought from heaven out of the heart of the crucified Christ, and that He gives in our heart, is first and foremost—love.

You know what John says: "No man hath seen God at any time. If we love one another; God dwelleth in us" (I John 4:12). That is, I cannot see God, but as a compensation I can see my brother, and if I love him, God dwells in me. Is that really true? That I cannot see God, but I must love my brother, and God will dwell in me? Loving my brother is the way to real fellowship with God. You know what John further says in that most solemn test, "If a man say, I love God, and hateth his brother, he is a liar; for he that loveth not his brother whom he hath seen, how can he love God whom he hath not seen?" (I John 4:20). There is a brother, a most unlovable man. He worries you every time you meet him. He is of the very opposite disposition to yours. You are a careful businessman, and you have to associate with him in your business. He is most untidy, unbusiness-like. You say:

"I cannot love him."

Oh, friend, you have not learned the lesson that Christ wanted to teach above everything. Let a man be what he will, you are to love him. Love is to be the fruit of the Spirit all the day and every day. Yes, listen! If you don't love that unlovable man whom you have seen, how can you love God whom you have not seen? You can deceive yourself with beautiful thoughts about loving God. You must prove your love to God by your love to your brother; that is the one standard by which God will judge your love to Him. If the love of God is in your heart, you will love your brother. The fruit of the Spirit is love.

And what is the reason that God's Holy Spirit cannot come in power? Is it not possible?

You remember the comparison I used in speaking of the vessel. I can dip a little water into a small vessel, but if a vessel is to be full, it must be unbroken. And the children of God, wherever they come together, to whatever church or mission or society they belong, must love each other intensely, or the Spirit of God cannot do His work. We talk about grieving the Spirit of God by worldliness and ritualism and formality and error and indifference. But, I tell you, the one thing above everything that grieves God's Spirit is this lack of love. Let every heart search itself, and ask that God may search it.

Our Love Shows God's Power

Why are we taught that "the fruit of the Spirit is love"? Because the Spirit of God has come to make our daily life an exhibition of divine power and a revelation of what God can do for His children.

In the second and the fourth chapters of Acts, we read that the disciples were of one heart and of one soul. During the three years they had walked with Christ, they never had been in that spirit. All Christ's teaching could not make them of one heart and one soul. But the Holy Spirit came from heaven and shed the love of God in their hearts, and they were of one heart and one soul. The same Holy Spirit that brought the love of heaven into their hearts must fill us, too. Nothing less will do. Even as Christ did, one might preach love for three years with the tongue of an angel, but that would not teach any man to love unless the power of the Holy Spirit should come upon him to bring the love of heaven into his heart.

Think of the Church at large. What divisions! Think of the different bodies. Take the question of holiness, take the question of the cleansing blood, take the question of the baptism of the Spirit—what differences are caused among dear believers by such questions! That there are differences of opinion does not trouble me. We do not have the same constitution and temperament and mind. But how often hate, bitterness, contempt, separation, and unlovingness are caused by the holiest truths of God's Word! Our doctrines, our creeds, have been more important than love. We often think we are valiant for the truth, and we forget God's command to speak the truth in love. And it was so in the time of the Reformation between the Lutheran and Calvinistic churches. What bitterness there was in regard to communion, which was meant to be the bond of union among all believers! And so, through the ages, the very dearest truths of God have become mountains that have separated us.

If we want to pray in power, and if we want to expect the Holy Spirit to come down in power, and if we indeed want God to pour out His Spirit, we must enter into a covenant with God that we will love one another with a heavenly love.

Are you ready for that? Only that is true love that is large enough to take in all God's children, the most unloving and unlovable and unworthy and unbearable and trying. If my vow—absolute surrender to God—was sincere, then it must mean absolute surrender to the divine love to fill me. I must be a servant of love to love every child of God around me. "The fruit of the Spirit is love."

Oh, God did something wonderful when He gave Christ, at His right hand, the Holy Spirit to come down out of the heart of the Father and His everlasting love. And how we have degraded the Holy Spirit into a mere power by which we have to do our work! God forgive us! Oh, that the Holy Spirit might be held in honor as a power to fill us with the very life and nature of God and of Christ!

Christian Work Requires Love

"The fruit of the Spirit is love." I ask once again, Why is it so? And the answer comes: That is the only power in which Christians really can do their work. Yes, it is love that we need. We want not only love that is to bind us to each other, but we want a divine love in our work for the lost around us. Oh, do we not often undertake a great deal of work—just as men undertake work of philanthropy—from a natural spirit of compassion for our fellow-men? Do we not often undertake Christian work because our minister. or friend calls us to it? And do we not often perform Christian work with a certain zeal but without having had a baptism of love?

People often ask: "What is the baptism of fire?"

I have answered more than once: "I know no fire like the fire of God, the fire of everlasting love that consumed the sacrifice on Calvary." The baptism of love is what the Church needs, and to get that we must begin at once to get down on our faces before God in confession, and plead:

"Lord, let love from heaven flow down into my heart. I am giving up my life to pray and live as one who has, given himself up for the everlasting love to dwell in and fill him."

Ali, yes, if the love of God were in our hearts, what a difference it would make! There are hundreds of believers who say:

"I work for Christ, and I feel I could work much harder, but I do not have the gift. I do not know how or where to begin. I do not know what I can do."

Brother, sister, ask God to baptize you with the Spirit of love, and love will find its way. Love is a fire that will burn through every difficulty. You may be a shy, hesitating person, who cannot speak well, but love can burn through everything. God fills us with love! We need it for our work.

You have read many a touching story of love expressed, and you have said, How beautiful! I heard one not long ago. A lady had been asked to speak at a Rescue Home where there were a number of poor women. As she arrived there and passed by the window with the matron, she saw a wretched woman sitting outside, and asked:

"Who is that?"

The matron answered: "She has been into the house thirty or forty times, and she has always gone away again. Nothing can be done with her, she is so low and hard." But the lady said: "She must come in."

The matron then said: "We have been waiting for you, and the company is assembled, and you have only an hour for the address."

The lady replied: "No, this is of more importance"; and she went outside where the woman was sitting and said:

"My sister, what is the matter?"

"I am not your sister," was the reply.

The lady laid her hand on her, and said: "Yes, I am your sister, and I love you"; and so she spoke until the heart of the poor woman was touched.

The conversation lasted some time, and the company was waiting patiently. Ultimately, the lady brought the woman into the room. There was the poor, wretched, degraded creature, full of shame. She would not sit on a chair, but sat down on a stool beside the speaker's seat, and she let her lean against her, with her arms around the poor woman's neck, while, she spoke to the assembled people. And that love touched the woman's heart; she had found one who really loved her, and that love gave access to the love of Jesus.

Praise God! there is love on earth in the hearts of God's children; but oh, that there were more!

O God, baptize our ministers with a tender love, and our missionaries, our Bible readers, our workers, and our young men's and young women's associations. Oh, that God would begin with us now, and baptize us with heavenly love!

Love Inspires Intercession

Once again. It is only love that can fit us for the work of intercession.

I have said that love must fit us for our work. Do you know what the hardest and the most important work is that has to be done for this sinful world? It is the work of intercession, the work of going to God and taking time to lay hold of Him.

A man may be an earnest Christian, an earnest minister, and a man may do good, but alas! how often he has to confess that he knows little of what it is to tarry with God. May God give us the great gift of an intercessory spirit, a spirit of prayer and supplication! Let me ask you in the name of Jesus not to let a day pass without praying for all saints, and for all God's people.

I find there are Christians who think little of that. I find there are prayer unions where they pray for the members, and not for all believers. I pray you, take time to pray for the Church of Christ. It is right to pray for the heathen, as I have already said. God help us to pray more for them. It is right to pray for missionaries and for evangelistic work and for the unconverted. But Paul did not tell people to pray for the heathen or the unconverted. Paul told them to pray for believers. Do make this your first prayer every day: "Lord, bless Thy saints everywhere."

The state of Christ's Church is indescribably low. Plead for God's people that He would visit them, plead for each other, plead for all believers who are trying to work for God. Let love fill your heart. Ask Christ to pour fresh love into you everyday. Try to grasp, by the Holy Spirit of God: I am separated unto the Holy Spirit, and the fruit of the Spirit is love. God help us to understand it.

May God grant that we learn day by day to wait more quietly upon Him. We must not wait upon God only for ourselves, or the power to do so will soon be lost. But, we must give ourselves up to the ministry and the love of intercession, and pray more for God's people in general, for God's people around us, for the Spirit of love in ourselves and in them, and for the work of God we are connected with. The answer will surely come, and our waiting upon God will be a source of untold blessing and power. "The fruit of the Spirit is love."

Have you a lack of love to confess before God? Then make confession and say before Him, "O Lord, my lack of heart, my lack of love—I confess it." And then, as you cast that lack at His feet, believe that the blood cleanses you, that Jesus comes in His mighty, cleansing, saving power to deliver you, and that He will give His Holy Spirit. "The Fruit of the Spirit is love."

Separated unto the Holy Spirit

"Now there were in the church that was at Antioch certain prophets and teachers; as Barnabas, and Simeon that was called Niger, and Lucius of Cyrene, and Manaen ... and Saul. "As they ministered to the Lord, and fasted, the Holy Ghost said, Separate me —Barnabas and Saul for the work whereunto I have called them.

"And when they had fasted and prayed, and laid their hands on them, they sent them away. So they, being sent forth by the Holy Ghost, departed unto Seleucia" (Acts 13:1-4).

In the story of our text, we find some precious thoughts to guide us to what God would have of us, and what God would do for us. The great lesson of the verses quoted is this: The Holy Spirit is the director of the work of God upon the earth. And what we should do if we are to rightly work for God, and if God is to bless our work, is to see that we stand in a right relationship with the Holy Spirit. We must see that we give Him the place of honor that belongs to Him everyday. In all our work and (what is more) in all our Private, inner life, the Holy Spirit must always have the first place. Let me point out to you some of the precious thoughts our passage suggests.

First of all, we see that God has His own plans with regard to His Kingdom. His church at Antioch had been established. God had certain plans and intentions with regard to Asia and with regard to Europe. He had conceived them; they were His, and He made them known to His servants.

Our great Commander organizes every campaign, and His generals and officers do not always know the great plans. They often receive sealed orders, and they have to wait for Him to reveal their contents. God in heaven has wishes and a will, in regard to any work that ought to be done, and to the way in which it has to be done. Blessed is the man who receives God's secrets and works under Him.

Some years ago, at Wellington, South Africa, where I live, we opened a Mission Institute—what is counted there a fine, large building. At our opening services, the principal said something that I have never forgotten. He remarked:

"Last year we gathered here to lay the foundation stone, and what was there then to be seen? Nothing but rubbish and stones and bricks and ruins of an old building that had been pulled down. There we laid the foundation stone, and very few knew what the building was that was to rise. No one knew it perfectly in every detail except one man, the architect. In his mind it was all clear, and as the contractor and the mason and the carpenter came to do their work, they took their orders from him. The humblest laborer had to be obedient to orders. The structure rose, and this beautiful building has been completed. And just so," he added, "this building that we open today is but laying the foundation of a work of which only God knows what is to become."

But God has His workers and His plans clearly mapped out. Our position is to wait so that God may communicate to us as much of His will as is needful.

We simply have to be faithful in obedience, carrying out His orders. God has a plan for His Church on earth. But alas! we too often make our own plan. We think that we know what ought to be done. We ask God first to bless our feeble efforts, instead of absolutely refusing to go unless God goes before us. God has planned for the work and the extension of His Kingdom. The Holy Spirit has had that work given in charge to Him, "The work whereunto I have called them." May God, therefore, help us all to be afraid of touching "the ark of God" (2 Samuel 6:6), except as we are led by the Holy Spirit.

Then the second thought—God is willing and able to reveal to His servants what His will is.

Yes, blessed be God, communications still come down from heaven! As we read here what the Holy Spirit said, so the Spirit will still speak to His Church and His people. In these latter days, He has often done it. He has come to individual men, and by His divine teaching He has led them out into fields of labor that others could not at first understand or approve. He has led them into ways and methods that did not appeal to the majority. But the Holy Spirit still, in our time, teaches His people. Thank God, in our foreign missionary societies and in our home missions, and in a thousand forms of work, the guiding of the Holy Spirit is known. But (we are all ready, I think, to confess) He is too little known. We have not learned to wait upon Him enough, and so we should make a solemn declaration before God: Oh God, we want to wait more for You to show us Your will.

Do not ask God only for power. Many a Christian has his own plan of working, but God must send the power. The man works in his own will, and

God must give the grace—the one reason why God often gives so little grace and so little success. But let us all take our place before God, and say:

"What is done in the will of God, the strength of God will not be withheld from it. What is done in the will of God must have the mighty blessing of God."

And so let our first desire be to have the will of God revealed.

If you ask me, Is it any easy thing to get these communications from heaven, and to understand them? I can give you the answer. It is easy to those who are in proper fellowship with heaven, and who understand the art of waiting on God in prayer. How often we ask: How can a person know the will of God? And people want, when they are in perplexity, to pray very earnestly so that God would answer them at once. But God can only reveal His will to a heart that is humble and tender and empty. God can only reveal His will in perplexities and special difficulties to a heart that has learned to obey and honor Him loyally in little things and in daily life.

That brings me to the third thought—Note the disposition to which the Spirit reveals God's will.

What do we read here? There were a number of men ministering to the Lord and fasting, and the Holy Spirit came and spoke to them. Some people understand this passage as they would in reference to a missionary committee of our day. We see there is an open field, and we have had our missions in other fields. We are going to get on to that field. We have virtually settled that, and we pray about it. But the position was a very different one in those former days. I doubt whether any of them thought of Europe (for later on even Paul himself tried to go back into Asia) until the night vision called him by the will of God. Look at those men. God had done wonders. He had extended the Church to Antioch, and He had given rich and large blessing. Now, here were these men ministering to the Lord, serving Him with prayer and fasting. What a deep conviction they have—"It must all come directly from heaven. We are in fellowship with the risen Lord; we must have a close union with Him, and somehow He will let us know what He wants." And there they were, empty, ignorant, helpless, glad, and joyful, but deeply humbled.

"O Lord," they seem to say, "we are Your servants, and in fasting and prayer we wait upon You. What is Your will for us?"

Was it not the same with Peter? He was on the housetop, fasting and praying, and little did he think of the vision and the command to go to Caesarea. He was ignorant of what his work might be.

It is in hearts entirely surrendered to the Lord Jesus, separating themselves from the world, and even from ordinary religious exercises, and giving themselves up in intense prayer to look to their Lord, that the heavenly will of God will be made manifest.

You know that word fasting occurs a second time (in the third verse): "They fasted and prayed." When you pray, you love to go into your closet, according to the command of Jesus, and shut the door. You shut out business and company and pleasure and anything that can distract, and you want to be alone with God. But in one way, even the material world follows you there. You must eat. These men wanted to shut themselves out from the influences of the material and the visible, and they fasted. What ,they ate was simply enough to supply the wants of nature. In the intensity of their souls, they thought to give expression to their letting go of everything on earth in their fasting before God. Oh, may God give us that intensity of desire—that separation from everything—because we want to wait upon God, that the Holy Spirit may reveal to us God's blessed will.

The fourth thought—What is now the will of God as the Holy Spirit reveals it? It is contained in one phrase: Separation unto the Holy Spirit. That is the keynote of the message from heaven.

"Separate me Barnabas and Saul for the work whereunto I have called them. The work is mine; and I care for it; and I have chosen these men and called them; and I want you who represent the Church of Christ upon earth to set them apart unto me."

Look at this heavenly message in its twofold aspect. The men were to be set apart to the Holy Spirit, and the Church was to do this separating work. The Holy Spirit could trust these men to do it in a right spirit. There they were abiding in fellowship with the heavenly. The Holy Spirit could say to them, "Do the work of separating these men." And these were the men the Holy Spirit had prepared, and He could say of them, "Let them be separated unto me."

Here we come to the very root—the very life of the need of Christian workers. The question is: What is needed so that the power of God would rest on us more mightily? What is needed so that the blessing of God would be poured out more abundantly among those poor, wretched people and perishing sinners among whom we labor? And the answer from heaven is:

"I want men separated unto the Holy Spirit."

What does that imply? You know that there are two spirits on earth. Christ said, when He spoke about the Holy Spirit: "The world cannot receive him" (John 14:17). Paul said: "We have received not the spirit of the world, but the Spirit that is of God" (I Corinthians 2:12). That is the great want in every worker—the spirit of the world going out, and the Spirit of God coming in to take possession of the inner life and of the whole being.

I am sure there are workers who often cry to God for the Holy Spirit to come upon them as a Spirit of power for their work. When they feel that measure of power, and receive blessing, they thank God for it. But God wants something more and something higher. God wants us to seek for the Holy Spirit as a Spirit of power in our own heart and life, to conquer self and cast out sin, and to work the blessed and beautiful image of Jesus into us.

There is a difference between the power of the Spirit as a gift and the power of the Spirit for the grace of a holy life. A man may often have a measure of the power of the Spirit, but if there is not a large measure of the Spirit as the Spirit of grace and holiness, the defect will be evident in his work. He may be made the means of conversion, but he never will help people on to a higher standard of spiritual life. When he passes away, a great deal of his work may pass away, too. But a man who is separated unto the Holy Spirit is a man who is given up to say:

"Father, let the Holy Spirit have full dominion over me, in my home, in my temper, in every word of my tongue, in every thought of my heart, in every feeling toward my fellow-men. Let the Holy Spirit have entire possession."

Is that what has been the longing and the convenant of your heart with your God—to be a man or a woman separated and given up unto the Holy Spirit? I pray you listen to the voice of heaven: "Separate me," said the Holy Spirit. Yes, separated unto the Holy Spirit. May God grant that the Word may enter into the very depths of our being to search us, and if we discover that we have not come out from the world entirely—if God discloses to us that self-life, self-will, self-exaltation are there—let us humble ourselves before Him.

Man, woman, brother, sister, you are a worker separated unto the Holy Spirit. Is that true? Has that been your longing desire? Has that been your surrender? Has that been what you have expected through faith in the power of our Risen and Almighty Lord Jesus? If not, here is the call of faith, and here is the key of blessing—separated unto the Holy Spirit. God write the word in our hearts!

I said the Holy Spirit spoke to that church as a church capable of doing that work. The Holy Spirit trusted them. God grant that our churches, our missionary societies, and our workers' unions, that all our directors and councils and committees may be men and women who are fit for the work of separating workers unto the Holy Spirit. We can ask God for that, too.

Then comes my fifth thought, and it is this: This holy partnership with the
Holy Spirit in this work becomes a matter of consciousness and of action.

These men, what did they do? They set apart Paul and Barnabas, and then
it is written of the two that they, being sent forth by the Holy Spirit, went
down to Silica. Oh, what fellowship! The Holy Spirit in heaven doing part of
the work, men on earth doing the other part. After the ordination of the men
on earth, it is written in God's inspired Word that they were sent forth by the
Holy Spirit.

And see how this partnership calls to new prayer and fasting. They had for
a certain time been ministering to the Lord and fasting, perhaps days. The
Holy Spirit speaks, and they have to do the work and to enter into partnership, and at once they come together for more prayer and fasting. That is the
spirit in which they obey the command of their Lord. And that teaches us
that it is not only in the beginning of our Christian work, but all along, that
we need to have our strength in prayer. If there is one thought with regard to
the Church of Christ which at times comes to me with overwhelming sorrow;
if there is one thought in regard to my own life of which I am ashamed; if
there is one thought of which I feel that the Church of Christ has not
accepted and not grasped; if there is one thought which makes me pray to
God: "Oh, teach us by Your grace, new things"—it is the wonderful power
that prayer is meant to have in the Kingdom. We have so little availed
ourselves of it.

We have all—read the expression of Christian in Bunyan's great work,
when he found he had the key in his breast that should unlock the dungeon.
We have the key that can unlock the dungeon of atheism for us. The Holy
Spirit, into whose hands God has put the work, has been called "the
executive of the Holy Trinity." The Holy Spirit has not only power, but He
has the Spirit of love. He is brooding over this dark world and every sphere
of work in it, and He is willing to bless. And why is there not more blessing?
There can be only one answer. We have not honored the Holy Spirit as we
should have done. Is there one who can say that that is not true? Is not every
thoughtful heart ready to cry: "God forgive me that I have not honored the
Holy Spirit as I should have done, that I have grieved Him, that I have
allowed self, the flesh, and my own will to work where the Holy Spirit should
have been honored! May God forgive me that I have allowed self, the flesh,
and the will to actually have the place that God wanted the Holy Spirit to
have."

Oh, the sin is greater than we know! No wonder that there is so much
feebleness and failure in the Church of Christ!

Peter's Repentance

"And the Lord turned, and looked upon Peter. And Peter remembered the word of the Lord, how he had said unto him, Before the cock crow, thou shalt deny me thrice. And Peter went out, and wept bitterly" (Luke 22:61, 62).

That was the turning point in the life of Peter. Christ had said to him: "Thou canst not follow me now" (John 13:36). Peter was not in a fit state to follow Christ, because he had not been brought to an end of himself. He did not know himself, and he therefore could not follow Christ. But when he went out and wept bitterly, then came the great change. Christ previously said to him: "When thou art converted, strengthen thy brethren" (Luke 22:32). Here is the point Where Peter was converted from self to Christ.

I thank God for the story of Peter. I do not know a man in the Bible who gives us greater comfort. When we look at his character, so full of failures, and at what Christ made him by the power of the Holy Spirit, there is hope for every one of us. But remember, before Christ could fill Peter with the Holy Spirit and make a new man of him, he had to go out and weep bitterly; he had to be humbled. If we want to understand this, I think there are four points that we must look at. First, let us look at Peter the devoted disciple of Jesus; next, at Peter as he lived the life of self; then, at Peter in his repentance; and last, at what Christ made of Peter by the Holy Spirit.

Peter the Devoted Disciple of Christ

Christ called Peter to forsake his nets and follow Him. Peter did it at once, and afterward he could rightly say to the Lord:

"We have forsaken all and followed thee" (Matthew 19:27).

Peter was a man of absolute surrender; he gave up all to follow Jesus. Peter was also a man of ready obedience. You remember Christ said to him, "Launch out into the deep, and let down your nets." Peter the fisherman knew there were no fish there, for they had been fishing all night and had caught nothing; but he said: "At thy word I will let down the net" (Luke 5:4,5). He submitted to the word of Jesus. Further, he was a man of great faith. When he saw Christ walking on the sea, he said: "Lord, if it be thou, bid me come unto thee" (Matthew 14:-28). At the voice of Christ, he stepped out of the boat and walked on the water.

And Peter was a man of spiritual insight. When Christ asked the disciples: "Whom say ye that I am?"

Peter was able to answer: "Thou art the Christ, the Son of the living God." And Christ said: "Blessed art thou, Simon Barjona; for flesh and blood hath not revealed it unto thee, but my Father which is in heaven" (Matthew 16:15-17). And Christ spoke of him as the rock man, and of his having the keys of the Kingdom. Peter was a splendid man, a devoted disciple of Jesus, and if he were living now, everyone would say that he was an advanced Christian. And yet how much there was wanting in Peter!

Peter Living the Life of Self

You recollect that just after Christ had said to him: "Flesh and blood hath not revealed it unto thee, but my Father which is in heaven," Christ began to speak about His sufferings, and Peter dared to say, "Be it far from thee, Lord; this shall not be unto thee." Then Christ had to say: "Get thee behind me, Satan; for thou savorest not the things that be of God, but those that be of men" (Matthew 16:22-23).

There was Peter in his self-will, trusting his own wisdom, and actually forbidding Christ to go and die. Where did that come from? Peter trusted in himself and his own thoughts about divine things. We see later on, more than once, that the disciples questioned who should be the greatest among them. Peter was one of them, and he thought he had a right to the very first place. He sought his own honor above the others. The life of self was strong in Peter. He had left his boats and his nets, but not his old self.

When Christ had spoken to him about His sufferings, and said: "Get thee behind me, Satan," He followed it up by saying: "If any man will come after me, let him deny himself, and take up his cross, and follow me" (Matthew 16:24). No man can follow Him unless he does that. Self must be utterly denied. What does that mean? When Peter denied Christ, we read that he said three times: "I know Him not" (Luke 22:57). In other words he said, "I have nothing to do with Him; He and I are not friends. I deny having any connection with Him." Christ told Peter that he must deny self. Self must be ignored, and its every claim rejected. That is the root of true discipleship. But Peter did not understand it and could not obey it. And what happened? When the last night came, Christ said to him:

"Before the cock crow twice thou shalt deny me thrice" (Mark 14:30).

But with self-confidence Peter said: "Though all shall be offended, yet will not !. I am ready to go with thee, to prison and to death" (Mark 14:29; Luke 22:33).

Peter meant it honestly, and he really intended to do it; but Peter did not know himself. He did not believe he was as bad as Jesus said he was.

We perhaps think of individual sins that come between us and God. But what are we to do with that self-life which is all unclean—our very nature? What are we to do with that flesh that is entirely under the power of sin? Deliverance from that is what we need. Peter knew it not, and therefore it was in self-confidence that he went forth and denied his Lord.

Notice how Christ uses that word deny twice. He said to Peter the first time, "Deny himself" (Matthew 16:24); He said to Peter the second time, "Thou shalt deny me" (Matthew 26:34). It is either of the two. There is no other choice for us; we must either deny self or deny Christ. There are two great powers fighting each other the self-nature in the power of sin, and Christ in the power of God. Either of these must rule within us.

It was self that made the devil. He was an angel of God, but he wanted to exalt self. He became a devil in hell. Self was the cause of the fall of man. Eve wanted something for herself, and so our first parents fell into all the wretchedness of sin. We, their children, have inherited an awful nature of sin.

Peter's Repentance

Peter denied his Lord three times, and then the Lord looked upon him. That look of Jesus broke Peter's heart. The terrible sin that he had committed, the terrible failure that had come, and the depth into which he had fallen suddenly opened up before him. Then, "Peter went out and wept bitterly."

Oh! who can tell what that repentance must have been? During the following hours of that night, and the next day—when he saw Christ crucified and buried, and the next day, the Sabbath—oh, what hopeless despair and shame he must have felt!

"My Lord is gone; my hope is gone; and I denied my Lord. After that life of love, after that blessed fellowship of three years, I denied my Lord. God have mercy upon me!"

I do not think we can imagine the depth of humiliation Peter sank into then. But that was the turning point and the change. On the first day of the week, Christ was seen by Peter, and in the evening He met him with the others. Later on at the Sea of Galilee, He asked him: "Lovest thou me?" (John 21:17). Peter was made sad by the thought that the Lord reminded him of having denied Him three times, and said in sorrow, but in uprightness: "Lord, thou knowest. all things; thou knowest that I love thee" (John 21:17).

Peter Transformed

Now, Peter was prepared for deliverance from self, and that is my last thought. You know Christ took him with the others to the footstool of the throne, and told them to wait there. Then, on the day of Pentecost, the Holy Spirit came, and Peter was a changed man. I do not want you to think only of the change in Peter, in that boldness, that power, that insight into the Scriptures, and that blessing with which he preached that day. Thank God for that. But there was something deeper and better which happened to Peter. His whole nature was changed. The work that Christ began in Peter when He looked upon him was perfected when he was filled with the Holy Spirit.

If you want to see that, read the first epistle of Peter. You know wherein Peter's failings lay. When he said to Christ, in effect: "Thou never canst suffer; it cannot be"—it showed he did not have a conception of what it was to pass through death into life. Christ said: "Deny thyself," and in spite of that he denied his Lord. When Christ warned him: "Thou shalt deny me" (Matthew 26:34), and he insisted that he never would, Peter showed how little he understood what there was in himself. But when I read his epistle and hear him say: "If ye be reproached for the name of Christ, happy are ye, for the spirit of glory and of God resteth upon you" (I Peter 4:14), then I say that it is not the old Peter, but that it is the very Spirit of Christ breathing and speaking within him.

I read again how he says: "Hereunto were ye called, to suffer, because Christ also suffered" (I Peter 2:21). I understand what a change had come over Peter. Instead of denying Christ, he found joy and pleasure in having self denied, crucified, and given up to the death. And therefore, we read in Acts that when he was called before the Council he could boldly say: "We ought to obey God rather than men" (Acts 5:29), and that he could return with the other disciples and rejoice that they were counted worthy to suffer for Christ's name.

You remember his self-exaltation; but now he has found out that "the ornament of a meek and quiet spirit is in the sight of God of great price" (I Peter 3:4). Again he tells us to be "subject one to another, and be clothed with humility" (I Peter 5:5).

Dear friend, I implore you, look at Peter utterly changed—the self-pleasing, the self-trusting, the self-seeking Peter, full of sin, continually getting into trouble, foolish and impetuous, now filled with the Spirit and the life of Jesus. Christ had done it for him by the Holy Spirit.

And now, what is the point in my having thus very briefly pointed to the story of Peter? That story must be the history of every believer who is really to be made a blessing by God. That story is a prophecy of what everyone can receive from God in heaven.

Now, let us just glance hurriedly at what these lessons teach us.

The first lesson is this—You may be a very earnest, godly, devoted believer, in whom the power of the flesh is still very strong.

That is a very solemn truth. Peter, before he denied Christ, had cast out devils and had healed the sick. Yet, the flesh had power; and, the flesh had room in him. Oh, beloved, we have to realize that it is because there is so much of that self-life in us that the power of God cannot work in us as mightily as He desires that it should work. Do you realize that the great God is longing to double His blessing, to give tenfold blessing through us? But there is something hindering Him, and that something is a proof of nothing but the self-life. We talk about the pride of Peter, and the impetuosity of Peter, and the self-confidence of Peter. It is all rooted in that one word, self Christ had said, "Deny self," and Peter had never understood, and never obeyed. Every failing came out of that.

What a solemn thought, and what an urgent plea for us to cry: Oh God, do show this to us so that none of us may be living the self-life! It has happened to people who have been Christians for years; it has happened to people who have perhaps occupied prominent positions—God found them out and taught them to find out about themselves. They became utterly ashamed and fell broken before God. Oh, the bitter shame and sorrow and pain and agony that came to them, until at last they found that there was deliverance! Peter went out and wept bitterly. There may be many godly people in whom the power of the flesh still rules.

And then my second lesson is—It is the work of our blessed Lord Jesus to disclose the power of self.

How was it that Peter—the carnal Peter, self-willed Peter, Peter with the strong self-love—ever became a man of Pentecost and the writer of his epistles? It was because Christ placed him in charge, and Christ watched over him, and Christ taught and blessed him. The warnings that Christ had given him were part of the training. Last of all, there came that look of love. In His suffering, Christ did not forget him, but turned around and looked upon him, and "Peter went out and wept bitterly." And the Christ who led Peter to

Pentecost is waiting today to take charge of every heart that is willing to surrender itself to Him.

Are there not some saying: "Ah! that is the problem with me; it is always the self-life, self-comfort, self-consciousness, self-pleasing, and self will. How am I to get rid of it?"

My answer is: It is Christ Jesus who can rid you of it. No one else but Christ Jesus can give deliverance from the power of self. And what does He ask you to do? He asks that you should humble yourself before Him.

Impossible with Man, Possible with God

"And he said, the things which are impossible with men are possible with God" (Luke 18:27).

Christ had said to the rich young ruler, "Sell all that thou hast ... and come, follow me." The young man went away sorrowful. Christ then turned to the disciples,: and said: "How hardly shall they that have riches enter into the kingdom of God!" The disciples, we read, were greatly astonished, and answered: "Who, then, can be saved?" And Christ gave this blessed answer: "The things which are impossible with men are possible with God" (Luke 18:2227).

The text contains two thoughts—that in the question of salvation and of following Christ by a holy life, it is impossible for man to do it. And then alongside that is the thought— What is impossible with man is possible with God.

These two thoughts mark the two great lessons that man has to learn in the Christian life. It often takes a long time to learn the first lesson—that in the Christian life man can do nothing, that salvation is impossible to man. And often a man learns that, and yet he does not learn the second lesson—what has been impossible to him is possible with God. Blessed is the man who learns both lessons! The learning of them marks stages in the Christian's life.

Man Cannot

The one stage is when a man is trying to do his utmost and fails, when a man tries to do better and falls again, when a man tries much more and always fails. And yet, very often he does not even then learn the lesson: With man it is impossible to serve God and Christ. Peter spent three years in Christ's school, and he never learned, it is impossible, until he had denied his Lord, went out, and wept bitterly. Then he learned it.

Just look for a moment at a man who is learning this lesson. At first, he fights against it. Then, he submits to it, but reluctantly and in despair. At last, he accepts it willingly and rejoices in it. At the beginning of the Christian life, the young convert has no conception of this truth. He has been converted; he has the joy of the Lord in his heart; he begins to run the race and fight the battle. He is sure he can conquer, for he is earnest and honest, and God will help him. Yet, somehow, very soon he fails where he did not expect it, and sin gets the better of him. He is disappointed, but he thinks: "I was not cautious enough. I did not make my resolutions strong enough." And again he vows, and again he prays, and yet he fails. He thinks: "Am I not, a redeemed man? Have I not the life of God within me?" And he thinks again: "Yes, and I have Christ to help me. I can live the holy life."

At a later period, he comes to another state of mind. He begins to see such a life is impossible, but he does not accept it. There are multitudes of Christians who come to this point: "I cannot." They then think that God never expected them to do what they cannot do. If you tell them that God does expect it, it is a mystery to them. A good many Christians are living a low life—a life of failure and of sin—instead of rest and victory, because they began to say: "I cannot, it is impossible." And yet they do not understand it fully. So, under the impression, I cannot, they give way to despair. They will do their best, but they never expect to get on very far.

But God leads His children on to a third stage. A man comes to take, it is impossible, in its full truth, and yet at the same time says: "I must do it, and I will do it—it is impossible for man, and yet I must do it." The renewed will begins to exercise its whole power, and in intense longing and prayer begins to cry to God: "Lord, what is the meaning of this? How am I to be freed from the power of sin?"

It is the state of the regenerate man in Romans, chapter seven. There you will find the Christian man trying his very utmost to live a holy life. God's law has been revealed to him as reaching down into the very depth of the desires of the heart. The man can dare to say:

"I delight in the law of God after the inward man. To will what is good is present with me. My heart loves the law of God, and my will has chosen that law."

Can a man like that fail, with his heart full of delight in God's law and with his will determined to do 'What is right? Yes. That is what Romans, chapter seven teaches us. There is something more needed. Not only must I delight in the law of God after the inward man and will what God wills, but I need a divine omnipotence to work it in me. And that is what the apostle Paul teaches in Philippians 2:13: "It is God which worketh in you, both to will and to do of his good pleasure."

Note the contrast. In Romans, chapter seven, the regenerate man says: "To will is present with me, but how to perform that which is good I find not" (Romans 7:18). But in Philippians, chapter two, you have a man who has been led on farther. He is a man who understands that when God has worked the renewed will, God will give the power to accomplish what that will desires. Let us receive this as the first great lesson in the spiritual life: "It is impossible for me, my God. Let there be an end of the flesh and all its powers, an end of self, and let it be my glory to be helpless.

Praise God for the divine teaching that makes us helpless!

When you thought of absolute surrender to God, were you not brought to an end of yourself? Did you not feel that you could see how you actually could live as a man absolutely surrendered to God every moment of the day—at your table, in your house, in your business, in the midst of trials and temptations? I pray you learn the lesson now. If you felt you could not do it, you are on the right road, if you let yourselves be led. Accept that position, and maintain it before God: "My heart's desire and delight, O God, is absolute surrender, but I cannot perform it. It is impossible for me to live that life. it is beyond me." Fall down and learn that when you are utterly helpless, God will come to work in you not only to will, but also to do.

God Can

Now comes the second lesson. "The things which are impossible with men are possible with God."

I said a little while ago that there is many a man who has learned the lesson, it is impossible with men, and then he gives up in helpless despair. He lives a wretched Christian life, without joy or strength or victory. And why? Because he does not humble himself to learn that other lesson: With God all things are possible.

Your Christian life is to be a continuous proof that God works impossibilities. Your Christian life is to be a series of impossibilities made possible and actual by God's almighty power. That is what the Christian needs. He has an almighty God that he worships, and he must learn to understand that he does not need a little of God's power. But, he needs—with reverence be it said—the whole of God's omnipotence to keep him right, and to live like a Christian.

The whole of Christianity is a work of God's omnipotence. Look at the birth of Christ Jesus. That was a miracle of divine power, and it was said to Mary: "With God nothing shall be impossible" (Luke 1:37). It was the omnipotence of God. Look at Christ's resurrection. We are taught that it was according to the exceeding greatness of His mighty power that God raised Christ from the dead.

Every tree must grow on the root from which it springs. An oak tree three hundred years old grows all the time on the one root from which it had its beginning. Christianity had its beginning in the omnipotence of God. In every soul, Christianity must have its continuance in that omnipotence. All the possibilities of the higher Christian life have their origin in a new understanding of Christ's power to work all God's will in us.

I want to call on you now to come and worship an almighty God. Have you learned to do it? Have you learned to deal so closely with an almighty God that you know omnipotence is working in you? In outward appearance there is often little sign of it.

The apostle Paul said: "I was with you in weakness and in fear and in much trembling, and ... my preaching was ... in demonstration of the Spirit and of power" (I Corinthians 2:3,4). From the human side there was feebleness; from the divine side there was divine omnipotence. And that is true of every godly life. If we would only learn that lesson better, and give a wholehearted, undivided surrender to it, we would learn what blessedness there is in dwelling every hour and every moment with an almighty God. Have you ever studied in the Bible the attribute of God's omnipotence? You know that it was God's omnipotence that created the world, and created light out of darkness, and created man. But have you studied God's omnipotence in the works of redemption?

Look at Abraham. When God called him to be the father of that people out of which Christ was to be born, He said to him: "I am the Almighty God, walk before me and be thou perfect" (Genesis 17: 1)'. And God trained Abraham to trust Him as the omnipotent One. Whether it was his going out to a land that he did not know, or his faith as a pilgrim midst the thousands of Canaanites—his faith said: "This is my land." Whether it was his faith in waiting twenty-five years for a son in his old age, against all hope, or whether it was the raising up of Isaac from the dead on Mount Moriah when he was going to sacrifice him—Abraham believed God. He was strong in faith, giving glory to God, because he accounted Him who had promised able to perform.

The cause of the weakness of your Christian life is that you want to work it out partly, and to let God help you. And that cannot be. You must come to be utterly helpless, to let God work. He will work gloriously. It is this that we need if we are indeed to be workers for God. I could go through Scripture and prove to you how Moses, when he led Israel out of Egypt; how Joshua, when he brought them into the land of Canaan; how all God's servants in the

Old Testament counted on the omnipotence of God doing impossibilities. And this God lives today; and this God is the God of every child of His. And yet some of us want God to give us a little help while we do our best, instead of coming to understand what God wants, and to say: "I can do nothing. God must and will do all." Have you said: "In worship, in work, in sanctification, in obedience to God, I can do nothing of myself, and so my place is to worship God, and to believe that He will work in me every moment"? Oh, may God teach us this! Oh, that God would by His grace show you what a God you have, and to what a God you have entrusted yourself—an omnipotent God. He is willing, with His whole omnipotence, to place Himself at the disposal of every child of His! Will we not take the lesson of the Lord Jesus, and say: "Amen; the things which are impossible with men are possible with God"?

Remember what we have said about Peter, his self-confidence, self-power, self-will, and how he came to deny his Lord. You feel, "Ah! there is the self-life; there is the flesh-life that rules in me!" And now, have you believed that there is deliverance from that? Have you believed that Almighty God is able to reveal Christ in your heart, to let the Holy Spirit rule in you so that the self-life will not have power or dominion over you? Have you coupled the two together—and, with tears of penitence and with deep humiliation and feebleness, cried out: "O God, it is impossible to me; man cannot do it, but glory to Your name, it is possible with God"? Have you claimed deliverance? Do it now. Put yourself afresh in absolute surrender into the hands of a God of infinite love. As infinite as His love is His power to do it.

God Works in Man

But again, we come to the question of absolute surrender, and feel that that is lacking in the Church of Christ. That is why the Holy Spirit cannot fill us, and why we cannot live as people entirely separated unto the Holy Spirit. That is why the flesh and the self-life cannot be conquered. We have never understood what it is to be absolutely surrendered to God as Jesus was. I know that many earnestly and honestly say: "Amen, I accept the message of absolute surrender to God." Yet they think: "Will that ever be mine? Can I count on God to make me one of whom it will be said in heaven, on earth, and in hell, he lives in absolute surrender to God?" Brother, sister, "the things which are impossible with men are possible with God." Do believe that, when He takes charge of you in Christ, it is possible for God to make you a man of absolute surrender. And God is able to maintain that. He is able to let you rise from bed every morning of the week with that blessed thought directly or indirectly: "I am in God's charge. My God is working out my life for me."

Some are weary of thinking about sanctification. You pray; you have longed and cried for it; and yet, it appeared so far off! You are so conscious of how distant the holiness and humility of Jesus is. Beloved friends, the one doctrine of sanctification that is scriptural and real and effectual is: "The things which are impossible with men are possible with God." God can sanctify men. By His almighty and sanctifying power, God can keep them every moment. Oh, that we might get a step nearer to our God now! Oh, that the light of God might shine, and that we might know our God better!

I could go on to speak about the life of Christ in us—living like Christ, taking Christ as our Savior from sin, and as our life and strength. It is God in heaven who can reveal that in you. What does that prayer of the apostle Paul say: "That he would grant you according to riches of his glory, to be strength—ened with might by his Spirit in the inner man" (Ephesians 3:16)? Do you not see that it is an omnipotent God working by His omnipotence in the heart of His believing children, so that Christ can become an indwelling Savior? You have tried to grasp it, understand it, and to believe it, and it would not come. It was because you had not been brought to believe that "the things which are impossible with men are possible with God."

And so I trust that the word spoken about love may have brought many to see that we must have an inflowing of love in quite a new way. Our heart must be filled with life from above—from the Fountain of everlasting love—if it is going to overflow all day. Then it will be just as natural for us to love our fellow-men as it is natural for the lamb to be gentle and the wolf to be cruel. When I am brought to such a state that the more a man hates and speaks evil of me—the more unlikable and unlovable a man is the more I will love him. When I am brought to such a state that the more obstacles, hatred, and ingratitude surround me, the more the power of love can triumph in me. Until I am brought to see these, I am not saying: "It is impossible with men." But if you have been led to say: "This message has spoken to me about a love utterly beyond my power. It is absolutely impossible"—then we can come to God and say: "It is possible with You."

Some are crying to God for a great revival. I can say that this is the unceasing prayer of my heart. Oh, if God would only revive His believing people! I cannot think of the unconverted formalists of the Church or of the infidels and skeptics or of all the wretched and perishing around me, without my heart pleading: "My God, revive Your Church and people." It is not for a lack of reason that thousands of hearts yearn after holiness and consecration. It is a forerunner of God's power. God works to will and then He works to do. These yearnings are a witness and a proof that God has worked to will.

Oh, let us in faith believe that the omnipotent God will work to do among His people more than we can ask. "Unto him," Paul said, "that is able to do exceeding abundantly above all that we ask or think,. unto him be glory" (Ephesians 3:20,21). Let our hearts say that. Glory to God, the omnipotent One, who can do above what we dare to ask or think!

"The things which are impossible with men are possible with God." All around you there is a world of sin and sorrow, and Satan is there. But remember, Christ is on the throne; Christ is stronger; Christ has conquered; and Christ will conquer. But wait on God. My text casts us down: "The things which are impossible with men", but it ultimately lifts us up high—"are possible with God." Get linked to God. Adore and trust Him as the omnipotent One, not only for your own life, but for all the souls that are entrusted to you. Never pray without adoring His omnipotence, saying: "Mighty God, I claim Your almightiness." And the answer to the prayer will come. Like Abraham you will become strong in faith, giving glory to God, because you account Him who has promised able to perform.

"O Wretched Man That I Am!"

"O wretched man that I am! who shall deliver me from the body of this death? I thank God through Jesus Christ our Lord" (Romans 7:24,25).

You know the wonderful location that this text has in the epistle to the Romans. It stands here at the end of the seventh chapter as the gateway into the eighth. In the first sixteen verses of the eighth chapter, the name of the Holy Spirit is found sixteen times. You have there the description and promise of the life that a child of God can live in the power of the Holy Spirit. This begins in the second verse: "The law of the Spirit of life in Christ Jesus hath made me free from the law of sin and death" (Romans 8:2). From that, Paul goes on to speak of the great privileges of the child of God who is to be led by the Spirit of God. The gateway into all this is found at the end of chapter seven: "O wretched man that I am!" There you have the words of a man who has come to the end of himself. He has in the previous verses described how he had struggled and wrestled in his own power to obey the holy law of God, and had failed. But in answer to his own questions, he now finds the true answer and cries out: "I thank God through Jesus Christ our Lord." From that he goes on to speak of what that deliverance is that he has found.

I want, from these words, to describe the path by which a man can be led out of the spirit of bondage into the spirit of liberty. You know how distinctly it is said: "Ye have not received the spirit of bondage again to fear" (Romans 8:15). We are continually warned that this is the great danger of the Christian life, to go again into bondage. I want to describe the path by which a man can get out of bondage into the glorious liberty of the children of God. Rather, I want to describe the man himself.

First, these words are the language of a regenerate man; second, of a weak man; third, of a wretched man; and fourth, of a man on the border of complete liberty.

The Regenerate Man

There is much evidence of regeneration from the fourteenth verse of chapter seven on to the twenty-third verse. "It is no more I that do it, but sin that dwelleth in me" (Romans 7:17). That is the language of a regenerate man—a man who knows that his heart and nature have been renewed, and that sin is now a power in him that is not himself. "I delight in the law of God after the inward man" (Romans 7:22). That again is the language of a regenerate man. He dares to say when he does evil: "It is no more I that do it, but sin that dwelleth me." It is of great importance to understand this,

In the first two great sections of the epistle, Paul deals with justification and sanctification. In dealing with justification, he lays the foundation of the doctrine in the teaching about sin. He does not speak of the singular sin, but of the plural, sins—the actual transgressions. In the second part of the fifth chapter, he begins to deal with sin, not as actual transgression, but as a power. Just imagine what a loss it would have been to us if we did not have this second half of the seventh chapter of the epistle to the Romans—if Paul had omitted in his teaching this vital question of the sinfulness of the believer. We should 'have missed the question we all want answered as to sin in the believer. What is the answer? The regenerate man is one in whom the will has been renewed, and who can say: "I delight in the law of God after the inward man."

The Weak Man

Here is the great mistake made by many Christian people—they think that when there is a renewed ,will, it is enough. But that is not the case. This regenerate man tells us: "I will to do what is good, but the power to perform I find not." How often people tell us that if you set yourself determinedly, you can perform what you will! But this man was as determined as any man can be, and yet he made the confession: "To will is present with me; but how to perform that which is good, I find not" (Romans 7:18).

But, you ask: "How is it God makes a regenerate man utter such a confession? He being with a right will, with a heart that longs to do good, and longs to do its very utmost to love God?"

Let us look at this question. What has God given us our will for? Had the angels who fell, in their own will, the strength to stand? Surely, no. The will of man is nothing but an empty vessel in which the power of God is to be made manifest. Man must seek in God all that is to be. You have it in the second chapter of the epistle to the Philippians, and you have it here also, that God's work is to work in us both to will and to do of His good pleasure. Here is a man who appears to say: "God has not worked to do in me." But we are taught that God works both to will and to do. How is the apparent contradiction to be reconciled?

You will find that in this passage (Romans 7:6-25), the name of the Holy Spirit does not occur once, nor does the name of Christ occur. The man is wrestling and struggling to fulfill God's law. Instead of the Holy Spirit and of Christ, the law is mentioned nearly twenty times. In this chapter, it shows a believer doing his very best to obey the law of God with his regenerate will. Not only this; but you will find the little words, I, me, my, occur more than forty times. It is the regenerate I in its weakness seeking to obey the law without being filled with the Spirit. This is the experience of almost every saint. After conversion, a man begins to do his best, and he fails. But if we are brought into the full light, we no longer need to fail. Nor need we fail at all if we have received the Spirit in His fullness at conversion.

God allows that failure so that the regenerate man should be taught his own utter inability. It is in the course of this struggle that the sense of our utter sinfulness comes to us. It is God's way of dealing with us. He allows man to strive to fulfill the law so that, as he strives and wrestles, he may be brought to this: "I am a regenerate child of God, but I am utterly helpless to obey His law." See what strong words are used all through the chapter to describe this condition: "I am carnal, sold under sin" (Romans 7:14); "I see another law in my members bringing me into captivity" (Romans 7:23); and last of all, "O wretched man that I am! who shall deliver me from the body of this death?" (Romans 7:24). This believer who bows here in deep contrition is utterly unable to obey the law of God.

The Wretched Man

Not only is the man who makes this confession a regenerate and a weak man, but he is also a wretched man. He is utterly unhappy and miserable. What is it that makes him so utterly miserable? It is because God has given him a nature that loves Himself. He is deeply wretched because he feels he is not obeying his God. He says, with brokenness of heart: "It is not I that do it, but I am under the awful power of sin, which is holding me down. It is I, and yet not I: alas! alas! it is myself; so closely am I bound up with it, and so closely is it intertwined with my very nature." Blessed be God when a man learns to say: "O wretched man that I am!" from the depth of his heart. He is on the way to the eighth chapter of Romans.

There are many who make this confession a pillow for sin. They say that if Paul had to confess his weakness and helplessness in this way, who are they that they should try to do better? So the call to holiness is quietly set aside. Pray God that every one of us would learn to say these words in the very spirit in which they are written here! When we hear sin spoken of as the abominable thing that God hates, do not many of us wince before the word? If only all Christians who go on sinning and sinning would take this verse to heart. If ever you utter a sharp word say: "O wretched man that I am!" And every time you lose your temper, kneel down and under stand that God never meant His child to remain in this state. If only we would take this word into our daily life, and say it every time we are touched about our own honor! If only we would take it into our hearts every time we say sharp things, and every time we sin against the Lord God, and against the Lord Jesus Christ in His humility and in His obedience and in His self-sacrifice! Pray God that we could forget everything else, and cry out: "O wretched man that I am! who shall deliver me from the body of this death?"

Why should you say this whenever you commit sin? Because it is when a man is brought to this confession that deliverance is at hand. And remember, it was not only the sense of being weak and taken captive that made him wretched. It was, above all, the sense of sinning against his God. The law was doing its work, making sin exceedingly sinful in his sight. The thought of continually grieving God became utterly unbearable. It was this that brought forth the piercing cry: "O wretched man!" As long as we talk and reason about our inability and our failure, and only try to find out what Romans, chapter seven, means, it will profit us little. But once every sin gives new intensity to the sense of wretchedness, and we feel our whole state as one of not only helplessness, but actual, exceeding sinfulness, we will be pressed not only to ask: "Who shall deliver us?" but to cry: "I thank God through Jesus Christ my Lord."

The Almost-Delivered Man

The man has tried to obey the beautiful law of God. He has loved it; he has wept over his sin; and he has tried to conquer. He has tried to overcome fault after fault, but every time he has ended in failure. What did he mean by "the body of this death"? Did he mean, my body when I die? Surely not. In the eighth chapter, you have the answer to this question in the words: "If ye through the Spirit do mortify the deeds of the body, ye shall live" (Romans 8:13). That is the body of death from which he is seeking deliverance.

And now he is on the brink of deliverance! In, the twenty-third verse of the seventh chapter, we have the words: "I see another law in my members, warring against the law of my mind, and bringing me into captivity to the law of sin which is in my members." It is a captive that cries: "O wretched man that I am! who shall deliver me from the body I of this death?" He is a man who feels himself bound. But look to.the contrast in the second verse of the eighth chapter: "The law of the Spirit of life in Christ Jesus hath made me free from the law of sin and death." That is the deliverance through Jesus Christ our Lord, the liberty to the captive which the Spirit brings. Can you keep captive any longer a man made free by the "law of the Spirit of life in Christ Jesus"?

But you say, the regenerate man did not have the Spirit of Jesus when he spoke in the sixth chapter. Yes, he did not know what the Holy Spirit could do for him.

God does not work by His Spirit as He works by a blind force in nature. He leads His people on as reasonable, intelligent beings. Therefore, when He wants to give us that Holy Spirit whom He has promised, He first brings us to the end of sel brings us to the conviction that though we have been striving to obey the law, we have failed. When we have come to the end of that, then He shows us that in the Holy Spirit we have the power of obedience, the power of victory, and the power of real holiness. God works to will, and He is ready to work to do, but many Christians misunderstand this. They think because they have the will, it is enough, and that now they are able to do. This is not so. The new will is a permanent gift, an attribute of the new nature. The power to do is not a permanent gift, but must be received each moment from the Holy Spirit. It is the man who is conscious of his own weakness as a believer who will learn that by the Holy Spirit he can live a holy life. This man is on the brink of that great deliverance; the way has been prepared for the glorious eighth chapter. I now ask this solemn question: Where are you living? With you, is it, "O wretched man that I am! who shall deliver me?" with now and then a little experience of the power of the Holy Spirit? Or is it, "I thank God through Jesus Christ! The law of the Spirit hath set me free from the law of sin and of death"?

What the Holy Spirit does is to give the victory. "If ye through the Spirit do mortify the deeds of the body, ye shall live" (Romans 8:13). It is the Holy Spirit who does this—the third Person of the Godhead. It is He who, when the heart is opened wide to receive Him, comes in and reigns there, and mortifies the deeds of the body, day by day, hour by hour, and moment by moment.

I want to bring this to a point. Remember, dear friend, what we need is to come to decision and action. There are in Scripture two very different sorts of Christians. The Bible speaks in Romans, Corinthians, and Galatians about yielding to the flesh; and that is the life of tens of thousands of believers. All their lack of joy in the Holy Spirit, and their lack of the liberty He gives, is just owing to the flesh. The Spirit is within them, but the flesh rules the life. To be led by the Spirit of God is what they need. If only I could make every child of His realize what it means that the everlasting God has given His dear Son, Christ Jesus, to watch over you every day, and that what you have to do is to trust. If only I could make His children understand that the work of the Holy Spirit is to enable you every moment to remember Jesus, and to trust Him! The Spirit has come to keep the link with Him unbroken every moment. Praise God for the Holy Spirit! We are so accustomed to thinking of the Holy Spirit as a luxury, for special times, or for special ministers and men. But the Holy Spirit is necessary for every believer, every moment of the day. Praise God you have Him, and that He gives you the full experience of the deliverance in Christ as He makes you free from the power of sin.

Who longs to have the power and the liberty of the Holy Spirit? Oh, brother, bow before God in one final cry of despair: "O God, must I go on sinning this way forever? Who shall deliver me, O wretched man that I am! from the body of this death?"

Are you ready to sink before God in that cry and seek the power of Jesus to live and work in you? Are you ready to say: "I thank God through Jesus Christ"?

What good does it do that we go to church or attend conventions, 'that we study our Bibles and pray, unless our lives are filled with the Holy Spirit? That is what God wants. Nothing else will enable us to live a life of power and peace. When a minister or parent is using the catechism, and a question is asked, an answer is expected. How sad that many Christians are content with the question put here: "O wretched man that I am! who shall deliver me from the body of this death?" but never give the answer.

Instead of answering, they are silent. Instead of saying: "I thank God through Jesus Christ our Lord," they are forever repeating the question without the answer. If you want the path to the full deliverance of Christ, and the liberty of the Spirit—the glorious liberty of the children of God—take it through the seventh chapter of Romans. Then say: "I thank God through Jesus Christ our Lord." Do not be content to remain ever groaning, but say: "I, a wretched man, thank God, through Jesus Christ. Even though I do not see it all, I am going to praise God."

There is deliverance; there is the liberty of the Holy Spirit. The Kingdom of God is "Joy in the Holy Spirit" (Romans 14:17).

"Having Begun in the Spirit"

The words from which I wish to address you, you will find in the epistle to the Galatians, the third chapter, the second and third verses: "This only would I learn of you, Received ye the Spirit by the works of the law, or by the hearing of faith?

Are ye so foolish?" And then comes my text—"Having begun in the Spirit, are ye now made perfect by the flesh?"

When we speak of the quickening or the deepening or the strengthening of the spiritual life, we are thinking of something that is feeble and wrong and sinful. It is a great thing to take our place before God with the confession: "Oh, God, our spiritual life is not what it should be!" May God work that in your heart, reader.

As we look around at the Church, we see so many indications of feebleness, failure, sin, and shortcoming. They compel us to ask: Why is it? Is there any necessity for the Church of Christ to be living in such a low state? Or is it actually possible that God's people should be living always in the joy and strength of their God?

Every believing heart must answer: It is possible.

Then comes the great question: Why is it, how is it to be accounted for, that God's Church as a whole is so feeble, and that the great majority of Christians are not living up to their privileges? There must be a reason for it. Has God not given Christ His Almighty Son to be the Keeper of every believer, to make Christ an ever-present reality, and to impart and communicate to us all that we have in Christ? God has given His Son, and God has given His Spirit. How is it that believers do not live up to their privileges?

In more than one of the epistles, we find a very solemn answer to that question. There are epistles, such as the first to the Thessalonians, where Paul writes to the Christians, in effect: "I want you to grow, to abound, to increase more and more." They were young, and there were things lacking in their faith. But their state was so far satisfactory, gave him such great joy, that he writes time after time: "I pray God that you may abound more and more; I write to you to increase more and more" (1 Thessalonians 4: 1,10). But there are other epistles where he takes a very different tone, especially the epistle to the Corinthians and to the Galatians, and he tells them in many different ways what the one reason was that they were .not living as Christians ought to live. Many were under the power of the flesh. My text is one example. He reminds them that by the preaching of faith they had received the Holy Spirit. He had preached Christ to them; they had accepted that Christ and had received the Holy Spirit in power.

But what happened? Having begun in the Spirit, they tried to perfect the work that the Spirit had begun in the flesh by their own effort. We find the same teaching in the epistle to the Corinthians.

Now, we have here a solemn discovery of what the great need is in the Church of Christ. God has called the Church of Christ to live in the power of the Holy Spirit. But the Church is living, .for the most part, in the power of human flesh, and of will and energy and effort apart from the Spirit of God. I do not doubt that this is the case with many individual believers. And oh, if God will use me to give you a message from Him, my one message will be this: "If the Church will return to acknowledge that the Holy Spirit is her strength and her help, and if the Church will return to give up everything, and wait on God to be filled with the Spirit, her days of beauty and gladness will return. We will see the glory of God revealed among us." This is my message to every individual believer: "Nothing will help you unless you come to understand that you must live every day under the power of the Holy Spirit." God wants you to be a living vessel in whom the power of the Spirit is to be manifested every hour and every moment of your life. God will enable you to be that.

Now, let us try to learn what this word to the Galatians teaches us—some very simple thoughts. It shows us how (1) the beginning of the Christian life is receiving the Holy Spirit. It shows us (2) what great danger there is of forgetting that we are to live know what it is, since that time, to walk in the power of the Holy Spirit. Let us try to take hold of this great truth: The beginning of the true Christian life is to receive the Holy Spirit. And the work of every Christian minister is that which was the work of Paul—to remind his people that they received the Holy Spirit, and must live according to His guidance and in His power.

If those Galatians who received the Holy Spirit in power were tempted to go astray by that terrible danger of perfecting in the flesh what had been begun in the Spirit, how much more danger do those Christians run who hardly ever know that they have received the Holy Spirit. How much more danger is there for those who, if they know it as a matter of belief, hardly ever think of the gift of the Holy Spirit, and hardly ever praise God for it!

Neglecting the Holy Spirit

But now look, in the second place, at the great danger.

You may all know what shunting is on a railway. A locomotive with its train may be traveling in a certain direction, and the points at some place may not be properly opened or closed, and unobservingly it is shunted off to the right or to the left. And if that takes place, for instance, on a dark night, the train goes in the wrong direction, and the people might never know it until they have gone some distance.

And just so, God gives Christians the Holy Spirit with this intention—that every day, all their life, should be lived in the power of the Spirit. A man cannot live one hour of a godly life unless by the power of the Holy Spirit. He may live a proper, consistent life, as people call it, an irreproachable life, a life of virtue and diligent service. But to live a life acceptable to God, in the enjoyment of God's salvation and God's love, to live and walk in the power of the new life—he cannot do it unless he is guided by the Holy Spirit every day and every hour.

But now listen to the danger. The Galatians received the Holy Spirit, but what was begun by the Spirit they tried to perfect in the flesh. How? They fell back again under Judaizing teachers who told them they must be circumcised. They began to seek their religion in external observances. And so Paul uses that expression about those teachers who had them circumcised so "that they may glorify in your flesh" (Galatians 6:13).

You sometimes hear the expression used, religious flesh. What is meant by that? It is simply an expression made to give utterance to these thoughts: My human nature and my human will and my human effort can be very active in religion. After being converted, and after receiving the Holy Spirit, I may begin in my own strength to try to serve God.

I may be very diligent and doing a great deal, and yet all the time it is more the work of human flesh than of God's Spirit. What a solemn thought, that man can, without noticing, be shunted off from the line of the Holy Spirit onto the line of the flesh.

How solemn it is that man can be most diligent and make great sacrifices, and yet it is all in the power of the human will! Ah, the great question for us to ask of God in self-examination is that we may be shown whether our Christian life is lived more in the power of the flesh than in the power of the Holy Spirit. A man may be a preacher, he may work most diligently in his ministry, a man may be a Christian worker, and others may say of him that he makes great sacrifices, and yet you can feel there is something lacking. You feel that he is not a spiritual man; there is no spirituality about his life. How many Christians there are about whom no one would ever think of saying: "What a spiritual man he is!" Ah! there is the weakness of the Church of Christ. It is all in that one word—flesh.

Now, the flesh may manifest itself in many ways. It may be manifested in fleshly wisdom. My mind may be most active about Christianity. I may preach or write or think or meditate, and delight in being occupied with things in God's Book and in God's Kingdom. Yet, the power of the Holy Spirit may be markedly absent. I fear that if you take the preaching throughout the Church of Christ and ask why there is so little converting power in the preaching of the Word, why there is so much work and often so little result for eternity, why the Word has so little power to build up believers in holiness and in consecration—the answer will be: It is the absence of the power of the Holy Spirit. And why is this? There can be no other reason except that the flesh and human energy have taken the place that the Holy Spirit ought to have. That was true of the Galatians; it was true of the Corinthians. You know Paul said to them: "I could not speak unto you as unto spiritual men, but as unto carnal" (1 Corinthians 3:1). And you know how often in the course of his epistle he had to reprove and condemn them for strife and for divisions.

Lacking the Fruit of the Holy Spirit

A third thought: What are the proofs or indications that a church like the Galatians, or a Christian, is serving God in the power of the flesh—is perfecting in the flesh what was begun in the Spirit? The answer is very easy. Religious self-effort always ends in sinful flesh. What was the state of those Galatians? They were striving to be justified by the works of the law. And yet they were quarreling and in danger of devouring one another. Count the number of expressions that the apostle uses to indicate their want of love. You will find more than twelve—envy, jealousy, bitterness, strife, and all sorts of others. Read in the fourth and fifth chapters what he says about that. You see how they tried to serve God in their own strength, and they failed utterly. All this religious effort resulted in failure. The power of sin and the sinful flesh got the better of them. Their whole condition was one of the saddest that could be thought of.

This comes to us with unspeakable solemnity.

There is a complaint everywhere in the Christian Church of the lack of a high standard of integrity and godliness, even among the professing members of Christian churches. I remember a sermon which I heard preached on commercial morality. But let us not speak only of the commercial morality or immorality; let us go into the homes of Christians. Think of the life to which God has called His children, and which He enables them to live by the Holy Spirit. Think of how much there is of unlovingness, temper, sharpness, and bitterness. Think how often there is strife among the members of churches, and how much there is of envy, jealousy, sensitiveness, and pride. Then we are compelled to say: "Where are marks of the presence of the Spirit of the Lamb of God?" Wanting, sadly wanting!

Many people speak of these things as though they were the natural result of our feebleness and cannot be helped. Many people speak of these things as sins, yet have given up the hope of conquering them. Many people speak of these things in the church around them, and do not see the least prospect of ever having the things changed. There is no prospect until there is a radical change, until the Church of God begins to see that every sin in the believer comes from the flesh—from a fleshly life midst our Christian activities, from a striving in self-effort to serve God. We will fail until we learn to make confession, and until we begin to see that we must somehow or other get God's Spirit in power back to His Church. Where did the Church begin in Pentecost? There they began in the Spirit. But, how the Church of the next century went off into the flesh! They thought to perfect the Church in the flesh.

Do not let us think, because the blessed Reformation restored the great doctrine of justification by faith, that the power of the Holy Spirit was then fully restored. If it is our belief that God is going to have mercy on His Church in these last ages, it will be because the doctrine and the truth about the Holy Spirit will not only be studied, but sought after with a whole heart. It is not only because that truth will be sought after, but because ministers and congregations will be found bowing before God in deep abasement with one cry: "We have grieved God's Spirit. We have tried to be Christian churches with as little as possible of God's Spirit. We have not sought to be churches filled with the Holy Spirit."

All the feebleness in the Church is owing to the refusal of the Church to obey its God. And why is that so? I know your answer. You say: "We are too feeble and too helpless, and we vow to obey, but somehow we fail." Ah yes, you fail because you do not accept the strength of God. God alone can work out His will in you. You cannot work out God's will, but His Holy Spirit can. Until the Church and the believers grasp this, and cease trying by human effort to do God's will, and wait upon the Holy Spirit to come with all His omnipotent and enabling power, the Church will never be what God wants her to be. It will never be what God is willing to make of her.

Yielding to the Holy Spirit

I come now to my last thought, that question: What is the way to restoration?

Beloved friend, the answer is simple and easy. If that train has been shunted off, there is nothing for it to do but to come back to the point at which it was led away. The Galatians had no other way in returning but to come back to where they had gone wrong. They had to come back from all religious effort in their own strength, and from seeking anything by their own work, and to yield themselves humbly to the Holy Spirit. There is no other way for us as individuals.

Is there any brother or sister whose heart is conscious: "My life knows little of the power of the Holy Spirit"? I come to you with God's message that you can have no conception of what your life would be in the power of the Holy Spirit. It is too high, too blessed, and too wonderful. But I bring you the message that just as truly as the everlasting Son of God came to this world and did His wonderful works, that just as truly as on Calvary He died and brought about your redemption by His precious blood, so can the Holy Spirit come into your heart. With His divine power, He may sanctify you and enable you to do God's blessed will, and fill your heart with joy and strength. But, we have forgotten; we have grieved; we have dishonored the Holy Spirit; and, He has not been able to do His work. But I bring you the message: The Father in heaven loves to fill His children with His Holy Spirit. God longs to give each one individually, separately, the power of the Holy Spirit for daily life. The command comes to us individually, unitedly. God wants us as His children to arise and place our sins before Him, and to call on Him for mercy. Oh, are you so foolish? Having begun in the Spirit, are you perfecting in the flesh that which was begun in the Spirit? Let us bow in shame, and confess before God how our fleshly religion, our self-effort and self-confidence, have been the cause of every failure.

I have often been asked by young Christians: "Why is it that I fail so? I did so solemnly vow with my whole heart, and did desire to serve God. Why have I failed?" To such I always give this answer: "My dear friend, you are trying to do in your own strength what Christ alone can do in you." And when they tell me: "I am sure I knew Christ alone could do it; I was not trusting in myself," my answer is: "You were trusting in yourself, or you could not have failed. If you had trusted Christ, He could not fail." Oh, this perfecting in the flesh what was begun in the Spirit runs far deeper through us than we know. Let us ask God to show us that it is only when we are brought to utter shame and emptiness that we will be prepared to receive the blessing that comes from on high.

And so I come with these two questions. Are you living, beloved brother—minister—I ask it of every minister of the Gospel—under the power of the Holy Spirit? Are you living as an anointed, Spirit-filled man in your ministry and your life before God? Oh friends, our place is an awful one. We have to show people what God will do for us, not in our words and teaching, but in our life. God help us to do it!

I ask it of every member of Christ's Church and of every believer: Are you living a life under the power of the Holy Spirit day by day? Or are you attempting to live without that? Remember, you cannot. Are you conse-crated, given up to the Spirit to work in you and to live in you? Oh, come and confess every failure of temper, every failure of tongue however small. Confess every failure owing to the absence of the Holy Spirit and the presence of the power of self. Are you consecrated, are you given up to the Holy Spirit?

If your answer is no, then I come with a second question—Are you willing to be consecrated? Are you willing to give yourself up to the power of the Holy Spirit? You well know that the human side of consecration will not help you. I may consecrate myself a hundred times with all the intensity of my being, and that will not help me. What will help me is this—that God from heaven accepts and seals the consecration.

And now are you willing to give yourselves up to the Holy Spirit? You can do it now. A great deal may still be dark and dim, and beyond what we understand. You may feel nothing; but come. God alone can work the change. God alone, who gave us the Holy Spirit, can restore the Holy Spirit in power into our life. God alone can "strengthen us with might by his Spirit in the inner man" (Ephesians 3:16). And to every waiting heart that will make the sacrifice, and give up everything, and give time to cry and pray to God, the answer will come. The blessing is not far off. Our God delights in helping us. He will enable us to perfect, not in the flesh, but in the Spirit, what was begun in the Spirit.

Kept by the Power of God

The words from which I speak, you will find in 1 Peter, chapter one, verse five. The third, fourth, and fifth verses are: "Blessed be the God and Father of our Lord Jesus Christ, which ...hath begotten us again unto a lively hope by the resurrection of Jesus Christ from the dead, to an inheritance incorruptible . . . reserved in heaven for you, who are kept by the power of God through faith unto salvation." The words of my text are: "Kept by the power of God through faith."

There we have two wonderful, blessed truths about the way a believer is kept unto salvation. One truth is, Kept by the power of God; and the other truth is, Kept through faith. We should look at the two sides—at God's side and His almighty power, offered to us to be our Keeper every moment of the day; and at the human side, we have nothing to do but in faith to let God do His keeping work. We are begotten again to an inheritance kept in heaven for us. We are kept here on earth by the power of God.

We see there is a double keeping—the inheritance kept for me in heaven, and I on earth kept for the inheritance there. Now, as to the first part of this —keeping, there is no doubt and no question. God keeps the inheritance in heaven very wonderfully and perfectly, and it is waiting there safely. And the same God keeps me for the inheritance. That is what I want to understand. It is very foolish for a father to take great trouble to have an inheritance for his children, and to keep it for them, if he does not keep them for it. Think of a man spending all of his time and making every sacrifice to amass money, and as he gets his tens of thousands, you ask him why it is that he sacrifices himself so. His answer is: "I want to leave my children a large inheritance, and I am keeping it for them." If you were then to hear that that man takes no trouble to educate his children, that he, allows them to run around the street wild, and to go in paths of sin and ignorance and folly, what would you think of him? Would you not say: "Poor man! he is keeping an inheritance for his children, but he is not keeping or preparing his children for the inheritance!" And there are so many Christians who think: "My God is keeping the inheritance for me." But they cannot believe: "My God is keeping me for that inheritance." The same power, the same love, the same God doing the double work.

Now, I want to speak about a work God does upon us, keeping us for the inheritance. I have already said that we have two very simple truths: the one, the divine side—we are kept by the power of God; the other, the human side—we are kept through faith.

Kept by the Power of God

Look at the divine side: Christians are kept by the power of God. Keeping Includes All. Think, first of all, that this keeping is all inclusive.

What is kept? You are kept. How much of you? The whole being. Does God keep one part of you and not another? No. Some people have an idea that this is a sort of vague, general keeping, and that God will keep them in such a way that when they die they will get to heaven. But they do not apply that word kept to everything in their being and nature. And yet that is what God wants.

Here I have a watch. Suppose that this watch had been borrowed from a friend, and he said to me: "When you go to Europe, I will let you take it with you, but mind you keep it safely and bring it back." And suppose I damage the watch, and had the hands broken, and the face defaced, and some of the wheels and springs spoiled, and took it back in that condition, and handed it to my friend. He would say: "Ah, but I gave you that watch on condition that you would keep it."

"Have I not kept it? There is the watch."

"But I did not want you to keep it in that general way, so that you should bring me back only the shell of the watch, or the remains. I expected you to keep every part of it." And so God does not want to keep us in this general way, so that at the last, somehow or other, we will be saved as by fire, and just get into heaven. But the keeping power and the love of God applies to every part of our being.

There are some people who think God will keep them in spiritual things, but not in temporal things. This latter, they say, lies outside of His realm. Now, God sends you to work in the world, but He did not say: "I must now leave you to go and earn your own money, and to get your livelihood for yourself." He knows you are not able to keep yourself. But God says: "My child, there is no work you are to do, and no business in which you are engaged, and not a cent which you are to spend, but I, your Father, will take that up into my keeping." God not only cares for the spiritual, but for the temporal, also. The greater part of the life of many people must be spent, sometimes eight or nine or ten hours a day, amid the temptations and distractions of business. But God will care for you there. The keeping of God includes all.

There are other people who think: "Ah! in time of trial God keeps me. But in times of prosperity I do not need. His keeping; then I forget Him and let Him go." Others, again, think the very opposite. They think: "In time of prosperity, when things are smooth and quiet, I am able to cling to God. But when heavy trials come, somehow or other my will rebels, and God does not keep me then."

Now, I bring you the message that in prosperity as in adversity, in the sunshine as in the dark, your God is ready to keep you all the time. Then again, there are others who think of this keeping thus: "God will keep me from doing very great wickedness, but there are small sins I cannot expect God to keep me from. There is the sin of temper. I cannot expect God to conquer that."

When you hear of some man who has been tempted and gone astray or fallen into drunkenness or murder, you thank God for His keeping power. "I might have done the same as that man," you say, "if God had not kept me." And you believe He kept you from drunkenness and murder. And why do you not believe that God can keep you from outbreaks of temper? You thought that this was of less importance. You did not remember that the great commandment of the New Testament is—"Love one another as I have loved you" (John 13:34). And when your temper and hasty judgment and sharp words came out, you sinned against the highest law—the law of God's love. And yet you say: "God will not, God cannot"—no, you will not say, God cannot; but you say, "God does not keep me from that." You perhaps say: "He can; but there is something in me that cannot attain to it, and which God does not take away."

I want to ask you, Can believers live a holier life than is generally lived? Can believers experience the keeping power of God all day, to keep them from sin? Can believers be kept in fellowship with God? And I bring you a message from the Word of God, in these words: Kept by the power of God. There is no qualifying clause to them. The meaning is, that if you will entrust yourself entirely and absolutely to the omnipotence of God, He will delight in keeping you.

Some people think that they can never reach the point that every word of their mouth would be to the glory of God. But it is what God wants of them; it is what God expects of them. God is willing to set a watch at the door of their mouth. If God will do that, can He not keep their tongue and their lips?

He can. That is what God is going to do for those who trust Him. God's keeping is all-inclusive. Let everyone who longs to live a holy life think about all their needs, their weaknesses, their shortcomings, and their sins, and say deliberately: "Is there any sin that my God cannot keep me from?" And the heart will have to answer: "No, God can keep me from every sin."

2) Keeping Requires Power. Second, if you want to understand this keeping, remember that it is not only an all-inclusive keeping, but it is an almighty keeping.

I want to get that truth burned into my soul. I want to worship God until my whole heart is filled with the thought of His omnipotence. God is almighty, and the Almighty God offers Himself to work in my heart—to do the work of keeping me. I want to get linked .with omnipotence, or rather, linked to the omnipotent One—the living God—and to have my place in the hollow of His hand. You read the Psalms, and you think of the wonderful thoughts in many of the expressions that David uses. For instance, when he speaks about being our God, our Fortress, our Refuge, our strong Tower, our Strength, and our Salvation. David had wonderful views of how the everlasting God is Himself the hiding place of the believing soul. David had a beautiful understanding of how God takes the believer and keeps him in the very hollow of His hand—in the secret of His pavilion—under the shadow of His wings, under His very feathers. And there David lived. And we, who are the children of Pentecost, who have known Christ, His blood, and the Holy Spirit sent down from heaven, why is it that we know so little of what it is to walk step by step with the Almighty God as our Keeper?

Have you ever thought that, in every action of grace in your heart, you have the whole omnipotence of God engaged to bless you? When I come to a man and he gives me a gift of money; I get it and go away with it. He has given me something of his. The rest he keeps for himself. But that is not the way with the power of God. God can part with nothing of His own power, and therefore I can experience the power and goodness of God only so far as I am in contact and fellowship with Him. And when I come into contact and fellowship with Him, I come into contact and fellowship with the whole omnipotence of God. I have the omnipotence of God to help me every day.

A son has, perhaps, a very rich father, and as the former is about to commence business the father says: "You can have as much money as you want for your undertaking." All the father has is at the disposal of the son. And that is the way with God, your Almighty God. You can hardly take it in; you feel like such a little worm. His omnipotence is needed to keep a little worm! Yes, His omnipotence is needed to keep every little worm that lives in the dust, and also to keep the universe. Therefore, His omnipotence is much more needed in keeping your soul and mine from the power of sin.

Oh, if you want to grow in grace, do learn to begin here. In all your judgings and meditations and thoughts and deeds and questions and studies and prayers, learn to be kept by your Almighty God. What is the Almighty God not going to do for the child that trusts Him? The Bible says: "Above all that we ask or think" (Ephesians 3:20). It is omnipotence you must learn to know and trust. Then you will live as a Christian ought to live. How little we have learned to study God, and to understand that a godly life is a life full of God. It is a life that loves God and waits on Him, trusts Him, and allows Him to bless it! We cannot do the will of God except by the power of God. God gives us the first experience of His power to prepare us to long for more, and to come and claim all that He can do. God helps us to trust Him every day.

3) Keeping Is Continuous

Another thought. This keeping is not only all inclusive and omnipotent, but also continuous and unbroken.

People sometimes say: "For a week or a month God has kept me very wonderfully. I have lived in the light of His countenance, and I can say what joy I have had in fellowship with Him. He has blessed me in my work for others. He has given me souls, and at times I felt as if I were carried heavenward on eagle wings. But it did not continue. It was too good; it could not last." And some say: "It was necessary that I should fall to keep me humble." And others say: "I know it was my own fault; but somehow you cannot always live up in the heights." Oh, beloved, why is it? Can there be any reason why the keeping of God should not be continuous and unbroken? Just think. All life is in unbroken continuity. If my life were stopped for half an hour, I would be dead, and my life gone. Life is a continuous thing, and the life of God is the life of His Church. The life of God is His almighty power working in us. And God comes to us as the Almighty One, and without any condition He offers to be my Keeper. His keeping means that day by day, moment by moment, God is going to keep us.

If I were to ask you the question: "Do you think God is able to keep you one day from actual transgression?" you would answer: "I not only know He is able to do it, but I think He has done it. There have been days in which He has kept my heart in His holy presence. There have also been days when, though I have always had a sinful nature within me, He has kept me from conscious, actual transgression."

Now, if He can do that for an hour or a day, why not for two days? Oh! let us make God's omnipotence as revealed in His Word the measure of our expectations. Has God not said in His Word: "I, the Lord, do keep it, and will water it every moment" (Isaiah 27:3)? What can that mean? Does "every moment" mean every moment? Did God promise of that vineyard or red wine that every moment He would water it so that the heat of the sun and the scorching wind might never dry it up? Yes. In South Africa, they sometimes make a graft, and above it they tie a bottle of water, so that now and then there will be a drop to saturate what they have put about it. And so the moisture is kept there unceasingly until the, graft has had time to take, and resist the heat of the sun.

Will our God, in His tenderhearted love toward us, not keep us every moment when He has promised to do so? Oh! if we once got hold of the thought: Our whole spiritual life is to be God's doing—"It is God which worketh in you both to will and to do of his pleasure" (Philippians 2:13). Once we get faith to expect that from God, God will do all for us.

The keeping is to be continuous. Every morning, God will meet you as you wake. It is not a question: If I forget to wake in the morning with the thought of Him, what will come of it? If you trust your waking to God, God will meet you in the mornings as you wake with His divine sunshine and life. He will give you the consciousness that through the day you have got God to continually take charge of you with His almighty power. And God will meet you the next day and every day. Never mind if, in the practice of fellowship, failure sometimes comes. If you maintain your position—and say: "Lord, I am going to expect You to do Your utmost, and I am going to trust You day by day to keep me absolutely," your faith will grow stronger and stronger. You will know the keeping power of God in unbrokenness.

Kept Through Faith

And now the other side—Believing. "Kept by the power of God through faith." How must we look at this faith?

4) Faith Implies Helplessness

Let me say, first of all, that this faith means utter inability and helplessness before God.

At the bottom of all faith there is a feeling of helplessness. If I have a bit of business to transact, perhaps to buy a house, the lawyer must do the work of getting the transfer of the property in my name. He must make all the arrangements. I cannot do that work, and, in trusting that agent, I confess I cannot do it. And so faith always means helplessness. In many cases it means: I can do it with a great deal of trouble, but another can do it better. But in most cases it is utter helplessness: another must do it for me. And that is the secret of the spiritual life. A man must learn to say: "I give up everything. I have tried and longed and thought and prayed, but failure has come. God has blessed me and helped me, but still, in the long run, there has been so much sin and sadness." What a change comes when a man is thus broken down into utter helplessness and self-despair, and says, "I can do nothing!"

Remember Paul. He was living a blessed life, and he had been taken up into the third heaven. Then the thorn in the flesh came, "a messenger of Satan to buffet me" (2 Corinthians 12:7). And what happened? Paul could not understand it, and three times he prayed to the Lord to take it away. But the Lord said, in effect: "No, it is possible that you might exalt yourself. Therefore, I have sent you this trial to keep you weak and humble." And Paul then learned a lesson that he never forgot—to rejoice in his infirmities. He said that the weaker he was the better it was for him. For when he was weak, he was strong in his Lord Christ.

Do you want to enter what people call "the higher life"? Then go a step lower down. I remember Dr. Boardman telling how once he was invited by a gentleman to go to a factory where they made fine shot. I believe the workmen did so by pouring down molten lead from a great height. This gentleman wanted to take Dr. Boardman up to the top of the tower to see how the work was done. The doctor came to the tower, he entered by the door, and began going upstairs. But when he had gone a few steps, the gentleman called out: "That is the wrong way. You must come down this way. That stair is locked up." The gentleman took him downstairs a good many steps, and there an elevator was ready to take him to the top. He said: "I have learned a lesson that going down is often the best way to get up."

Ah, yes, God will have to bring us down very low. A sense of emptiness and despair and nothingness will have to come upon us. It is when we sink down in utter helplessness that the everlasting God will reveal Himself in His power. Then our hearts will learn to trust God alone.

What is it that keeps us from trusting Him perfectly?

Many say: "I believe what you say, but there is one difficulty. If my trust were perfect and always abiding, all would come right, for I know God will honor trust. But how am I to get that trust?"

My answer is: "By the death of self. The great hindrance to trust is self-effort. So long as you have got your own wisdom and thoughts and strength, You cannot fully trust God. But when God breaks you down, when everything begins to grow dim before your eyes and you see that you understand nothing, then God is coming near. If you will bow down in nothingness and wait on God, He will become all."

As long as we are something, God cannot be all. His omnipotence cannot do its full work. That is the beginning of faith—utter despair of self, a ceasing from man and everything on earth and finding our hope in God alone.

5) Faith Is Rest

And then, next, we must understand that faith is rest.

In the beginning of the faith—life, faith is struggling. But as long as faith is struggling, faith has not attained its strength. But when faith in its struggling gets to the end of itself, and throws itself upon God and rests on Him, then joy and victory come.

Perhaps I can make it plainer if I tell the story of how the Keswick Convention began. Canon Battersby was an evangelical clergyman of the Church of England for more than twenty years. He was a man of deep and tender godliness, but he did not have the consciousness of rest and victory over sin. He was often deeply saddened by the thought of stumbling and failure and sin. When he heard about the possibility of victory, he felt it was desirable, but it was as if he could not attain it. On one occasion, he heard an address on "Rest and Faith" from the story of the nobleman who came from Capernaum to Cana to ask Christ to heal his child. In the address, it was shown that the nobleman believed that Christ could help him in a general way. But he came to Jesus a good deal by way of an experiment. He hoped Christ would help him, but he did not have any assurance of that help. But what happened? When Christ said to him: "Go thy way, for thy child liveth" (John 4:50), that man believed the word that Jesus spoke. He rested in that word. He had no proof that his child was well again, and he had to walk back seven hours' journey to Capernaum. He walked back, and on the way met his servant, and got the first news that the child was well. The servant told him that at one o'clock on the afternoon of the previous day, at the very time that Jesus spoke to him, the fever left the child. That father rested on the word of Jesus and His work, and he went down to Capernaum and found his child well. He praised God, and he and his whole house became believers and disciples of Jesus. Oh, friends, that is faith! When God comes to me with the promise of His keeping, and I have nothing on earth to trust in, I say to God: "Your word is enough. I am kept by the power of God." That is faith, that is rest. When Canon Battersby heard that address, he went home that night, and in the darkness of the night he found rest. He rested on the word of Jesus. And the next morning, in the streets of Oxford, he said to a friend: "I have found it!" Then he went and told others, and asked that the Keswick Convention might commence. He said that those at the convention, along with himself, should simply testify what God had done.

It is a great thing when a man comes to rest on God's almighty power for every moment of his life. It is also great when he does so in the midst of temptations to temper and haste and anger and unlovingness and pride and sin. It is a great thing in the face of these to enter into a covenant with the omnipotent Jehovah—not on account of anything that any man says, or of anything that my heart feels—but on the strength of the Word of God: "Kept by the power of God through faith."

Oh, let us say to God that we are going to prove Him to the very utmost. Let us say: We ask You for nothing more than You can give, but we want nothing less. Let us say: My God, let my life be a proof of what the omnipotent God can do. Let these be the two dispositions of our souls every day—deep helplessness, and simple, childlike rest.

6) Faith Needs Fellowship

That brings me to just one more thought in regard to faith. Faith implies fellowship with God.

Many people want to take the Word and believe that, but do not think it is so necessary to fellowship with God. Ah, no! you cannot separate God from His Word. No goodness or power can be received separate from God. If you want to get into this life of godliness, you must take time for fellowship with God. People sometimes tell me: "My life is one of such scurry and bustle that I have no time for fellowship with God." A dear missionary said to me: "People do not know how we missionaries are tempted. I get up at five o'clock in the morning, and there are the natives waiting for their orders for work. Then, I have to go to the school and spend hours there. Then, there is other work, and sixteen hours rush along. I hardly get time to be alone with God."

Ah! there is the need. I pray you, remember two things. I have not told you to trust the omnipotence of God as a thing, and I have not told you to trust the Word of God as a written book. I have told you to go to the God of omnipotence and the God of the Word. Deal with God as that nobleman dealt with the living Christ. Why was he able to believe the word that Christ spoke to him? Because in the very eyes and tone and voice of Jesus, the Son of God, he saw and heard something which made him feel that he could trust Him. And that is what Christ can do for you and me. Do not try to stir and arouse faith from within. How often I have tried to do that, and made a fool of myself! You cannot stir up faith from the depths of your heart. Leave your heart, and look into the face of Christ. Listen to what He tells you about how He will keep you. Look up into the face of your loving Father, and take time every day with Him. Begin a new life with the deep emptiness and poverty of a man who has got nothing, and who wants to get everything from

Him—with the deep restfulness of a man who rests on the living God, the omnipotent Jehovah. Try God, and prove Him if He will not open the windows of heaven and pour out a blessing that there will not be room to receive it.

I close by asking if you are willing to fully experience the heavenly keeping for the heavenly inheritance? Robert Murray M'Cheyne says, somewhere: "Oh, God, make me as holy as a pardoned sinner can be made." And if that prayer is in your heart, come now, and let us enter into a covenant with the everlasting and omnipotent Jehovah afresh. In great helplessness, but in great restfulness, let us place ourselves in His hands. And then, as we enter into our covenant, let us have the one prayer—that we may fully believe that the everlasting God is going to be our companion. Let us believe that He will hold our hand every moment of the day. He is our Keeper, watching over us without a moment's interval. He is our Father, delighting to reveal Himself in our souls always. He has the power to let the sunshine of His love be with us all day. Do not be afraid that because you have your business you cannot have God with you always. Learn the lesson that the natural sun shines on you all day, and you enjoy its light. Wherever you are you have got the sun; God makes certain that it shines on you. And God will make certain that His own divine light shines on you, and that you will abide in that light, if you will only trust Him for it. Let us trust God to do that with a great and entire trust. Here is the omnipotence of God, and here is faith reaching out to the measure of that omnipotence. We can say: "All that that omnipotence can do, I am going to trust my God for." Are not the two sides of this heavenly life wonderful? God's omnipotence covers me, and my will in its littleness rests in that omnipotence, and rejoices in it!

Moment by moment, I'm kept in His love;
Moment by moment, I've life from above;
Looking to Jesus, the glory doth shine;
Moment by moment, Oh, Lord, I am thine!

"Ye Are the Branches"

An Address to Christian Workers

Everything depends on our being right in Christ. If I want good apples, I must have a good apple tree. If I care for the health of the apple tree, the apple tree will give me good apples. And it is just so with our Christian life and work. If our life with Christ is right, all will come out right. Instruction and suggestion and help and training in the different departments of the work may be needed; all that has value. But in the long run, the greatest essential is to have the full life in Christ—in other words, to have Christ in us, working through us. I know how much there is to disturb us, or to cause anxious questionings. But the Master has such a blessing for every one of us and such perfect peace and rest. He has such joy and strength if we can only come into, and be kept in, the right attitude toward Him.

I will take my text from the parable of the Vine and the Branches, in John, chapter fifteen, verse five: "I am the vine, ye are the branches." Especially these words: "Ye are the branches."

What a simple thing it is to be a branch, the branch of a tree, or the branch of a vine! The branch grows out of the vine, or out of the tree, and there it lives and grows and, in due time, bears fruit. It has no responsibility except to receive sap and nourishment from the root and stem. And if only we knew, by the Holy Spirit, about our relationship to Jesus Christ, our work would be changed into the brightest and most heavenly thing on earth. Instead of there ever being soul-weariness or exhaustion, our work would be like a new experience, linking us to Jesus as nothing else can. For, is it not true that often our work comes between us and Jesus? What folly! The very work that He has to do in me, and I for Him, I take up in such a way that it separates me from Christ. Many a laborer in the vineyard has complained that he has too much work, and not enough time for close communion with Jesus. He complains that his usual work weakens his inclination for prayer, and that his many conversations with men darken the spiritual life. Sad thought, that the bearing of fruit should separate the branch from the vine! That must be because we have looked on our work as something other than the branch bearing fruit. May God deliver us from every false .thought about the Christian life.

Now, just a few thoughts about this blessed branch—life.

Absolute Dependence

In the first place, it is a life of absolute dependence. The branch has nothing; it just depends on the vine for everything. Absolute dependence is one of the most solemn and precious of thoughts. A great German theologian wrote two large volumes some years ago to show that the whole of Calvin's theology is summed up in that one principle of absolute dependence upon God; and he was right. Another great writer has said that absolute, unalterable dependence upon God alone is the essence of the religion of angels. It should also be that of men. God is everything to the angels, and He is willing to be everything to the Christian. If I can learn to depend on God every moment of the day, everything will come right. You will receive the higher life if you depend absolutely on God.

Now, here we find it with the vine and the branches. Every vine you ever see, or every bunch of grapes that come to your table, let it remind you that the branch is absolutely dependent on the vine. The vine has to do the work, and the branch enjoys the fruit of it.

What has the vine to do? It has to do a great work. It has to send its roots out into the soil and hunt under the ground—the roots often extend a long way out—for nourishment, and to drink in the moisture. Put certain elements of manure in certain directions, and the vine sends its roots there. Then, its roots or stems turn the moisture and manure into that special sap which makes the fruit that is borne. The vine does the work, and the branch has just to receive the sap from the vine. The sap is then changed into grapes. I have been told that at Hampton Court, London, there was a vine that sometimes bore a couple of thousand bunches of grapes. People were astonished at its large growth and rich fruitage. Afterward, the cause was discovered. The Thames River flows nearby, so the vine had stretched its roots hundreds of yards under the ground until it had come to the riverside. There, in all the rich slime of the riverbed, it had found rich nourishment, and obtained moisture. The roots had drawn the sap all that distance up and up into the vine. As a result, there was the abundant, rich harvest. The vine had the work to do, and the branches had just to depend on the vine and receive what it gave.

Is that literally true of my Lord Jesus? Must I understand that when I have to work, when I have to preach a sermon or address a Bible class or go out and visit the poor, neglected ones, that all the responsibility of the work is on Christ? That is exactly what Christ wants you to understand. Christ desires that in all your work the very foundation should be the simple, blessed consciousness: Christ must care for all. And how does He fulfill the trust of that dependence? He does it by sending down the Holy Spirit—not now and then only as a special gift. But remember, the relationship between the vine and the branches is such that hourly, daily, unceasingly, the living connection is maintained. The sap does not flow for a time, and then stop, and then flow again. Instead, moment to moment, the sap flows from the vine to the branches. And just so, my Lord Jesus wants me to take that blessed position as a worker. Morning by morning and day by day and hour by hour and step by step—in every work—I have to go out to abide before Him in the simple, utter helplessness of one who knows nothing. I must be as one who is nothing, and can do nothing. Oh, beloved workers, study that word nothing. You sometimes sing: "Oh, to be nothing, nothing"; but have you really studied that word and prayed every day and worshipped God in the light of it? Do you know the blessedness of that word nothing?

If I am something, then God is not everything; but when I become nothing, God can become all. The everlasting God in Christ can reveal Himself fully. That is the higher life. We need to become nothing. Someone has well said that the seraphim and cherubim are flames of fire because they know they are nothing, and they allow God to put His fullness and His glory and brightness into them. Oh, become nothing in deep reality, and, as a worker, study only one thing—to become poorer and lower and more helpless, that Christ may work all in you.

Workers, here is your first lesson: learn to be nothing, learn to be helpless. The man who has got something is not absolutely dependent. But the man who has got nothing is absolutely dependent. Absolute dependence on God is the secret of all power in work. The branch has nothing but what it gets from the vine. You and I can have nothing but what we get from Jesus.

Deep Restfulness

But second, the life of the branch is not only a life of entire dependence, but also of deep restfulness.

That little branch, if it could think, feel, and speak, and if we could say: "Come, branch of the vine, I want to learn from you how I can be a true branch of the living Vine," what would it answer? The little branch would whisper: "Man, I hear that you are wise, and I know that you can do a great many wonderful things. I know you have much strength and wisdom given to you, but I have one lesson for you. With all your hurry and effort in Christ's work, you never prosper. The first thing you need is to come and rest in your Lord Jesus. That is what I do. Since I grew out of that vine, I have spent years and years, and all I have done is just to rest in the vine. When the time of spring came I had no anxious thought or care. The vine began to pour its sap into me, and to give the bud and leaf. And when summer came, I had no care; and in the great heat, I trusted the vine to bring moisture to keep me fresh. And in the time of harvest, when the owner came to pluck the grapes, I had no care. If there was anything in the grapes not good, the owner never blamed the branch; the blame was always on the vine. And if you would be a true branch of Christ, the living Vine, just rest on Him. Let Christ bear the responsibility."

You say: "Won't that make me slothful?"

I tell you it will not. No one who learns to rest on the living Christ can become slothful. The closer your contact with Christ, the more the Spirit of His zeal and love will be borne in upon you. But, oh, begin to work in the midst of your entire dependence by adding to that deep restfulness. A man sometimes tries and tries to be dependent on Christ, but he worries himself about this absolute dependence. He tries and he cannot get it. But let him sink down into entire restfulness every day.

In Thy strong hand I lay me down.
So shall the work be done;
For who can work so wondrously
As the Almighty One?

Workers, take your place every day at the feet of Jesus, in the blessed peace and rest that come from the knowledge—I have no care, my cares are His! I have no fear, He cares for all my fears.

Come, children of God, and understand that it is the Lord Jesus who wants to work through you. You complain of the lack of fervent love. It will come from Jesus. He will give the divine love in your heart with which you can love people. That is the meaning of the assurance: "The love of God is shed abroad in our hearts by the Holy Spirit" (Romans 5:5); and of that other word: "The love of Christ constraineth us" (2 Corinthians 5:14). Christ can give you a fountain of love so that you cannot help loving the most wretched and the most ungrateful, or those who have wearied you. Rest in Christ, who can give wisdom and strength. You do not know how that restfulness will often prove to be the very best part of your message. You plead with people and you argue, and they get the idea: "There is a man arguing and striving with me." But if you will let the deep rest of God come over you—the rest in Christ Jesus, the peace and the rest and holiness of heaven—that restfulness will bring a blessing to the heart, even more than the words you speak.

Much Fruitfulness

But third, the branch teaches a lesson of much fruitfulness.

The Lord Jesus Christ repeated the word fruit often in that parable. He spoke, first, of fruit, and then of more fruit, and then of much fruit. Yes, you are ordained not only to bear fruit, but to bear much fruit. "Herein is my Father glorified, that ye bear much fruit" (John 15:8). In the first place, Christ said: "I am the true Vine, and my Father is the Husbandman" (John 15:1). God will watch over the connection between Christ and the branches. It is in the power of God through Christ that we are to bear fruit.

Oh, Christians, you know this world is perishing for lack of workers. And it lacks more than workers. Many workers are saying, some more earnestly than others: "We need not only more workers, but we need our workers to have a new powera different life—so that we workers would be able to bring more blessing." Children of God, I appeal to you. You know what trouble you take, say, in a case of sickness. You have a beloved friend apparently in danger of death, and nothing can refresh that friend so much as a few grapes. But, they are out of season. Still, what trouble you will take to get the grapes that are to be the nourishment of this dying friend! And, there are people around who never go to church, and so many who go to church, but do not know Christ. And yet, the heavenly grapes—the grapes of the heavenly Vine—are not to be had at any price except as the child of God bears them out of his inner life in fellowship with Christ. Except the children of God are filled with the sap of the heavenly Vine, except they are filled with the Holy Spirit and the love of Jesus, they cannot bear much of the real heavenly grape. We all confess there is a great deal of work, a great deal of preaching, teaching, and visiting, a great deal of machinery, and a great deal of earnest effort of every kind. But, there is not much manifestation of the power of God in it.

What is wanting? The close connection between the worker and the heavenly Vine is lacking. Christ, the heavenly Vine, has blessings that He could pour on tens of thousands who are perishing. Christ, the heavenly Vine, has power to provide the heavenly grapes. But "Ye are the branches," and you cannot bear heavenly fruit unless you are in close connection with Jesus Christ.

Do not confuse work and fruit. There may be a good deal of work for Christ that is not the fruit of the heavenly Vine. Do not seek for work only. Oh! study this question of fruit-bearing. It means the very life, power, spirit, and love within the heart of the Son of God. It means the heavenly Vine Himself coming into your hearts and mine.

You know there are different sorts of grapes, each with a different name. Every vine provides exactly that peculiar aroma and juice which gives the grape its particular flavor and taste. Just so, there is in the heart of Christ Jesus a life, a love, a Spirit, a blessing, and a power for men, that are entirely heavenly and divine, and that will come down into our hearts. Stand in close connection with the heavenly Vine and say: "Lord Jesus, nothing less than the sap that flows through You, nothing less than the Spirit of Your divine life is what we ask. Lord Jesus, I pray, let Your Spirit flow through me in all my work for You." I tell you again that the sap of the heavenly Vine is nothing but the Holy Spirit. The Holy Spirit is the life of the heavenly Vine. What you must get from Christ is nothing less than a strong inflow of the Holy Spirit. You need it exceedingly, and you want nothing more than that. Remember that. Do not expect Christ to give a bit of strength here, and a bit of blessing yonder, and a bit of help over there. As the vine does its work in giving its own peculiar sap to the branch, so expect Christ to give His own Holy Spirit into your heart. Then you will bear much fruit. Perhaps you have only begun to bear fruit, and are listening to the word of Christ in the parable, "more fruit," "much fruit." Remember, that in order for you to bear more fruit, you just require more of Jesus in your life and heart.

We ministers of the Gospel, how we are in danger of getting into a condition of work, work, work! And we pray over it, but the freshness, buoyancy, and joy of the heavenly life are not always present. Let us seek to understand that the life of the branch is a life of much fruit, because it is a life rooted in Christ, the living, heavenly Vine.

Close Communion

And fourth, the life of the branch is a life of close communion.

Let us again ask: What has the branch to do? You know that precious, inexhaustible word that Christ used—Abide. Your life is to be an abiding life. And how is the abiding to be? It is to be just like the branch in the vine, abiding every minute of the day. The branches are in close communion, in unbroken communion, with the vine, from January to December. And can I not live every day—it is to me an almost terrible thing that we should ask the question—in abiding communion with the heavenly Vine?

You say: "But I am so occupied with other things."

You may have ten hours' hard work daily, during which your brain has to be occupied with temporal things. God orders it so. But the abiding work is the work of the heart, not of the brain. It is the work of the heart clinging to and resting in Jesus, a work in which the Holy Spirit links us to Christ Jesus. Oh, do believe that deeper down than the brain, deep down in the inner life, you can abide in Christ, so that every moment you are free, the consciousness will come: "Blessed Jesus, I am still in You." If you will learn for a time to put aside other work and to get into this abiding contract with the heavenly Vine, you will find that fruit will come. What is the application to our life of this abiding communion? What does it mean? It means close fellowship with Christ in secret prayer. I am sure there are Christians who do long for the higher life, and who sometimes have received a great blessing. I am sure there are those who have at times found a great inflow of heavenly joy and a great outflow of heavenly gladness. Yet, after a time, it has passed away. They have not understood that close, personal communion with Christ is an absolute necessity for daily life. Take time to be alone with Christ. Nothing in heaven or earth can free you from the necessity for that, if you are to be happy and holy Christians.

Oh! how many Christians look on it as a burden and a tax, a duty and a difficulty, to often be alone with God! That is the great hindrance to our Christian life everywhere. We need more quiet fellowship with God. I tell you in the name of the heavenly Vine that you cannot be healthy branches—branches into which the heavenly sap can flow—unless you take plenty of time for communion with God. If you are not willing to sacrifice time to get alone with Him, and to give Him time everyday to work in you, and to keep up the link of connection between you and Himself, He cannot give you that blessing of His unbroken fellowship. Jesus Christ asks you to live in close communion with Him. Let every heart say: "O Christ, it is this I long for. It is this I choose." And He will gladly give it to you.

Absolute Surrender

And then finally, the life of the branch is a life of absolute surrender.

These words, absolute surrender, are great and solemn. I believe we do not fully understand their meaning. But yet the little branch preaches it. "Have you anything to do, little branch, besides bearing grapes?" "No, nothing."

"Are you fit for nothing?"

Fit for nothing! The Bible says that a bit of vine cannot even be used as a pen. It is fit for nothing but to be burned. "And now, what do you understand, little branch, about your relationship to the vine?" "My relationship is just this: I am utterly given up to the vine, and the vine can give me as much or as little sap as it chooses. Here I am, at its disposal, and the vine can do with me what it likes."

Oh, friends, we need this absolute surrender to the Lord Jesus Christ. The more I speak, the more I feel that this is one of the most difficult points to make clear. It is also one of the most important and needful points to explain what this absolute surrender is. It is often an easy thing for a man or a number of men to come out and offer themselves up God for entire consecration, saying: "Lord, it is my desire to give myself up entirely to You." That is of great value, and often brings very rich blessing. But the one question I ought to study quietly is: What is meant by absolute surrender?

It means that, as literally as Christ was given up entirely to God, I am given up entirely to Christ. Is that too strong? Some think so. Some think that can never be. They cannot believe that just as entirely and absolutely as Christ gave up His life to do nothing but seek the Father's pleasure, and depend on the Father absolutely and entirely, I am to do nothing but to seek the pleasure of Christ. But that is actually true. Christ Jesus came to breathe His own Spirit into us. He came to help us find our very highest happiness in living entirely for God, just as He did. Oh, beloved brethren, if that is the case, then I ought to say: "Yes, as true as it is of that little branch of the vine, by God's grace, I would have it to be true of me. I would live day by day that Christ may be able to do with me what He will."

Ah! here comes the terrible mistake that lies at the bottom of so much of our own Christianity. A man thinks: "I have my business and family duties, and my responsibilities as a citizen. All this I cannot change. And now alongside all this, I am to take Christianity and the service of God as something that will keep me from sin. God help me to perform my duties properly!"

This is not right. When Christ came, He bought the sinner with His blood. If there was a slave market here and I were to buy a slave, I would take that slave away to my own house from his old surroundings. He would live at my house as my personal property, and I could order him about all day. And if he were a faithful slave, he would live as having no will and no interests of his own. His one care would be to promote the well-being and honor of his master. And in like manner I, who have been bought with the blood of Christ, have been bought to live every day with the one thought—How can I please my Master? Oh, we find the Christian life so difficult because we seek God's blessing while we live in our own will. We desire to live the Christian life according to our own liking. We make our own plans and choose our own work. Then, we ask the Lord Jesus to come in and make sure that sin will not conquer us too much, and that we will not go too far wrong. We ask Him to come in and give us so much of His blessing. But our relationship to Jesus ought to be such that we are entirely at His disposal. Every day we are to come to Him humbly and straightforwardly and say: "Lord, is there anything in me that is not according to Your will, that has not been ordered by You, or that is not entirely given up to You?"

Oh, if we could wait patiently, I tell you what the result would be. A relationship between us and Christ would spring up. It would be so close and so tender that afterward we would be amazed at how we formerly could have lived with the idea: "I am surrendered to Christ." We would feel how distant our fellowship with Him had previously been. We would understand that He can, and does indeed, come and take actual possession of us, and give us unbroken fellowship all day. The branch calls us to absolute surrender.

Now I do not speak so much about the giving up of sins. There are people who need that, people who have got violent tempers, bad habits, and actual sins which they from time to time commit, and which they have never given up into the very bosom of the Lamb of God. I pray you, if you are branches of the living Vine, do not keep one sin back. I know there are a great many difficulties about this question of holiness. I know that all do not think exactly the same with regard to it. To me, that would be a matter of comparative indifference if I could see that all are honestly longing to be free from every sin. But I am afraid that unconsciously there are often compromises in hearts, with the idea that we cannot be without sin. There are those who think that we must sin a little every day; we cannot help it. Oh, that people would actually cry to God: "Lord, do keep me from sin!" Give yourself utterly to Jesus, and ask Him to do His very utmost for you in keeping you from sin.

There is a great deal in our work, in our church, and in our surroundings that we found in the world when we were born into it. It has grown all around us and we think that it is all right, that it cannot be changed. We do not come to the Lord Jesus and ask Him about it. Oh! I advise you, Christians, bring everything into relationship with Jesus, and say: "Lord, everything in my life has to be in most complete harmony with my position as a branch of You, the blessed Vine."

Let your surrender to Christ be absolute. I do not understand that word surrender fully. It gets new meanings every now and then. It enlarges immensely from time to time. But I advise you to speak it out: "Absolute surrender to You, Oh Christ, is what I have chosen." And Christ will show you what is not according to His mind, and lead you on to deeper and higher blessedness.

In conclusion, let me gather up all in one sentence. Christ Jesus said: "I am the Vine, ye are the branches." In other words: "I, the living One who have so completely given Myself to you, am the Vine. It is impossible to trust Me too much. I am the Almighty Worker, full of a divine life and power."

You are the branches of the Lord Jesus Christ. If there is in your heart the consciousness that you are not a strong, healthy, fruit-bearing branch—not closely linked with Jesus, not living in Him as you should be—then listen to Him say: "I am the Vine; I will receive you. I will draw you to Myself; I will bless you. I will strengthen you; I will fill you with My Spirit. I, the Vine, have taken you to be My branches. I have given Myself utterly to you; children, give yourselves utterly to Me. I have surrendered Myself as God absolutely to you. I became man and died for you that I might be entirely yours. Come and surrender yourselves entirely to be Mine."

What shall our answer be? Oh, let it be prayer from the depths of our heart, that the living Christ may take each one of us and link us closely to Himself. Let our prayer be that He, the living Vine, will so link each of us to Himself that we will go away with our hearts singing: "He is my Vine, and I am His branch—I want nothing more—now that I have the everlasting Vine."Then, when you get alone with Him, worship and adore Him; praise and trust Him; love Him and wait for His love. "You are my Vine, and I am Your branch. It is enough; my soul is satisfied."

Glory to His blessed name!

The Master's Indwelling

Table of Contents

Carnal Christians

1 Corinthians 3: 1.—And I, brethren, could not speak unto you as unto spiritual, but as unto carnal.

The apostle here speaks of two stages of the Christian life, two types of Christians: "I could not speak unto you as unto spiritual, but as unto carnal, even as unto babes in Christ." They were Christians, in Christ, but instead of being spiritual Christians, they were carnal. "I have fed you with milk, and not with meat, for hitherto ye were not able to bear it, neither yet are ye able, for ye are yet carnal." Here is that word a second time. "For whereas"—this is the proof—"there is among you envying, and strife, and divisions, are ye not carnal, and walk as men? For while one saith, I am of Paul, and another, I am of Apollos, are ye not carnal?" Four times the apostle uses that word carnal. In the wisdom which the Holy Ghost gives him, Paul feels:—I can not write to these Corinthian Christians unless I know their state, and unless I tell them of it. If I give spiritual food to men who are carnal Christians, I am doing them more harm than good, for they are not fit to take it. I cannot feed them with meat, I must feed them with milk. And so he tells them at the very outset of the epistle what he sees to be their state. In the two previous chapters he had spoken about his ministry being by the Holy Spirit; now he begins to tell them what must be the state of a people in order to accept spiritual truth, and he says: "I have not liberty to speak to you as I would, for you are carnal, and you cannot receive Spiritual truth." That suggests to us the solemn thought, that in the Church of Christ there are two classes of Christians. Some have lived many years as believers, and yet always remain babes; others are spiritual men, because they have given themselves up to the power, the leading and to the entire rule of the Holy Ghost. If we are to obtain a blessing, we must first decide to which of these classes we belong. Are we, by the grace of God, in deep humility living a spiritual life, or are we living a carnal life? Then, let us first try to understand what is meant by the carnal state in which believers may be living.

We notice from what we find in Corinthians, four marks of the carnal state. First: It is simply a condition of protracted infancy. You know what that means. Suppose a beautiful babe, six months old. It cannot speak, it cannot walk, but we do not trouble ourselves about that; it is natural, and ought to be so. But suppose a year later we find the child not grown at all, and three years later still no growth; we would at once say: "There must be some terrible disease;" and the baby that at six months old was the cause of joy to every one who saw him, has become to the mother and to all a source of anxiety and sorrow. There is something wrong; the child can not grow. It was quite right at six months old that it should eat nothing but milk; but years have passed by, and it remains in the same weakly state. Now this is just the condition of many believers. They are converted; they know what it is to have assurance and faith; they believe in pardon for sin; they begin to work for God; and yet, somehow, there is very little growth in spirituality, in the real heavenly life. We come into contact with them, and we feel at once there is something wanting; there is none of the beauty of holiness or of the power of God's Spirit in them. This is the condition of the carnal Corinthians, expressed in what was said to the Hebrews: "You have had the Gospel so long that by this time you ought to be teachers, and yet you need that men should teach you the very rudiments of the oracles of God." Is it not a sad thing to see a believer who has been converted five, ten, twenty years, and yet no growth, and no strength, and no joy of holiness?

What are the marks of a little child? One is, a little child cannot help himself, but is always keeping others occupied to serve him. What a tyrant a baby in a house often is! The mother cannot go out, there must be a servant to nurse it; it needs to be cared for constantly. God made a man to care for others, but the baby was made to be cared for and to be helped. So there are Christians who always want help. Their pastor and their Christian friends must always be teaching and comforting them. They go to church, and to prayer-meetings, and to conventions, always wanting to be helped,—a sign of spiritual infancy.

The other sign of an infant is this: he can do nothing to help his fellow-man. Every man is expected to contribute something to the welfare of society; every one has a place to fill and a work to do, but the babe can do nothing for the common weal. It is just so with Christians. How little some can do! They take a part in work, as it is called, but there is little of exercising spiritual power and carrying real blessing. Should we not each ask, "Have I outgrown my spiritual infancy?" Some must reply, "No, instead of having gone forward, I have gone backward, and the joy of conversion and the first love is gone." Alas! They are babes in Christ; they are yet carnal.

The second mark of the carnal state is this: that there is sin and failure continually. Paul says: "Whereas there is strife and division among you, and envying, are ye not carnal?" A man gives way to temper. He may be a minister, or a preacher of the Gospel, or a Sunday-school teacher, most earnest at the prayer-meeting, but yet strife or bitterness or envying is often shown by him. Alas! Alas! In Gal. 3:5 we are told that the works of the flesh are specially hatred and envy. How often among Christians, who have to work together, do we see divisions and bitterness! God have mercy upon them, that the fruit of the Spirit, which is love, is so frequently absent from His own people. You ask, "Why is it, that for twenty years I have been fighting with my temper, and can not conquer it?" It is because you have been fighting with the temper, and you have not been fighting with the root of the temper. You have not seen that it is all because you are in the carnal state, and not properly given up to the Spirit of God. It may be that you never were taught it; that you never saw it in God's Word; that you never believed it. But there it is; the truth of God remains unchangeable. Jesus Christ can give us the victory over sin, and can keep us from actual transgression. I am not telling you that the root of sin will be eradicated, and that you will have no longer any natural tendency to sin; but when the Holy Spirit comes not only with His power for service as a gift, but when He comes in Divine grace to fill the heart, there is victory over sin; power not to fulfill the lusts of the flesh. And you see a mark of the carnal state not only in unlovingness, self-consciousness and bitterness, but in so many other sins. How much worldliness, how much ambition among men, how much seeking for the honor that comes from man—all the fruit of the carnal life—to be found in the midst of Christian activity! Let us remember that the carnal state is a state of continual sinning and failure, and God wants us not only to make confession of individual sins, but to come to the acknowledgment that they are the sign that we are not living a healthy life,—we are yet carnal.

A third mark which will explain further what I have been saying, is that this carnal state may be found in existence in connection with great spiritual gifts. There is a difference between gifts and graces. The graces of the Spirit are humility and love, like the humility and love of Christ. The graces of the Spirit are to make a man free from self; the gifts of the Spirit are to fit a man for work. We see this illustrated among the Corinthians. In the first chapter Paul says, "I thank God that you are enriched unto all utterance, and all knowledge, and all wisdom." In the 12th and 14th chapters we see that the gifts of prophecy and of working miracles were in great power among them; but the graces of the Spirit were noticeably absent.

And this may be in our days as well as in the time of the Corinthians. I may be a minister of the Gospel; I may teach God's Word beautifully; I may have influence, and gather a large congregation, and yet, alas! I may be a carnal man; a man who may be used by God, and may be a blessing to others, and yet the carnal life may still mark me. You all know the law that a thing is named according to what is its most prominent characteristic. Now, in these carnal Corinthians there was a little of God's Spirit, but the flesh predominated; the Spirit had not the rule of their whole life. And the spiritual men are not called so because there is no flesh in them, but because the Spirit in them has obtained dominance, and when you meet them and have intercourse with them, you feel that the Spirit of God has sanctified them. Ah, let us beware lest the blessing God gives us in our work deceive us and lead us to think that because he has blessed us, we must be spiritual men. God may give us gifts that we use, and yet our lives may not be wholly in the power of the Holy Ghost.

My last mark of the carnal state is that it makes a man unfit for receiving spiritual truths. That is what the apostle writes to the Corinthians: "I could not preach to you as unto spiritual; you are not fit for spiritual truth after being Christians so long; you can not yet bear it; I have to feed you with milk." I am afraid that in the church of the nineteenth century we often make a terrible mistake. We have a congregation in which the majority are carnal men. We give these men spiritual teaching, and they admire it, understand it, and rejoice in such ministry; yet their lives are not practically affected. They work for Christ in a certain way, but we can scarce recognize the true sanctification of the Spirit; we dare not say they are spiritual men, full of the Holy Spirit.

Now, let us recognize this with regard to ourselves. A man may become very earnest, may take in all the teaching he hears; he may be able to discern, for discernment is a gift; he may say, "That man helps me in this line, and that man in another direction, and a third man is remarkable for another gift;" yet, all the time, the carnal life may be living strongly in him, and when he gets into trouble with some friend, or Christian worker, or worldly man, the carnal root is bearing its terrible fruit, and the spiritual food has failed to enter his heart. Beware of that. Mark the Corinthians and learn of them. Paul did not say to them, "You can not bear the truth as I would speak it to you," because they were ignorant or a stupid people. The Corinthians prided themselves on their wisdom, and sought it above everything, and Paul said:

"I thank God that you are enriched in utterance, in knowledge, and in wisdom; nevertheless, you are yet carnal, your life is not holy; your life is not sanctified unto the humility of the life of the Lamb of God, you can not yet take in real spiritual truth."

We find the carnal state not only at Corinth, but throughout the Christian world to-day. Many Christians are asking, "What is the reason there is so much feebleness in the Church?" We can not ask this question too earnestly, and I trust that God Himself will so impress it upon our hearts that we shall say to Him, "It must be changed. Have mercy upon us." But, ah! that prayer and that change can not come until we have begun to see that there is a carnal root ruling in believers; they are living more after the flesh than the Spirit; they are yet carnal Christians.

There is a passage "from carnal to spiritual." Did Paul find any spiritual believers? Undoubtedly he did. Just read the 6th chapter of the Epistle to the Galatians! That was a church where strife, and bitterness, and envy were terrible. But the apostle says in the first verse: "Brethren, if a man be overtaken in a fault, ye which are spiritual restore such an one in the spirit of meekness." There we see that the marks of the spiritual man are that he will be a meek man; and that he will have power, and love to help and restore those that are fallen. The carnal man can not do that. If there is a true spiritual life that can be lived, the great question is: Is the way open, and how can I enter into the spiritual state? Here, again, I have four short answers.

First, we must know that there is such a spiritual life to be lived by men on earth. Nothing cuts the roots of the Christian life so much as unbelief. People do not believe what God has said about what He is willing to do for His children. Men do not believe that when God says, "Be filled with the Spirit," He means it for every Christian. And yet Paul wrote to the Ephesians each one: "Be filled with the Spirit, and do not be drunk with wine." Just as little as you may be drunk with wine, so little may you live without being filled with the Spirit. Now, if God means that for believers, the first thing that we need is to study, and to take home God's Word, to our belief until our hearts are filled with the assurance that there is such a life possible which it is our duty to live; that we can be spiritual men. God's Word teaches us that God does not expect a man to live as he ought for one minute unless the Holy Spirit is in him to enable him to do it.

We do not want the Holy Spirit only when we go to preach, or when we have some special temptation of the devil to meet, or some great burden to bear; God says: "My child can not live a right life unless he is guided by my Spirit every minute." That is the mark of the child of God: "As many as are led by the Spirit of God, they are the sons of God." In Romans V. we read: "The love of God is shed abroad in our hearts by the Holy Spirit given unto us." That is to be the common, every-day experience of the believer, not his life at set times only. Did ever a father or mother think, "For to-day I want my child to love me?" No, they expect the love every day. And so God wants His child every moment to have a heart filled with love of the Spirit. In the eyes of God, it is most unnatural to expect a man to love as he should if he is not filled with the Spirit. Oh, let us believe a man can be a spiritual man. Thank God, there is now the blessing waiting us. "Be filled with the Spirit." "Be led by the Spirit." There is the blessing. If you have to say, "Oh, God, I have not this blessing," say it; but say also, "Lord, I know it is my duty, my solemn obligation to have it, for without it I can not live in perfect peace with Thee all the day; without it I can not glorify Thee, and do the work Thou wouldst have me do." This is our first step from carnal to spiritual,—to recognize a spiritual life, a walk in the Spirit, is within our reach. How can we ask God to guide us into spiritual life, if we have not a clear, confident conviction that there is such a life to be had?

Then comes the second step; a man must see the shame and guilt of his having lived such a life. Some people admit there is a spiritual life to live, and that they have not lived it, and they are sorry for themselves, and pity themselves, and think, "How sad that I am too feeble for it! How sad that God gives it to others, but has not given it to me!" They have great compassion upon themselves, instead of saying, "Alas! it has been our unfaithfulness, our unbelief, our disobedience, that has kept us from giving ourselves utterly to God. We have to blush and to be ashamed before God that we do not live as spiritual men."

A man does not get converted without having conviction of sin. When that conviction of sin comes, and his eyes are opened, he learns to be afraid of his sin, and to flee from it to Christ, and to accept Christ as a mighty deliverer. But a man needs a second conviction of sin; a believer must be convicted of his peculiar sin. The sins of an unconverted man are different from the sins of a believer. An unconverted man, for instance, is not ordinarily convicted of the corruption of his nature; he thinks principally about external sins,—"I have sworn, been a liar, and I am on the way to hell." He is then convicted for conversion. But the believer is in quite a different condition. His sins are far more blamable, for he has had the light and the love and the Spirit of God given to him. His sins are far deeper. He has striven to conquer them and he has grown to see that his nature is utterly corrupt, that the carnal mind, the flesh, within him, is making his whole state utterly wretched. When a believer is thus convicted by the Holy Spirit, it is specially his life of unbelief that condemns him, because he sees that the great guilt connected with this has kept him from receiving the full gift of God's Holy Spirit. He is brought down in shame and confusion of face, and he begins to cry: "Woe is me, for I am undone. I have heard of God by the hearing of the ear; I have known a great deal of Him and preached about Him, but now mine eye seeth Him." God comes near him. Job, the righteous man, whom God trusted, saw in himself the deep sin of self and its righteousness that he had never seen before. Until this conviction of the wrongness of our carnal state as believers comes to each one of us; until we are willing to get this conviction from God, to take time before God to be humbled and convicted, we never can become spiritual men.

Then comes the third mark, which is that out of the carnal state into the spiritual is only one step. One step; oh, that is a blessed message I bring to you—it is only one step. I know many people will refuse to admit that it is only one step; they think it too little for such a mighty change. But was not conversion only one step?

So it is when a man passes from carnal to spiritual. You ask if when I talk of a spiritual man I am not thinking of a man of spiritual maturity, a real saint, and you say: "Does that come in one day? Is there no growth in holiness?" I reply that spiritual maturity cannot come in a day. We can not expect it. It takes growth, until the whole beauty of the image of Christ is formed in a man. But still I say that it needs but one step for a man to get out of the carnal life into the spiritual life. It is when a man utterly breaks with the flesh; when he gives up the flesh into the crucifixion death of Christ; when he sees that everything about it is accursed and that he can not deliver himself from it; and then claims the slaying power of Christ's cross within him,—it is when a man does this and says: "This spiritual life prepared for me is the free gift of my God in Christ Jesus," that he understands how one step can bring him out of the carnal into the spiritual state.

In that spiritual life there will be much still to be learned. There will still be imperfections. Spiritual life is not perfect; but the predominant characteristic will be spiritual. When a man has given himself up to the real, living, acting, ruling power of God's Spirit, he has got into the right position in which he can grow. You never think of growing out of sickness into health; you may grow out of feebleness into strength, as the little babe can grow to be a strong man; but where there is disease, there must healing come if there is to be a cure effected. There are Christians who think that they must grow out of the carnal state into the spiritual state. You never can. What could help those carnal Corinthians? To give them milk could not help them, for milk was a proof they were in the wrong state. To give them meat would not help them, for they were unfit to eat it. What they needed was the knife of the surgeon. Paul says that the carnal life must be cut out. "They that are Christ's have crucified the flesh." When a man understands what that means, and accepts it in the faith of what Christ can do, then one step can bring him from carnal to spiritual. One simple act of faith in the power of Christ's death, one act of surrender to the fellowship of Christ's death as the Holy Spirit can make it ours, will make it ours, will bring deliverance from the power of your efforts.

What brought deliverance to that poor condemned sinner who was most dark and wretched in his unconverted state? He felt he could do nothing good of himself. What did he do? He saw set before him the almighty Saviour and he cast himself into His arms; he trusted himself to that omnipotent love and cried, "Lord, have mercy upon me." That was salvation. It was not for what he did that Christ accepted him. Oh, believers, if any of us who are conscious that the carnal state predominates have to say: "It marks me; I am a religious man, an earnest man, a friend of missions; I work for Christ in my church, but, alas! temper and sin and worldliness have still the mastery over my soul," hear the word of God. If any will come and say: "I have struggled, I have prayed, I have wept, and it has not helped me," then you must do one other thing. You must see that the living Christ is God's provision for your holy, spiritual life. You must believe that that Christ who accepted you once, at conversion, in His wonderful love is now waiting to say to you that you may become a spiritual man, entirely given up to God. If you will believe that, your fear will vanish and you will say: "It can be done; if Christ will accept and take charge, it shall be done."

Then, my last mark. A man must take that step, a solemn but blessed step. It cost some of you five or ten years before you took the step of conversion. You wept and prayed for years, and could not find peace until you took that step. So, in the spiritual life, you may go to teacher after teacher, and say, "Tell me about the spiritual life, the baptism of the Spirit, and holiness," and yet you may remain just where you were. Many of us would love to have sin taken away. Who loves to have a hasty temper? Who loves to have a proud disposition? Who loves to have a worldly heart? No one. We go to Christ to take it away, and he does not do it; and we ask, "Why will he not do it? I have prayed very earnestly." It is because you wanted Him to take away the ugly fruits while the poisonous root was to stay in you. You did not ask Him that the flesh should be nailed to His cross, and that you should henceforth give up self entirely to the power of His Spirit.

There is deliverance, but not in the way we seek it. Suppose a painter had a piece of canvas, on which he desired to work out some beautiful picture. Suppose that piece of canvas does not belong to him, and any one has a right to take it and to use it for any other purpose; do you think the painter would bestow much work on that? No. Yet people want Jesus Christ to bestow His trouble upon them in taking away this temper, or that other sin, though in their hearts they have not yielded themselves utterly to His command and His keeping. It can not be. But if you will come and give your whole life into His charge, Christ Jesus is mighty to save; Christ Jesus waits to be gracious; Christ Jesus waits to fill you with His Spirit.

Will you not take the step? God grant that we may be led by His Spirit to a yielding up of ourselves to Him as never before. Will you not come in humble confession that, alas! the carnal life has predominated too much, has altogether marked you, and that you have a bitter consciousness that with all the blessing God has bestowed, He has not made you what you want to be—a spiritual man? It is the Holy Spirit alone who by His indwelling can make a spiritual man. Come then and cast yourself at God's feet, with this one thought, "Lord, I give myself an empty vessel to be filled with Thy Spirit." Each one of you sees every day at the tea table an empty cup set there, waiting to be filled with tea when the proper time comes. So with every dish, every plate. They are cleansed and empty, ready to be filled. Emptied and cleansed. Oh, come! and just as a vessel is set apart to receive what it is to contain, say to Christ that you desire from this hour to be a vessel set apart to be filled with His Spirit, given up to be a spiritual man. Bow down in the deepest emptiness of soul, and say, "Oh, God, I have nothing!" and then surely as you place yourself before Him you have a right to say, "My God will fulfill His promise! I claim from Him the filling of the Holy Spirit to make me, instead of a carnal, a spiritual Christian." If you place yourself at His feet, and tarry there; if you abide in that humble surrender and that childlike trust, as sure as God lives the blessing will come.

Oh, have we not to bow in shame before God, as we think of His whole Church and see so much of the carnal prevailing? Have we not to bow in shame before God, as we think of so much of the carnal in our hearts and lives? Then let us bow in great faith in God's mercy. Deliverance is nigh, deliverance is coming, deliverance is waiting, deliverance is sure. Let us trust; God will give it.

The Self Life

Matt. 16: 24.—If any man will come after me, let him deny himself, and take up his cross, and follow me.

In the 13th verse we read that Jesus at Caesarea Philippi asked His disciples, "Whom do men say that I, the Son of Man, am?" When they had answered, He asked them, "But whom say ye that I am?" And in verse 16 Peter answered and said, "Thou art the Christ, the Son of the Living God." Jesus answered and said unto him: "Blessed art thou, Simon Barjonas, for flesh and blood hath not revealed it unto thee, but my Father which is in Heaven. And I say also unto thee that thou art Peter, and upon this rock I will build my church and the gates of hell shall not prevail against it." Then in verse 21 we read how Jesus began to tell His disciples of His approaching death; and in verse 22 how Peter began to rebuke Him, saying, "Be it far from Thee, Lord; this shall not be unto Thee." But Jesus turned and said unto Peter, "Get thee behind me, Satan; thou art an offense unto me, for thou savorest not the things that be of God, but those that be of men." Then said Jesus unto His disciples, "If any man will come after me, let him deny himself, and take up his cross and follow me."

We often hear about the compromise life and the question comes up What lies at the root of it? What is the reason that so many Christians are wasting their lives in the terrible bondage of the world instead of living in the manifestation and the privilege and the glory of the child of God? And another question perhaps comes to us: What can be the reason that when we see a thing is wrong and strive against it we cannot conquer it? What can be the reason that we have a hundred times prayed and vowed, yet here we are still living a mingled, divided, half-hearted life? To those two questions there is one answer: it is self that is the root of the whole trouble. And therefore, if any one asks me, "How can I get rid of this compromise life?" the answer would not be, "You must do this, or that, or the other thing," but the answer would be, "A new life from above, the life of Christ, must take the place of the self-life; then alone can we be conquerors."

We always go from the outward to the inward; let us do so here; let us consider from these words of the text the one word, "self." Jesus said to Peter: "If any man will come after me let him deny himself, his own self, and take up the cross and follow me." That is a mark of the disciple; that is the secret of the Christian life—deny self and all will come right. Note that Peter was a believer, and a believer who had been taught by the Holy Spirit. He had given an answer that pleased Christ wonderfully: "Thou art the Christ, the Son of the living God." Do not think that that was nothing extraordinary. We learn it in our catechisms; Peter did not; and Christ saw that the Holy Spirit of the Father had been teaching him and He said: "Blessed art thou, Simon Barjonas." But note how strong the carnal man still is in Peter. Christ speaks of His cross; He could understand about the glory, "Thou art the Son of God;" but about the cross and the death he could not understand, and he ventured in his self-confidence to say, "Lord, that shall never be; Thou canst not be crucified and die." And Christ had to rebuke him: "Get thee behind me, Satan. Thou savorest not the things that be of God." You are talking like a mere carnal man, and not as the Spirit of God would teach you. Then Christ went on to say, "Remember, it is not only I who am to be crucified, but you; it is not only I who am to die, but you also. If a man would be my disciple, he must deny self, and he must take up his cross and follow me." Let us dwell upon this one word, "self." It is only as we learn to know what self is that we really know what is at the root of all our failure, and are prepared to go to Christ for deliverance.

Let us consider, first of all, the nature of this self life, then denote some of its works and then ask the question: "How may we be delivered from it?"

Self is the power with which God has created and endowed every intelligent creature. Self is the very center of a created being. And why did God give the angels or man a self? The object of this self was that we might bring it as an empty vessel unto God; that He might put into it His life. God gave me the power of self-determination, that I might bring this self every day and say: "Oh, God, work in it; I offer it to thee." God wanted a vessel into which He might pour out His divine fullness of beauty, wisdom and power; and so He created the world, the sun, and the moon, and the stars, the trees, and the flowers, and the grass, which all show forth the riches of His wisdom, and beauty, and goodness. But they do it without knowing what they do. Then God created the angels with a self and a will, to see whether they would come and voluntarily yield themselves to Him as vessels for Him to fill. But alas! they did not all do that. There was one at the head of a great company, and he began to look upon himself, and to think of the wonderful powers with which God had endowed him, and to delight in himself. He began to think: "Must such a being as I always remain dependent on God?" He exalted himself, pride asserted itself in separation from God, and that very moment he became, instead of an angel in Heaven, a devil in hell. Self turned to God is the glory of allowing the Creator to reveal Himself in us. Self turned away from God is the very darkness and fire of hell.

We all know the terrible story of what took place further; God created man, and Satan came in the form of a serpent and tempted Eve with the thought of becoming as God, having an independent self, knowing good and evil. And while he spoke with her, he breathed into her, in those words, the very poison and the very pride of hell. His own evil spirit, the very poison of hell, entered humanity, and it is this cursed self that we have inherited from our first parents. It was that self that ruined and brought destruction upon this world, and all that there has been of sin, and of darkness, and of wretchedness, and of misery; and all that there will be throughout the countless ages of eternity in hell, will be nothing but the reign of self, the curse of self, separating man and turning him away from his God. And if we are to understand fully what Christ is to do for us, and are to become partakers of a full salvation, we must learn to know, and to hate, and to give up entirely this cursed self.

Now what are the works of self? I might mention many, but let us take the simplest words that we are continually using,—self-will, self-confidence, self-exaltation. Self-will, pleasing self, is the great sin of man, and it is at the root of all that compromising with the world which is the ruin of so many. Men can not understand why they should not please themselves and do their own will. Numbers of Christians have never gotten hold of the idea that a Christian is a man who is never to seek his own will, but is always to seek the will of God, as a man in whom the very spirit of Christ lives. "Lo, I come to do Thy will, oh, my God!" We find Christians pleasing themselves in a thousand ways, and yet trying to be happy, and good, and useful; and they do not know that at the root of it all is self-will robbing them of the blessing. Christ said to Peter, "Peter, deny yourself." But instead of doing that, Peter said, "I will deny my Lord and not myself." He never said it in words, but Christ said to him in the last night, "Thou shalt deny Me," and he did it. What was the cause of this? Self-pleasing. He became afraid when the woman servant charged him with belonging to Jesus, and three times said, "I know not this man, I have nothing to do with Him." He denied Christ. Just think of it! No wonder Peter wept those bitter tears. It was a choice between self, that ugly, cursed self, and that beautiful, blessed Son of God; and Peter chose self. No wonder that he thought: "Instead of denying myself, I have denied Jesus; what a choice I have made!" No wonder that he wept bitterly.

Christians, look at your own lives in the light of the words of Jesus. Do you find there self-will, self-pleasing? Remember this: every time you please yourself, you deny Jesus. It is one of the two. You must please Him only, and deny self, or you must please yourself and deny Him. Then follows self-confidence, self-trust, self-effort, self-dependence. What was it that led Peter to deny Jesus? Christ had warned him; why did he not take warning? Self-confidence. He was so sure: "Lord, I love Thee. For three years I have followed Thee. Lord, I deny that it ever can be. I am ready to go to prison and to death." It was simply self-confidence. People have often asked me, "What is the reason I fail? I desire so earnestly, and pray so fervently, to live in God's will." And my answer generally is, "Simply because you trust yourself." They answer me: "No, I do not; I know I am not good; and I know that God is willing to keep me, and I put my trust in Jesus." But I reply, "No, my brother; no; if you trusted God and Jesus, you could not fall, but you trust yourself." Do let us believe that the cause of every failure in the Christian life is nothing but this. I trust this cursed self, instead of trusting Jesus. I trust my own strength, instead of the almighty strength of God. And that is why Christ says, "This self must be denied."

Then there is self-exaltation, another form of the works of self. Ah, how much pride and jealousy is there in the Christian world; how much sensitiveness to what men say of us or think of us; how much desire of human praise and pleasing men, instead of always living in the presence of God, with the one thought: "Am I pleasing to Him?" Christ said, "How can ye believe who receive honor one of another?" Receiving honor of one another renders a life of faith absolutely impossible. This self started from hell, it separated us from God, it is a cursed deceiver that leads us astray from Jesus.

Now comes the third point. What are we to do to get rid of it? Jesus answers us in the words of our text: "If any man will come after me, let him take up his cross and follow me." Note it well.—I must deny myself and take Jesus himself as my life,—I must choose. There are two lives, the self life and the Christ life; I must choose one of the two. "Follow me," says our Lord, "make me the law of your existence, the rule of your conduct; give me your whole heart; follow me, and I will care for all." Oh, friends, it is a solemn exchange to have set before us; to come and, seeing the danger of this self, with its pride and its wickedness, to cast ourselves before the Son of God, and to say, "I deny my own life, I take Thy life to be mine."

The reason why Christians pray and pray for the Christ life to come in to them, without result, is that the self life is not denied. You ask, "How can I get rid of this self life?" You know the parable: the strong man kept his house until one stronger than he came in and cast him out. Then the place was garnished and swept, but empty, and he came back with seven other spirits worse than himself. It is only Christ Himself coming in that can cast out self, and keep out self. This self will abide with us to the very end. Remember the Apostle Paul; he had seen the Heavenly vision, and lest he should exalt himself, the thorn in the flesh was sent to humble him. There was a tendency to exalt himself, which was natural, and it would have conquered, but Christ delivered him from it by His faithful care for His loving servant. Jesus Christ is able, by His divine grace, to prevent the power of self from ever asserting itself or gaining the upper hand; Jesus Christ is willing to become the life of the soul; Jesus Christ is willing to teach us so to follow Him, and to have heart and life set upon Him alone, that He shall ever and always be the light of our souls. Then we come to what the apostle Paul says; "Not I, but Christ liveth in me." The two truths go together. First "Not I," then, "but Christ liveth in me."

Look at Peter again. Christ said to him, "Deny yourself, and follow me." Whither had he to follow? Jesus led him, even though he failed; and where did he lead him? He led him on to Gethsemane, and there Peter failed, for he slept when he ought to have been awake, watching and praying; He led him on towards Calvary, to the place where Peter denied Him. Was that Christ's leading? Praise God, it was. The Holy Spirit had not yet come in His power; Peter was yet a carnal man; the Spirit willing, but not able to conquer; the flesh weak. What did Christ do? He led Peter on until he was broken down in utter self-abasement, and humbled in the depths of sorrow. Jesus led him on, past the grave, through the Resurrection, up to Pentecost, and the Holy Spirit came, and in the Holy Spirit Christ with His divine life came, and then it was, "Christ liveth in me."

There is but one way of being delivered from this life of self. We must follow Christ, set our hearts upon Him, listen to His teachings, give ourselves up every day, that He may be all to us, and by the power of Christ the denial of self will be a blessed, unceasing reality. Never for one hour do I expect the Christian to reach a stage at which he can say, "I have no self to deny;" never for one moment in which he can say, "I do not need to deny self." No, this fellowship with the cross of Christ will be an unceasing denial of self every hour and every moment by the grace of God. There is no place where there is full deliverance from the power of this sinful self. We are to be crucified with Christ Jesus. We are to live with Him as those who have never been baptized into His death. Think of that! Christ had no sinful self, but He had a self and that self He actually gave up unto death. In Gethsemane He said, "Father, not My will." That unsinning self He gave up unto death that He might receive it again out of the grave from God, raised up and glorified. Can we expect to go to Heaven in any other way than He went? Beware! remember that Christ descended into death and the grave, and it is in the death of self, following Jesus to the uttermost, that the deliverance and the life will come.

And now, what is the use that we are to make of this lesson of the Master? The first lesson will be that we should take time, and that we should humble ourselves before God, at the thought of what this self is in us; put down to the account of the self every sin, every shortcoming, all failure, and all that has been dishonoring to God, and then say, "Lord, this is what I am;" and then let us allow the blessed Jesus Christ to take entire control of our life, in the faith that His life can be ours.

Do not think it is an easy thing to get rid of self. At a consecration meeting, it is easy to make a vow, and to offer a prayer, and to perform an act of surrender, but as solemn as the death of Christ was on Calvary—His giving up of His unsinning self life to God,—just as solemn must it be between us and our God—the giving up of self to death. The power of the death of Christ must come to work in us every day. Oh, think what a contrast between that self-willed Peter, and Jesus giving up His will to God! What a contrast between that self-exaltation of Peter, and the deep humility of the Lamb of God, meek and lowly in heart before God and man! What a contrast between that self-confidence of Peter, and that deep dependence of Jesus upon the Father, when He said: "I can do nothing of myself." We are called upon to live the life of Christ, and Christ comes to live His life in us; but one thing must first take place; we must learn to hate this self, and to deny it. As Peter said, when he denied Christ, "I have nothing to do with him," so we must say, "I have nothing to do with self," that Christ Jesus may be all in all. Let us humble ourselves at the thought of what this self has done to us and how it has dishonored Jesus; and let us pray very fervently: "Lord, by Thy light discover this self; we beseech Thee to discover it to us. Open our eyes, that we may see what it has done, and that it is the only hindrance that has been keeping us back." Let us pray that fervently, and then let us wait upon God until we get away from all our religious exercises, and from all our religious experience, and from all our blessings, until we get close to God, with this one prayer: "Lord God, self changed an archangel into a devil, and self ruined my first parents, and brought them out of Paradise into darkness and misery, and self has been the ruin of my life and the cause of every failure; oh, discover it to me." And then comes the blessed exchange, that a man is made willing and able to say: "Another will live the life for me, another will live with me, another will do all for me," Nothing else will do. Deny self; take up the cross, to die with Jesus; follow Him only. May He give us the grace to understand, and to receive, and to live the Christ life.

Waiting on God

Psalms 62: 5.—My soul, wait thou only upon God, for my expectation is from Him.

The solemn question comes to us, "Is the God I have, a God that is to me above all circumstances, nearer to me than any circumstance can be?" Brother, have you learned to live your life having God so really with you every moment, that in circumstances the most difficult He is always more present and nearer than anything around you? All our knowledge of God's Word will help us very little, unless that comes to be the question to which we get an answer.

What can be the reason that so many of God's beloved children complain continually: "My circumstances separate me from God; my trials, my temptations, my character, my temper, my friends, my enemies, anything can come between my God and me?" Is God not able so to take possession that He can be nearer to me than anything in the world? Must riches or poverty, joy or sorrow, have a power over me that my God has not? No. But why, then, do God's children so often complain that their circumstances separate them from Him? There can be but one answer, "They do not know their God." If there is trouble or feebleness in the Church of God, it is because of this. We do not know the God we have. That is why in addition to the promise, "I will be thy God," the promise is so often added, "And ye shall know that I am your God." If I know that, not through man's teaching, not with my mind or my imagination; but if I know that, in the living evidence which God gives in my heart, then I know that the divine presence of my God will be so wonderful, and my God Himself will be so beautiful, and so near, that I can live all my days and years a conqueror through Him that loved me. Is not that the life which we need?

The question comes again: Why is it that God's people do not know their God? And the answer is: They take anything rather than God,—ministers, and preaching, and books, and prayers, and work, and efforts, any exertion of human nature, instead of waiting, and waiting long if need be, until God reveals Himself. No teaching that we may get, and no effort that we may put forth, can put us in possession of this blessed light of God, all in all to our souls. But still it is attainable, it is within reach, if God will reveal Himself. That is the one necessity. I would to God that every one would ask his heart whether he has said, and is saying every day: "I want more of God. Do not speak to me only of the beautiful truth there is in the Bible. That can not satisfy me. I want God." In our inner Christian life, in our every-day prayers, in our Christian living, in our churches, in our prayer-meetings, in our fellowship, it must come to that—that God always has the first place; and if that be given Him, He will take possession. Oh, if in our lives as individuals every eye were set upon God, upon the living God, every heart were crying, "My soul thirsteth for God," what power, what blessing and what presence of the everlasting God would be revealed to us! Let me use an illustration. When a man is giving an illustrated lecture he often uses a long pointer to indicate places on a map or chart. Do the people look at that pointer? No, that only helps to show them the place on the map, and they do not think of it,—it might be of fine gold; but the pointer can not satisfy them. They want to see what the pointer points at. And this Bible is nothing but a pointer, pointing to God; and,—may I say it with reverence—Jesus Christ came to point us, to show us the way, to bring us to God. I am afraid there are many people who love Christ and who trust in Him, but who fail of the one great object of His work; they have never learned to understand what the Scripture saith: "He died, that He might bring us unto God."

There is a difference between the way and the end which I am aiming at. I might be traveling amid most beautiful scenery, in the most delightful company; but if I have a home to which I want to go, all the scenery, and all the company, and all the beauty and happiness around me can not satisfy me; I want to reach the end; I want my home. And God is meant to be the home of our souls. Christ came into the world to bring us back to God, and unless we take Christ for what God intended we should, our religion will always be a divided one. What do we read in Hebrews vii? "He is able to save to the uttermost."—Whom? "Them that come to God by Him;" not them that only come to Christ. In Christ—bless His name—we have the graciousness, the condescension, and the tenderness of God. But we are in danger of standing there, and being content with that, and Christ wants to bring us back to rejoice as much as in the glory of God Himself, in His righteousness, His holiness, His authority, His presence and His power. He can save completely those who come to God through Him!

Now, just a very few thoughts on the way by which I can come to know God as this God above all circumstances, filling my heart and life every day. The one thing needful is: I must wait upon God. The original is,—it is in our Dutch version, and it is in the margin, too,—"My soul is silent into God." What ought to be the silence of the soul unto God? A soul conscious of its littleness, its ignorance, its prejudices and its dangers from passion, from all that is human and sinful,—a soul conscious of that, and saying, "I want the everlasting God to come in and to take hold of me and to take such hold of me that I may be kept in the hollow of His hand for my life long; I want Him to take such possession of me that every moment He may work all in all in me." That is what is implied in the very nature of our God. How we ought to be silent unto Him, and wait upon Him!

May I ask, with reverence: What is God for? A God is for this: to be the light and the life of creation, the source and power of all existence. The beautiful trees, the green grass, the bright sun, God created that they might show forth His beauty, His wisdom and His glory. The tree of one hundred years old—when it was planted God did not give it a stock of life by which to carry on its existence. Nay, verily, God clothes the lilies every year afresh with their beauty; every year God clothes the tree with its foliage and its fruit. Every day and every hour it is God who maintains the life of all nature. And God created us, that we might be the empty vessels in which He could work out His beauty, His will, His love, and the likeness of His blessed Son. That is what God is for, to work in us by His mighty operation, without one moment's ceasing. When I begin to get hold of that, I no longer think of the true Christian life as a high impossibility, and an unnatural thing, but I say, "It is the most natural thing in creation that God should have me every moment, and that my God should be nearer to me than all else." Just think, for a moment, what folly it is to imagine that I can not expect God to be with me every moment. Just look at the sunshine; have you ever had any trouble as you were working or as you were studying or reading a book in the light the sun gives? Have you ever said, "Oh, how can I keep that light, how can I hold it fast, how can I be sure that I shall continue to have it to use?" You never thought that. God has taken care that the sun itself should provide you with light, and without your care; the light comes unbidden. And I ask you: What think you? Has God arranged that the light of that sun that will one day be burned up, can come to you unconsciously and abide in you blessedly and mightily; and is God not willing, or is He not able, to let His light and His presence so shine through you that you can walk all the day with God nearer to you than anything in nature? Praise God for the assurance; He can do it.

And why does He not do it? Why so seldom, and why in such feeble measure? There is but one answer: you do not let Him. You are so occupied and filled with other things, religious things, preaching and praying, studying and working, so occupied with your religion, that you do not give God the time to make Himself known, and to enter in and to take possession. Oh, brother, listen to the word of the man who knew God so well, and begin to say: "My soul, wait thou only upon God."

I might show that this is the very glory of the Creator, the very life Christ brought into the world, the life He lived, and the very life Christ wants to lift us up to in its entire dependence on the Father. The very secret of the Christ-life is this: such a consciousness of God's presence that whether it was Judas, who came to betray Him, or Caiaphas, who condemned Him unjustly, or Pilate, who gave Him up to be crucified, the presence of the Father was upon Him, and within Him, and around Him, and man could not touch His spirit. And that is what God wants to be to you and to me. Does not all your anxious restlessness, and futile effort, prove that you have not let God do His work? God is drawing you to Himself. This is not your own wish, and the stirring of your own heart, but the everlasting Divine magnet is drawing you. These restless yearnings and thirstings, remember, are the work of God. Come and be still, and wait upon God. He will reveal Himself.

And how am I to wait on God? In answer I would say: first of all, in prayer take more time to be still before God without saying one word. What is, in prayer, the most important thing? That I catch the ear of Him to whom I speak. We are not ready to offer our petition until we are fully conscious of having secured the attention of God. You tell me you know all that. Yes, you know it; but you need to have your heart filled by the Holy Spirit with the holy consciousness that the everlasting, almighty God is indeed come very near you. The loving one is longing to have you for His own. Be still before God, and wait, and say: "Oh, God, take possession. Reveal Thyself, not to my thoughts or imaginations, but by the solemn, awe-bringing, soul-subduing consciousness that God is shining upon me bring me to the place of dependence and humility."

Prayer may be indeed waiting upon God, but there is a great deal of prayer that is not waiting upon God. Waiting on God is the first and the best beginning for prayer. When we bow in the humble, silent acknowledgment of God's glory and nearness, ere we begin to pray there will be the very blessing that we often get only at the end. From the very beginning I come face to face with God; I am in touch with the everlasting omnipotence of love and I know my God will bless me. Let us never be afraid to be still before

God; we shall then carry that stillness into our work; and when we go to church on Sunday, or to the prayer-meeting on week-days, it will be with the one desire that nothing may stand betwixt us and God, and that we may never be so occupied with hearing and listening as to forget the presence of God.

Oh, that God might make every minister what Moses was at the foot of Mount Sinai; "Moses led the people out to meet God," and they did meet Him until they were afraid. Let every minister ask with all the earnestness his soul can command, that God may deliver him from the sin of preaching and teaching without making the people feel first of all: "The man wants to bring us to God Himself." It can be felt, not only in the words, but in the very disposition of the humble, waiting, worshiping heart. We must carry this waiting into all our worship; we will have to make a study of it; we will have to speak about it; we will have to help each other, for the truth has been too much lost in the Church of Christ; we must wait upon God about it. Then we shall be able to carry it out into our daily life. There are so many Christians who wonder that they fail; but think of the ease with which they talk and join in conversation, spending hours in it, never thinking that all this may be dissipating the soul's power and leading them to spend hours not in the immediate presence of God. I am afraid this is the great difficulty: that we are not willing to make the needed sacrifice for a life of continual waiting upon God. Are there not some of us who would feel it an impossibility to spend every moment under the covering of the Most High, "in the secret of His pavilion?" Beloved, do not think it too high, or too difficult. It is too difficult for you and me to attain, but our God will give it to us. Let us begin even now to wait more earnestly and intensely upon God. Let us in our homes sometimes bow a little in silence; let us in our closets wait in silence, and make a covenant, it may be, without words, that with our whole hearts we will seek God's presence to come in upon us.

What is religion? Just as much as you have of God working in you, that alone is religion. And if you want more religion, more grace, more strength and more fruitfulness, you must have more of God. Let that be the cry of our hearts,—More of God! More of God! More of God! And let us say to our souls, "My soul, wait thou upon God, for my expectation is from Him."

Entrance into Rest

Hebrews 4: 1.—Let us therefore fear, lest, a promise being left us of entering into His rest, any of you should seem to come short of it.

Hebrews 4: 11.—Let us labor therefore to enter into that rest, lest any man fall after the same example of unbelief.

I want, in the simplest way possible, to answer the question: "How does a man enter into that rest?" and to point out the simple steps that he takes, all included in the one act of surrender and faith.

And the first step, I think, is this: that a man learns to say, "I believe, heartily, there is rest in a life of faith." Israel passed through two stages. This is beautifully expressed in the fifth of Deuteronomy: "He brought us out, that He might bring us in"—two parts of God's work of redemption—"He brought us out from Egypt, that He might bring us into Canaan." And that is applicable to every believer. At your conversion, God brought you out of Egypt, and the same almighty God is longing to bring you into the Canaan life. You know how God brought the Israelites out, but they would not let Him bring them in and they had to wander for forty years in the wilderness—the type, alas! of so many Christians. God brings them out in conversion, but they will not let Him bring them in into all that He has prepared for them. To a man who asks me, "How can I enter into the rest?" I say, first of all, speak this word, "I do believe that there is a rest into which Jesus, our Joshua, can bring a trusting soul." And if you would know what the difference is between the two lives—the life you have been leading, and the life you now want to lead, just look at the wilderness and Canaan. What are the points of difference? In the wilderness, wandering for forty years, backward and forward; in Canaan, perfect rest in the land that God gave them. That is the difference between the life of a Christian who has, and one who has not entered into Canaan. In wandering backward and forward; going after the world, and coming back and repenting; led astray by temptation, and returning only to go off again;—a life of ups and downs. In Canaan, on the other hand, a life of rest, because the soul has learned to trust: "God keeps me every hour in His mighty power." There is the second difference: the life in the wilderness was a life of want; in Canaan, a life of plenty. In the wilderness there was nothing to eat; there was often no water. God graciously supplied their wants by the manna, and the water from the rock. But, alas! they were not content with this, and their life was one of want and murmurings. But in Canaan God gave them vineyards that they had not planted, and the old corn of the land was there waiting for them; a land flowing with milk and honey; a land that lived by the rain of Heaven and had the very care of God Himself. Oh, Christian, come and say to-day, "I believe there is a possibility of such a change out of that life of spiritual death, and darkness, and sadness, and complaining, that I have often lived, into the land of supply of every want; where the grace of Jesus is proved sufficient every day, every hour." Say to-day: "I believe in the possibility that there is such a land of rest for me."

And then, the third difference: In the wilderness there was no victory. When they tried, after they had sinned at Kadesh, to go up against their enemies, they were defeated. In the land they conquered every enemy; from Jericho onward, they went from victory to victory. And so God waits, and Christ waits, and the Holy Spirit waits, to give victory every day; not freedom from temptation; no, not that; but in union with Christ a power that can say, "I can do all things through Him that strengtheneth me." "We are more than conquerors through Him that loved us." May God help every heart to say that.

Then comes the second step. I want you to say not only, "I believe there is such a life," but, second, "I have not had it yet." Say that. "I have never yet got that." Some may say, "I have sought it;" some may say, "I have never heard about it;" some may say, "At times I thought I had found it, but I lost it again." Let every one be honest with God.

And now, will all who have never yet found it honestly, begin to say, "Lord, up to this time I have never had it?" And why is it of such consequence to speak thus? Because, dear friends, some people want to glide into this life of rest gradually; and just quietly to steal in; and God won't have it. Your life in the wilderness has not only been a life of sadness to yourself, but of sin and dishonor to God. Every deeper entrance into salvation must always be by the way of conviction and confession; therefore, let every Christian be willing to say: "Alas! I have not lived that life, and I am guilty; I have dishonored God; I have been like Israel; I have provoked Him to wrath by my unbelief and disobedience. God have mercy upon me!" Oh, let it go up before God—the secret confession: "I haven't it; alas! I have not glorified God by a life in the land of rest."

Then comes the third word I want you to speak and that is: "Thank God, that life is for me." Some say, "I believe there is such a life, but not for me." There are people who continually say: "Oh, my character is so unstable; my will is naturally very weak; my temperament is nervous and excitable, it is impossible for me always to live without worry, resting in God." Beloved brother, do not say that. You say so only for one reason: You do not know what your God will do for you. Do begin to look away from self, and to look up to God, Take that precious word: "He brought them out that he might bring them in." The God who took them through the Red Sea was the God who took them through Jordan into Canaan. The God who converted you is the God who is able to give you every day this blessed life. Oh, begin to say, with the beginnings of a feeble faith, even before you claim it, begin even intellectually to say: "It is for me; I do believe that. God does not disinherit any of His children. What He gives is for every one. I believe that blessed life is waiting for me. It is meant for me. God is waiting to bestow it, and to work it in me. Glory be to His blessed name! My soul says it is for me, too." Oh, take that little word "me," and looking up in the very face of God dare to say: "This inestimable treasure—it is for me, the weakest and the unworthiest; it is for me." Have you said that? Say it now: "This life is possible to me, too."

And then comes the next step, and that is: "I can never, by any effort of mine, grasp it; it is God must bestow it on me." I want you to be very bold in saying, "It is for me." But then I want you to fall down very low and say, "I can not seize it; I can not take it to myself." And how can you then get it? Praise God, if once He has brought you down in the consciousness of utter helplessness and self-despair, then comes the time that He can draw nigh and ask you, "Will you trust your God to work this in you?" Dearly beloved Christians, say in your heart: "I never, by any effort, can take hold of God, or seize this for myself; it is God must give it." Cherish this blessed impotence. It is He who brought us out, who Himself must bring us in. It is your greatest happiness to be impotent. Pray God by the Holy Spirit to reveal to you this true impotence, and that will open the way for your faith to say, "Lord, Thou must do it, or it will never be done." God will do it. People wonder, when they hear so many sermons about faith, and such earnest pleading to believe, and ask why it is they can not believe. There is just one answer: It is self. Self is working; is trying; is struggling, and self must fail. But when you come to the end of self and can only cry, "Lord, help me! Lord, help me!"—then the deliverance is nigh; believe that. It was God brought the people in. It is God who will bring you in.

One should be willing, for the sake of this rest, to give up everything. The grace of God is very free. It is given without money and without price. And yet, on the other hand, Jesus said that every man who wants the pearl of great price must sacrifice his all, must sell all that he has to buy that pearl. It is not enough to see the beauty, the attractiveness and the glory, and almost to taste the gladness and the joy of this wonderful life as it has been set before you. You must become the possessor, the owner of the field. The man who found the field with a treasure, and the man who found the great pearl, were both glad; but they had not yet got it. They had found it, seen it, desired it, rejoiced in it; but they had not yet got it. Not until they went and sold all, gave up everything, and bought the ground, and bought the pearl. Ah, friends, there is a great deal that has to be given up: the world, its pleasures, its favor, its good opinion. You are to stand to the world in the same relation as Jesus did. The world rejected Him, and cast Him out, and you are to take up the position of your Lord, to whom you belong, and to follow with the rejected Christ. You have to give up everything. You have to give up all that is good in yourself and to be humbled in the dust of death. And that is not all. Your past religious life and experience and successes—you have to give all up and become nothing, that God alone may have the glory. God has brought you out in conversion; it was God's own life given you: but you defiled it with disobedience and with unbelief. Give it all up. Give up all your own wisdom, and your own thoughts about God's work. How hard it is for the minister of the Gospel to give up all his wisdom, and to lay it at the feet of Jesus, to become a fool and to say: "Lord, I know nothing as I should know it. I have been preaching the Gospel, and how little I have seen of the glory of the blessed land, and the blessed life!"

Why is it that the blessed Spirit can not teach us more effectually? No reason but this: the wisdom of man prevents it; the wisdom of man prevents the light of God from shining in. And so we could say of other things; give up all. Some may have an individual sin to give up. There may be a Christian man who is angry with his brother. There may be a Christian woman who has quarreled with her neighbor. There may be friends who are not living as they should. There may be Christians holding fast some little doubtful thing, not willing to surrender and leave behind the whole of the wilderness life and lust. Oh, do take this step and say: "I am ready to give up everything to have this pearl of great price; my time, my attention, my business, I count all subordinate to this rest of God as the first thing in my life; I yield all to walk in perfect fellowship with God." You can not get that and live every day in perfect fellowship with God, without giving up time to it. You take time for everything. How many hours a day has a young lady spent for years and years that she may become proficient on the piano? How many years does a young man study to fit himself for the profession of the law or medicine? Hours, and days, and weeks, and months, and years, gladly given up to perfect himself for his profession. And do you expect that religion is so cheap that without giving time you can find close fellowship with God? You can not. But, oh, my brothers and sisters, the pearl of great price is worth everything. God is worth everything. Christ is worth everything. Oh, come to-day, and say, "Lord, at any cost help me; I do want to live this life." And if you find it difficult to say this, and if there is a struggle within the heart, never mind; say to God, "Lord, I thought I was willing, but I see how much unwillingness there is; come and discover what the evil is still in the heart." By His grace, if you will lie at His feet and trust Him you may depend upon it deliverance will come.

Then comes the next step, and that is to say: "I do now give up myself to the holy and everlasting God, for Him to lead me into this perfect rest." Ah, friends, we must learn to meet God face to face. My sin has been against God. David felt that when he said, "Against Thee, Thee only, have I sinned." It is God on the judgment seat whose face you will have to meet personally. It is God Himself, personally, who met you to pardon your sins. Come to-day and put yourself into the hands of the living God. God is love. God is near. God is waiting to give you His blessing. The heart of God is yearning over you. "My child," God says, "you think you are longing for rest; it is I that am longing for you, because I desire to rest in your heart as My home, as My temple." You need your God. Yes, but your God needs you, to find the full satisfaction of His Father heart in Christ in you. Come to-day and say: "I do now give up myself to Christ. I have made the choice. I deliberately say, 'Lord God, I am the purchaser of the pearl of great price. I give up everything for it. In the name of Jesus I accept that life of perfect rest.'"

And then comes my last thought. When you have said that, then add: "And now, I trust God to make it all real to me in my experience. Whether I am to live one year, or thirty years, I have heard it to-day again: 'God is Jehovah, the great I AM of the everlasting future, the eternal One; and thirty years hence is to Him just the same as now;' and that God gives Himself to me, not according to my power to hold Him, but according to His almighty power of love to hold me." Will you trust God to-day for the future? Oh, will you look up to God in Christ Jesus once again? A thousand times you have heard, and thought, and thanked—"God has given us His Son;" but will you not to-day say, "How shall He not with Him give me all things, every moment and every day of my life?" Say that in faith. "How shall God not be willing to keep me in the light of His countenance, in the full experience of Christ's saving power? Did God make the sun to shine so brightly, and is the light so willing to pour itself into every nook and corner where it can find entrance? And will not my God, who is love, be willing all the day to shine into this heart of mine, from morning to night, from year's end to year's end?" God is love, and longs to give Himself to us.

Oh, come, Christians, you have hitherto lived a life in your own strength. Will you not begin to-day? Will you not choose a life in which God shall be all, and in which you rest in Him for all? Will you not choose a life in which you shall say: "Oh, God, I ask, I expect, I trust Thee for it. I enter this day into the rest of God to let God keep me; to let God keep me every hour. I enter into the rest of God." Are you ready to say that? Be of good courage; fear not, you can trust God. He brings into rest. Listen to God's word in the Prophets once again: "Take heed, and be quiet. Fear not, neither be faint-hearted." Joshua brought Israel into the land. God did it through Joshua; and Joshua is Jesus, your Jesus, who washed you in His blood; your Jesus, whom you have learned to know as a precious Saviour. Trust Him to-day afresh: "O my Joshua, take me, bring me in and I will trust Thee, and in Thee the Father." You may count upon it. He will take you and the work will be done.

The Kingdom First

Matt 6: 33.—Seek ye first the kingdom of God.

You have heard what need there is of unity in Christian life and Christian work. And where is the bond of unity between the life of the Church, the life of the individual believer and the work to be done among the heathen? One of the expressions for that unity is: "Seek first the Kingdom of God," That does not mean, as many people take it, "Seek salvation; seek to get into the Kingdom, and then thank God, and rest there." Ah, no; the meaning of that word is entirely different and infinitely larger. It means: Let the Kingdom of God, in all its breadth and length, in all its Heavenly glory and power; let the Kingdom of God be the one thing you live for, and all other things will be added unto you. "Seek first the Kingdom of God." Let me just try to answer two very simple questions; the one: "Why should the Kingdom of God be first?" and the other: "How can it be?" The one, "Why should it be so?" God has created us as reasonable beings, so that the more clearly we see that according to the law of nature, according to the fitness of things, something that is set before us is proper, and an absolute necessity, we so much the more willingly accept it, and aim after it. And now, why does Christ say this: "Seek first the Kingdom of God?" If you want to understand the reason, look at God, and look at man. Look at God. Who is God? The great Being for whom alone the universe exists; in whom alone it can have its happiness. It came from Him. It can not find any rest or joy but in Him. Oh, that Christians understood and believed that God is a fountain of happiness, perfect, everlasting blessedness! What would the result be? Every Christian would say, "The more I can have of God, the happier. The more of God's will, and the more of God's love, and the more of God's fellowship, the happier." How Christians, if they believed that with their whole heart, would, with the utmost ease, give up everything that would separate them from God! Why is it that we find it so hard to hold fellowship with God? A young minister once said to me, "Why is it that I have so much more interest in study than in prayer, and how can you teach me the art of fellowship with God?" My answer was: "Oh, my brother, if we have any true conception of what God is, the art of fellowship with Him will come naturally, and will be a delight." Yes, if we believed God to be only joy to the one who comes to Him, only a fountain of unlimited blessing, how we should give up all for Him! Has not joy a far stronger attraction than anything in the world? Is it not in every beauty, or in every virtue, in every pursuit, the joy that is set before us that draws? And if we believe that God is a fountain of joy, and sweetness, and power to bless, how our hearts will turn aside from everything, and say: "Oh, the beauty of my God! I rejoice in Him alone." But, alas! the Kingdom of God looks to many as a burden, and as something unnatural. It looks like a strain, and we seek some relaxation in the world, and God is not our chief joy. I come to you with a message. It is right, on account of what God is as Infinite Love, as Infinite Blessing; it is right and more, it is our highest privilege to listen to Christ's words, and to seek God and His Kingdom first and above everything.

And then look at man again; man's nature. What was man created for? To live in the likeness of God, and as His image. Now, if we have been created in the image and likeness of God, we can find our happiness in nothing except that in which God finds His happiness. The more like Him we are the happier. And in what does God find His happiness? In two things: Everlasting righteousness and everlasting beneficence. God is righteousness everlasting. "He is Light, and in Him is no darkness." The Kingdom, the domination, the rule of God will bring us nothing but righteousness. "Seek the Kingdom of God and His righteousness." If men but knew what sin is, and if men really longed to be free from everything like sin, what a grand message this would be! Jesus comes to lead me to God and His righteousness. We were created to be like God, in His perfect righteousness and holiness. What a prospect! And in His love too. The Kingdom of God means this: that there is in God a rule of universal love. He loves, and loves, and never ceases to love; and He longs to bless all who will yield to His pleadings. God is Light, and God is Love. And now the message comes to man. Can you think of a higher nobility; can you think of anything grander than to take the position that God takes, and to be one with God in His Kingdom; i.e., to have His Kingdom fill your heart; to have God Himself as your King and portion? Yes, my friends, let us remember that we must not just try to get here and there one and another of the blessings of the Kingdom. But the glory of the Kingdom is this: that it is the Kingdom of God where God is all in all. The French Empire, when Napoleon lived, had military glory as the ideal. Every Frenchman's heart thrilled at the name of Napoleon as the man who had given the empire its glory. If we realized what it means,—our God takes us up into His Kingdom and puts His Kingdom into us and with the Kingdom we have God Himself, that blessed One, possessing us—surely there would be nothing that could move our hearts to enthusiasm like this. The Kingdom of God first! Blessed be His name I Look at man. I don't speak about man's sins, and about man's wretchedness, and about man's seeking everywhere for pleasure, and for rest, and for deliverance from sin, but I just say: Think what man is by creation and think what man is now by redemption; and let every heart say: "It is right. There is no blessedness or glory like that of the Kingdom. The Kingdom of God ought to be first in my whole life and being."

But now comes the important question, "How can I attain this?" Here we come to the great question that is troubling the lives of tens of thousands of Christians throughout the world. And it is strange that it is so very difficult for them to find the answer; that tens of thousands are not able to give an answer; and others, when the answer is given, can not understand it; The day the centurion found his joy in being devoted to the Roman Empire, it took charge of him with all its power and glory. Dear friends, how are we to attain to this blessed position in which the Kingdom of God shall fill our hearts with such enthusiasm that it will spontaneously be first every day? The answer is, first of all give up everything for it. You have heard of the Roman soldier who gave up his soul, his affection, his life, who gave up everything, to be a soldier; and you have often seen, in history ancient and modern, how men who were not soldiers gave up their lives in sacrifice for a king or a country. You have heard how in the South African Republic not many years ago the war of liberty was fought. After three years of oppression by the English the people said they would endure it no longer, and so they gathered together to fight for their liberty. They knew how weak they were, as compared with the English power, but they said, "We must have our liberty." They bound themselves together to fight for it, and when that vow had been made, they went to their homes to prepare for the struggle. Such a thrill of enthusiasm passed through that country that in many cases women, when their husbands might have been allowed to stay at home, said to them: "No, go, even though you have not been commanded." And there were mothers who, when one son was called out to the front, said: "No, take two, three." Every man and woman was ready to die. It was in very deed "Our country first, before everything." And even so, friends, must it be with you if you want this wonderful Kingdom of God to take possession of you. I pray you by the mercies of God, give up every-thing for it. You do not know at once what that may mean, but take the words and speak them out at the footstool of God: "Anything, everything, for the Kingdom of God." Persevere in that, and by the Holy Spirit your God will begin to open to you the double blessing: on the one hand, the blessedness of the Kingdom which comes to possess your heart; and on the other hand, the blessedness of being surrendered to Him, and sacrificing and giving up all for Him.

"The Kingdom of God first!" How am I to reach that blessed life? The answer is: "Give up everything for it." And then a second answer would be this: Live every day and hour of your life in the humble desire to maintain that position. There are people who hear this test, and who say it is true, and that they want to obey it. But if you were to ask them how much time they spend with God day by day, you would be surprised and grieved to hear how little time they give up to Him. And yet they wonder that the blessedness of the divine life disappears. We prove the value we attach to things by the time we devote to them. The Kingdom should be first every day, and all the day. Let the Kingdom be first every morning. Begin the day with God, and God Himself will maintain His Kingdom in your heart. Do believe that. Rome did its utmost to maintain the authority of the man who gave himself to live for it. And God, the living God, will He not maintain His authority in your soul if you submit to Him? He will, indeed. Come to Him; only come, and give yourself up to Him in fellowship through Christ Jesus. Seek to maintain that fellowship with God all the day. Ah, friends, a man cannot have the Kingdom of God first, and at times, by way of relaxation, throw it off and seek his enjoyment in the things of this world. People have a secret idea life will become too solemn, too great a strain; it will be too difficult every moment of the day, from morning to evening, to have the Kingdom of God first. One sees at once how wrong it is to think thus. The presence of the love of God must every moment be our highest joy. Let us say: "By the help of God, it shall ever be the Kingdom of God first."

And then, my last remark, in answer to that question, "How can it be?" is this: it can be only by the power of the Holy Ghost. Let us remember that God's Word comes to us with the language, "Be filled with the Spirit;" and if you are content with less of the Spirit than God offers, not utterly and entirely yielding to be filled with the Spirit, you do not obey the command. But listen: God has made a wonderful provision. Jesus Christ came preaching the Gospel of the Kingdom, and proclaimed "The Kingdom is at hand." "Some," He said, "are standing here who will not see death until they see the Kingdom come in power." He said to the disciples, "The Kingdom is within you." And when did the Kingdom come—that Kingdom of God upon earth? When the Holy Ghost descended. On Ascension Day the King went and sat down upon the throne at the right hand of God, and the Kingdom of God, in Christ, the Kingdom of Heaven upon earth, was inaugurated. When the Holy Ghost came down He brought God into the heart, and Christ, and established the rule of God in power. I am afraid sometimes, that in speaking of the Holy Spirit we forget one thing. The Holy Spirit is very much spoken of in connection with power; and it is right that we should seek power. It is not so much spoken of in connection with the graces. And yet these are always more important than the gifts of power—the holiness, the humility, the meekness, the gentleness, and the lovingness; these are the true marks of the Kingdom. We speak rightly of the Holy Spirit as the only one who can breathe all this into us. But I think there is a third thing almost more important, that we forget, and that is: in the Spirit, the Father and the Son themselves come. When Christ first promised the Holy Spirit, and spoke about His approaching coming, He said: "In that day ye shall know that I am in the Father, and ye in me, and I in you. He that loveth me keepeth my commandments; and my Father will love him, and we will come and make our abode with him." Brother, would you have the Kingdom of God first in your life, you must have the Kingdom in your hearts. If my heart be set upon a thing I may be bound with chains, but the moment the chains are loosened I fly towards the object of my affection and desire. And just so the Kingdom must be within us, and then it is easy to say: "The Kingdom first." But to have the Kingdom within us in truth, we must have God the Father, and Christ the Son, by the Holy Ghost within us too. No Kingdom without the King.

You are called to likeness with Christ. Oh, how many Christians strive after this part and that part of the likeness of Christ, and forget the root of the whole! What is the root of all? That Christ gave Himself up utterly to God, and His Kingdom and glory. He gave His life, that God's Kingdom might be established. Do you the same to-day and give your life to God to be every moment a living sacrifice, and the Kingdom will come with power into your heart. Give yourself up to Christ. Let Christ the King reign in your heart, and the heavenly Kingdom will come there and the Presence and the Rule of God be known in power. Oh, think of that wonderful thing that is going to happen in the great eternity. We read of it in 1st Corinthians: God has entrusted Christ with the Kingdom, but there is coming a day when Christ shall come Himself again to be subjected unto the Father, and He shall give up the Kingdom to the Father, that God may be all, and in that day Christ shall say before the universe: "This is my glory, I give back the Kingdom to the Father!" Christians, if your Christ finds His glory here on earth in dying and sacrificing Himself for the Kingdom and then in eternity again in giving the

Kingdom to God, shall not you and I come to God to do the same and count anything we have as loss, that the Kingdom of God may be made manifest, and that God may be glorified.

Christ Our Life

Colossians 3: 4.—Christ who is our life.

One question that rises in every mind is this: "How can I live that life of perfect trust in God?" Many do not know the right answer, or the full answer. It is this: "Christ must live it in me." That is what He became man for; as a man to live a life of trust in God, and so to show to us how we ought to live. When He had done that upon earth, He went to heaven, that He might do more than show us, might give us, and live in us that life of trust. It is as we understand what the life of Christ is and how it becomes ours, that we shall be prepared to desire and to ask of Him that He would live it Himself in us. When first we have seen what the life is, then we shall understand how it is that He can actually take possession, and make us like Himself. I want especially to direct attention to that first question. I wish to set before you the life of Christ as He lived it, that we may understand what it is that He has for us and that we can expect from Him. Christ Jesus lived a life upon earth that He expects us literally to imitate. We often say that we long to be like Christ. We study the traits of His character, mark His footsteps, and pray for grace to be like Him, and yet, somehow, we succeed but very little. And why? Because we are wanting to pluck the fruit while the root is absent. If we want really to understand what the imitation of Christ means, we must go to that which constituted the very root of His life before God. It was a life of absolute dependence, absolute trust, absolute surrender, and until we are one with Him in what is the principle of His life, it is in vain to seek here or there to copy the graces of that life.

In the Gospel story we find five great points of special importance; the birth, the life on earth, the death, the resurrection, and the ascension. In these we have what an old writer has called "the process of Jesus Christ;" the process by which He became what He is to-day—our glorified King, and our life. In all this life process we must be made like unto Him. Look at the first. What have we to say about His birth? This: He received His life from God. What about His life upon earth? He lived that life in dependence upon God.

About His death? He gave up His life to God. About His resurrection? He was raised from the dead by God. And about His ascension? He lives His life in glory with God.

First, He received His life from God. And why is it of consequence that we should look to that? Because Christ Jesus had in that the starling-point of His whole life. He said: "The Father sent me;" "The Father hath given the Son all things;" "The Father hath given the Son to have life in Himself." Christ received it as His own life, just as God has His life in Himself. And yet, all the time it was a life given and received. "Because the Father almighty has given this life unto me, the Son of man on earth, I can count upon God to maintain it and to carry me through all." And that is the first lesson we need. We need often to meditate on it, and to pray, and to think, and to wait before God, until our hearts open to the wonderful consciousness that the everlasting God has a divine life within us which can not exist but through Him. I believe God has given His life, it roots in Him. I shall feel it must be maintained by Him. We often think that God has given us a life which is now our own, a spiritual life, and that we are to take charge; and then we complain that we can not keep it right. No wonder. We must learn to live, learn to live as Jesus did. I have a God-given treasure in this earthen vessel. I have the light of the knowledge of the glory of God in the face of Christ. I have the life of God's Son within me given me by God Himself, and it can only be maintained by God Himself as I live in fellowship with Him. What does the Apostle Paul teach us in Romans VI.; there where he has just told us that we must reckon ourselves dead unto sin, and alive unto God in Christ Jesus? He goes on at once to say: "Therefore yield, present yourselves unto God, as those that are alive from the dead." How often a Christian hears solemn words about his being alive to God, and his having to reckon himself dead indeed to sin, and alive to God in Christ! He does not know what to do; he immediately casts about: "How can I keep it, this death and this life?" Listen to what Paul says. The moment that you reckon yourself dead to sin and alive to God, go with that life to God Himself, and present yourself as alive from the dead, and say to God: "Lord, Thou hast given me this life. Thou alone canst keep it. I bring it to Thee. I cannot understand all. I hardly know what I have got, but I come to God to perfect what He has begun." To live like Christ, I must be conscious every moment that my life has come from God, and He alone can maintain it.

Then, secondly, how did Christ live out His life during the thirty-three years in which He walked here upon earth? He lived it in dependence on God. You know how continually He says: "The Son can do nothing of

Himself. The words that I speak, I speak not of Myself." He waited unceasingly for the teaching, and the commands, and the guidance of the Father. He prayed for power from the Father. Whatever He did, He did in the name of the Father. He, the Son of God, felt the need of much prayer, of persevering prayer, of bringing down from heaven and maintaining the life of fellowship with God in prayer. We hear a great deal about trusting God. Most blessed! And we may say: "Ah, that is what I want," and we may forget what is the very secret of all,—that God, in Christ, must work all in us. I not only need God as an object of trust, but I must have Christ within as the power to trust; He must live His own life of trust in me. Look at it in that wonderful story of Paul, the Apostle, the beloved servant of God. He is in danger of self-confidence, and God in heaven sends that terrible trial in Asia to bring him down, lest he trust in himself and not in the living God. God watched over his servant that he should be kept trusting. Remember that other story about the thorn in the flesh, in 2 Corinthians XII., and think what that means. He was in danger of exalting himself, and the blessed Master came to humble him, and to teach him: "I keep thee weak, that thou mayest learn to trust not in thyself, but in Me." If we are to enter into the rest of faith, and to abide there; if we are to live the life of victory in the land of Canaan, it must begin here. We must be broken down from all self-confidence and learn like Christ to depend absolutely and unceasingly upon God. There is a greater work to be done in that than we perhaps know. We must be broken down, and the habit of our souls must be unceasingly: "I am nothing; God is all. I cannot walk before God as I should for one hour, unless God keep the life He has given me." What a blessed solution God gives then to all our questions and our difficulties, when He says: "My child, Christ has gone through it all for thee. Christ hath wrought out a new nature that can trust God; and Christ the Living One in heaven will live in thee, and enable thee to live that life of trust." That is why Paul said: "Such confidence have we toward God, through Christ." What does that mean? Does it only mean through Christ as the mediator, or intercessor? Verily, no. It means much more; through Christ living in and enabling us to trust God as He trusted Him.

Then comes, thirdly, the death of Christ. What does that teach us of Christ's relation to the Father? It opens up to us one of the deepest and most solemn lessons of Christ life, one which the Church of Christ understands all too little. We know what the death of Christ means as an atonement, and we never can emphasize too much that blessed substitution and bloodshedding, by which redemption was won for us. But let us remember, that is only half the meaning of His death. The other half is this: just as much as Christ was my substitute, who died for me, just so much He is my head, in whom, and with whom, I die; and just as He lives for me, to intercede, He lives in me, to carry out and to perfect His life. And if I want to know what that life is which He will live in me, I must look at His death. By His death He proved that He possessed life only to hold it, and to spend it, for God. To the very uttermost; without the shadow of a moment's exception, He lived for God,—every moment, everywhere, He held life only for His God. And so, if one wants to live a life of perfect trust, there must be the perfect surrender of his life, and his will, even unto the very death. He must be willing to go all lengths with Jesus, even to Calvary. When a boy twelve years of age Jesus said: "Wist ye not that I must be about my Father's business?" and again when He came to Jordan to be baptized: "It becometh us to fulfill all righteousness." So on through all His life, He ever said: "It is my meat and drink to do the will of my Father. I come not to do my own will, but the will of Him that sent me." "Lo, I am come to do Thy will, O God." And in the agony of Gethsemane, His words were: "Not my will, but Thine, be done."

Some one says: "I do indeed desire to live the life of perfect trust; I desire to let Christ live it in me; I am longing to come to such an apprehension of Christ as shall give me the certainty that Christ will forever abide in me; I want to come to the full assurance that Christ, my Joshua, will keep me in the land of victory." What is needful for that? My answer is: "Take care that you do not take a false Christ, an imaginary Christ, a half Christ." And what is the full Christ? The full Christ is the man who said, "I give up everything to the death that God may be glorified. I have not a thought; I have not a wish; I would not live a moment except for the glory of God." You say at once, "What Christian can ever attain that?" Do not ask that question, but ask, "Has Christ attained it and does Christ promise to live in me?" Accept Him in His fullness and leave Him to teach you how far He can bring you and what He can work in you. Make no conditions or stipulations about failure, but cast yourself upon, abandon yourself to this Christ who lived that life of utter surrender to God that He might prepare a new nature which He could impart to you and in which He might make you like Himself. Then you will be in the path by which He can lead you on to blessed experience and possession of what He can do for you. Christ Jesus came into the world with a commandment from the Father that He should lay down His life, and He lived with that one thought in His bosom His whole life long. And the one thought that ought to be in the heart of every believer is this: "I am in the death with Christ; absolutely, unchangeably given up to wait upon God, that God may work out His purpose and glory in me from moment to moment."

Few attain the victory and the enjoyment and the full experience at once. But this you can do: Take the right attitude and as you look to Jesus and what He was, say: "Father, Thou hast made me a partaker of the divine nature, a partaker of Christ. It is in the life of Christ given up to Thee to the death, in His power and indwelling, in His likeness, that I desire to live out my life before Thee." Death is a solemn thing, an awful thing. In the Garden it cost Christ great agony to die that death; and no wonder it is not easy to us. But we willingly consent when we have learned the secret; in death alone the life of God will come; in death there is blessedness unspeakable. It was this made Paul so willing to bear the sentence of death in himself; he knew the God who quickeneth the dead. The sentence of death is on everything that is of nature. But are we willing to accept it, do we cherish it? and are we not rather trying to escape the sentence or to forget it? We do not believe fully that the sentence of death is on us. Whatever is of nature must die. Ask God to make you willing to believe with your heart that to die with Christ is the only way to live in Him. You ask, "But must it then be dying every day?" Yes, beloved; Jesus lived every day in the prospect of the cross, and we, in the power of His victorious life, being made conformable to His death, must rejoice every day in going down with Him into death. Take an illustration. Take an oak of some hundred years' growth. How was that oak born? In a grave. The acorn was planted in the ground, a grave was made for it that the acorn might die. It died and disappeared; it cast roots downward, and it cast shoots upward, and now that tree has been standing a hundred years. Where is it standing? In its grave; all the time in the very grave where the acorn died; it has stood there stretching its roots deeper and deeper into that earth in which its grave was made, and yet, all the time, though it stood in the very grave where it had died, it has been growing higher, and stronger, and broader, and more beautiful. And all the fruit it ever bore, and all the foliage that adorned it year by year, it owed to that grave in which its roots are cast and kept. Even so Christ owes everything to His death and His grave. And we, too, owe everything to that grave of Jesus. Oh! let us live every day rooted in the death of Jesus. Be not afraid, but say: "To my own will I will die; to human wisdom, and human strength, and to the world I will die; for it is in the grave of my Lord that His life has its beginning, and its strength and its glory."

This brings us to our next thought. First, Christ received life from the Father; second, Christ lived it in dependence on the Father; third, Christ gave it up in death to the Father; and now, fourth, Christ received it again raised by the Father, by the power of the glory of the Father. Oh, the deep meaning of the resurrection of Christ! What did Christ do when He died? He went down into the darkness and absolute helplessness of death. He gave up a life that was without sin; a life that was God-given; a life that was beautiful and precious; and He said, "I will give it into the hands of my Father if He asks it;" and He did it; and He was there in the grave waiting on God to do His will; and because He honored God to the uttermost in His helplessness, God lifted Him up to the very uttermost of glory and power. Christ lost nothing by giving up His life in death to the Father. And so, if you want the glory and the life of God to come upon you, it is in the grave of utter helplessness that that life of glory will be born. Jesus was raised from the dead, and that resurrection power, by the grace of God, can and will work in us. Let no one expect to live a right life until he lives a full resurrection life in the power of Jesus. Let me state in a different way what this resurrection means.

Christ had a perfect life, given by God. The Father said: "Will you give up that life to me? Will you part with it at my command?" And He parted with it, but God gave it back to Him in a second life ten thousand times more glorious than that earthly life. So God will do to every one of us who willingly consents to part with his life. Have you ever understood it? Jesus was born twice. The first time He was born in Bethlehem. That was a birth into a life of weakness. But the second time, He was born from the grave; He is the "first-born from the dead." Because He gave up the life that He had by His first birth, God gave him the life of the second birth, in the glory of heaven and the throne of God. Christians, that is exactly what we need to do. A man may be an earnest Christian; a man may be a successful worker; he may be a Christian that has had a measure of growth and advance; but if he has not entered this fullness of blessing, then he needs to come to a second and deeper experience of God's saving power; he needs, just as God brought him out of Egypt, through the Red Sea, to come to a point where God brings him through Jordan into Canaan. Beloved, we have been baptized into the death of Christ. It is as we say: "I have had a very blessed life, and I have had many blessed experiences, and God has done many things for me; but I am conscious there is something wrong still; I am conscious that this life of rest and victory is not really mine." Before Christ got His life of rest and victory on the throne, He had to die and give up all. Do you it, too, and you shall with Him share His victory and glory. It is as we follow Jesus in His death, that His resurrection, power and joy will be ours.

And then comes our last point. The fifth step in His wondrous path was: He was lifted up to be forever with the Father. Because He humbled Himself, therefore God highly exalted Him. Wherein cometh the beauty and the blessedness of that exaltation of Jesus? For Himself perfect fellowship with the

Father; for others participation in the power of God's omnipotence. Yes, that was the fruit of His death. Scripture promises not only that God will, in the resurrection life, give us joy, and peace that passeth all understanding, victory over sin, and rest in God, but He will baptize us with the Holy Ghost; or, in other words, will fill us with the Holy Ghost. Jesus was lifted to the throne of heaven, that He might there receive from the Father the Spirit in His new, divine manifestation, to be poured out in His fullness. And as we come to the resurrection life, the life in the faith of Him who is one with us, and sits upon the throne—as we come to that, we too may be partakers of the fellowship with Christ Jesus as He ever dwells in God's presence, and the Holy Spirit will fill us, to work in us, and out of us in a way that we have never yet known.

Jesus got this divine life by depending absolutely upon the Father all His life long, depending upon Him even down into death. Jesus got that life in the full glory of the Spirit to be poured out, by giving Himself up in obedience and surrender to God alone, and leaving God even in the grave to work out His mighty power; and that very Christ will live out His life in you and me. Oh, the mystery! Oh, the glory! And oh, the Divine certainty. Jesus Christ means to live out that life in you and me. What think you, ought we not to humble ourselves before God? Have we been Christians so many years, and realized so little what we are? I am a vessel set apart, cleansed, emptied, consecrated; just standing, waiting every moment for God, in Christ, by the Holy Spirit, to work out in me as much of the holiness and the life of His Son as pleases Him. And until the Church of Christ comes to go down into the grave of humiliation, and confession, and shame; until the Church of Christ comes to lay itself in the very dust before God, and to wait upon God to do something new, and something wonderful, something supernatural, in lifting it up, it will remain feeble in all its efforts to overcome the world. Within the Church what lukewarmness, what worldliness, what disobedience, what sin! How can we ever fight this battle, or meet these difficulties? The answer is: Christ, the risen One, the crowned One, the almighty One, must come, and live in the individual members. But we can not expect this except as we die with Him. I referred to the tree grown so high and beautiful, with its roots every day for a hundred years in the grave in which the acorn died. Children of God, we must go down deeper into the grave of Jesus. We must cultivate the sense of impotence, and dependence, and nothingness, until our souls walk before God every day in a deep and holy trembling. God keep us from being anything. God teach us to wait on Him, that He may work in us all He wrought in His Son, till Christ Jesus may live out His life in us! For this may God help us!

Christ's Humility Our Salvation

Philippians 2: 5-8.—"Let this mind be in you which was also in Christ Jesus. He humbled Himself and became obedient unto death, even the death of the cross."

All are familiar with this wonderful passage. Paul is speaking about one of the most simple, practical things in daily life,—humility; and in connection with that, he gives us a wonderful exhibition of divine truth. In this chapter we have the eternal Godhead of Jesus—He was in the form of God, and one with God. We have His incarnation—He came down, and was found in the likeness of man. We have his death with the atonement—He became obedient unto death. We have His exaltation—God hath highly exalted Him. We have the glory of His Kingdom,—that every knee shall bow, and every tongue confess Him. And in what connection? Is it a theological study? No. Is it a description of what Christ is? No; it is in connection with a simple, downright call to a life of humility in our intercourse with each other. Our life on earth is linked to all the eternal glory of the Godhead as revealed in the exaltation of Jesus. The very looking to Jesus, the very bowing of the knee to Jesus, ought to be inseparably connected with a spirit of the very deepest humility. Consider the humility of Jesus. First of all, that humility is our salvation; then, that humility is just the salvation we need; and again, that humility is the salvation which the Holy Spirit will give us.

Humility is the salvation that Christ brings. That is our first thought. We often have very vague,—I might also say visionary—ideas of what Christ is; we love the person of Christ, but that which makes up Christ, which actually constitutes Him the Christ, that we do not know or love. If we love Christ above everything, we must love humility above everything, for humility is the very essence of His life and glory, and the salvation He brings. Just think of it. Where did it begin? Is there humility in heaven? You know there is, for they cast their crowns before the throne of God and the Lamb. But is there humility on the throne of God? Yes, what was it but heavenly humility that made Jesus on the throne willing to say: "I will go down to be a servant, and to die for man; I will go and live as the meek and lowly Lamb of God?" Jesus brought humility from heaven to us. It was humility that brought Him to earth, or He never would have come. In accordance with this, just as Christ became a man in this divine humility, so His whole life was marked by it. He might have chosen another form in which to appear; He might have come in the form of a king, but He chose the form of a servant. He made Himself of no reputation; He emptied Himself; He chose the form of a servant. He said: "The Son of Man is not come to be ministered unto, to be served, but to serve, and to give His life a ransom for many." And you know, in the last night, He took the place of a slave, and girded Himself with a towel, and went to wash the feet of Peter and the other disciples. Beloved, the life of Jesus upon earth was a life of the deepest humility. It was this gave His life its worth and beauty in God's sight. And then His death—possibly you haven't thought of it much in this connection—but His death was an exhibition of unparalleled humility. "He humbled Himself, and became obedient unto death, even the death of the cross." My Lord Christ took a low place all the time of His walk upon earth; He took a very low place when He began to wash the disciples' feet; but when He went to Calvary, He took the lowest place there was to be found in the universe of God, the very lowest, and He let sin, and the curse of sin, and the wrath of God, cover Him. He took the place of a guilty sinner, that He might bear our load, that He might serve us in saving us from our wretchedness, that He might by His precious blood win deliverance for us, that He might by that blood wash us from our stain and our guilt.

We are in danger of thinking about Christ, as God, as man, as the atonement, as the Saviour, and as exalted upon the throne, and we form an image of Christ, while the real Christ, that which is the very heart of His character, remains unknown. What is the real Christ? Divine humility, bowed down into the very depths for our salvation. The humility of Jesus is our salvation. We read, "He humbled Himself, therefore God hath highly exalted Him." The secret of His exaltation to the throne is this: He humbled Himself before God and man. Humility is the Christ of God, and now in Heaven, to-day, that Christ, the Man of humility, is on the throne of God. What do I see? A Lamb standing, as it had been slain, on the throne; in the glory He is still the meek and gentle Lamb of God. His humility is the badge He wears there. You often use that name—the Lamb of God—and you use it in connection with the blood of the sacrifice. You sing the praise of the Lamb, and you put your trust in the blood of the Lamb. Praise God for the blood. You never can trust that too much. But I am afraid you forget that the word "Lamb" must mean to us two things: it must mean not only a sacrifice, the shedding of blood, but it must mean to us the meekness of God, incarnate upon earth, the meekness of God represented in the meekness and gentleness of a little Lamb.

But the salvation that Christ brought is not only a salvation that flows out of humility; it also leads to humility. We must understand that this is not only the salvation which Christ brought; but that it is exactly the salvation which you and I need. What is the cause of all the wretchedness of man? Primarily pride; man seeking his own will and his own glory. Yes, pride is the root of every sin, and so the Lamb of God comes to us in our pride, and brings us salvation from it. We need above everything to be saved from our pride and our self-will. It is good to be saved from the sins of stealing, murdering, and every other evil; but a man needs above all to be saved from what is the root of all sin, his self-will and his pride. It is not until man begins to feel that this is exactly the salvation he needs, that he really can understand what Christ is, and that he can accept Him as his salvation. This is the salvation that we as Christians and believers specially need. We know the sad story of Peter and John; what their self-will and pride brought upon them. They needed to be saved from nothing except themselves, and that is the lesson which we must learn, if we are to enter the life of rest. And how can we enter that life, and dwell there in the bosom of the Lamb of God, if pride rules? Have we not often heard complaints of how much there is of pride in the Church of Christ? What is the cause of all the division, and strife, and envying, that is often found even among God's saints? Why is it that often in a family there is bitterness—it may be only for half an hour, or half a day; but what is the cause of hard judgments and hasty words? What is the cause of estrangement between friends? What is the cause of evil speaking? What is the cause of selfishness and indifference to the feelings of others? Simply this: the pride of man. He lifts himself up, and he claims the right to have his opinions and judgments as he pleases. The salvation we need is indeed humility, because it is only through humility that we can be restored to our right relation to God.

"Waiting upon God,"—that is the only true expression for the real relation of the creature to God; to be nothing before God. What is the essential idea of a creature made by God? It is this: to be a vessel in which He can pour out His fullness, in which He can exhibit His life, His goodness, His power, and His love. A vessel must be empty if it is to be filled, and if we are to be filled with the life of God we must be utterly empty of self. This is the glory of God, that He is to fill all things, and more especially His redeemed people. And as this is the glory of the creature, so this is the only redemption, and the only glory of every redeemed soul, to be empty and as nothing before God; to wait upon Him, and to let God be all in all.

Humility has a prominent place in almost every epistle of the New Testament. Paul says: "Walk with all lowliness and meekness, with longsuffering, forbearing one another in love; endeavoring to keep the unity of the Spirit in the bond of peace." The nearer you get to God, and the fuller of God, the lowlier you will be; and equally before God and man, you will love to bow very low. We know of Peter's early self-confidence; but in his epistles what a different language he speaks! He wrote there: "Let the younger be subject to the elder, and all of you be subject one to another; humble yourselves under the mighty hand of God, that He may exalt you in His own time." He understood, and he dared to preach, humility to all. It is indeed the salvation we need. What is it that prevents people from coming to that entire surrender that we speak of? Simply that they dare not abandon themselves, and trust themselves, to God; that they are not willing to be nothing, to give up their wishes, and their will, and their honor to Christ. Shall we not accept the salvation that Jesus offers? He gave up His own will; He gave up His own honor; He gave up any confidence in Himself; He lived dependent upon God as a servant whom the Father had sent. There is the salvation we need, the Spirit of humility that was in Christ.

What is it that often disturbs our hearts, and our peace? It is pride seeking to be something. And God's decree is irreversible, "God resisteth the proud; He gives grace only to the humble." How often Jesus had to speak to his disciples about it! You will find repeatedly in the Gospel those simple words: "He that humbleth Himself shall be exalted; he that exalteth himself shall be humbled." He taught His disciples: "He that would be chiefest among you, let him be the servant of all." This should be our one cry before God: "Let the power of the Holy Ghost come upon me, with the humility of Jesus, that I may take the place that He took." Brother, do you want a better place than Jesus had? Are you seeking a higher place than Jesus? Or will you say: "Down, down, as deep as ever I can go. By the help of God I will be nothing before God; I will be where Jesus was."

And now comes the third thought,—This is the salvation the Holy Ghost brings. You know what a change took place in those disciples. Let us praise God for it; the Holy Spirit means this: the life, the disposition, the temper, and the inclinations of Jesus, brought down from heaven into our hearts. That is the Holy Ghost. He has His mighty workings to bestow as gifts; but the fullness of the Holy Ghost is this: Jesus Christ in His humility coming to dwell in us. When Christ was teaching His disciples, all His instructions may have helped in the way of preparation, breaking them down, and making them conscious of what was wrong, and awakening desire; but the instruction could not do it, and all their love to Jesus and their desire to please Him could not do it, until the Holy Ghost came. That is the promise Christ gave. He says, in connection with the coming of the Holy Ghost: "I will come again to you." Christ said to His disciples: "I have been three years with you, and you have been in the closest contact with me, and I have done the utmost to reach your hearts; I have sought to get into your hearts, yet I have failed; but fear not, I will come again. In that day ye shall see me, and your hearts shall rejoice, and no man shall take your joy from you. I will come again to dwell in you, and live my life in you." Christ went to heaven that He might get a power which He never had before. And what was that? The power of living in men. God be praised for this! It was because Jesus, the humble One, the Lamb of God, the meek, the lowly and gentle One, came down in the Holy Spirit into the hearts of His disciples, that the pride was expelled, and that the very breath of Heaven breathed through Him in the love that made them one heart and one soul.

Dear friends, Christ is yours. Christ as He comes in the power of the Holy Spirit is yours. Are you longing to have Him, to have the perfect Christ Jesus? Come, then, and see how, amid the glories of His Godhead—His having been in the form of God, and equal to God; amid the glories of His incarnation—His having become a man; amid the glories of His atonement—His having been obedient to death; and amid the glories of His exaltation, which is the chief and brightest glory, He humbled Himself from Heaven down to earth and on earth down to the cross. He humbled Himself to bear the name and show the meekness, and die the death of the Lamb of God. And what is it we now need to do? How are we to be saved by this humility of Jesus? It is a solemn question, but, thank God, the answer can be given. First we must desire it above everything. Let us learn to pray God to deliver us from every vestige of pride, for this is a cursed thing. Let us learn to set aside for a time other things in the Christian life, and begin to plead with the Lamb of God day by day, "O Lamb of God, I know Thy love, but I know so little of Thy meekness." Come day after day, and lay your heart against His heart, and say to Him with strong desire: "Jesus, Lamb of God, give, oh, give me Thyself, with Thy meekness and humility," and He will fulfill the desire of them that fear Him. It is not enough to desire it and to pray for it; claim and accept it as yours. This humility is given you in Christ Jesus. Christ is our life. What does that mean? Oh, that God might give you and me a vision of what that means. The air is our life, and the air is everywhere, universal. We breathe without difficulty because God surrounds us with the air; and is the air nearer to me than Christ is? The sun gives light to every green leaf and every blade of grass, shining hour by hour and moment by moment. And is the sun nearer to the blade of grass than Christ is to man's soul? Verily, no; Christ is around us on every side; Christ is pressing on us to enter, and there is nothing in heaven, or earth, or hell, that can keep the light of Christ from shining into the heart that is empty and open. If the windows of your room were closed with shutters, the light could not enter; it would be on the outside of the building, streaming and streaming against the shutters; but it could not enter. But leave the windows without shutters, and the light comes, it rejoices to come in and fill the room. Even so, children of God, Jesus and His light, Jesus and His humility, are around you on every side, longing to enter into your hearts. Come and take Him to-day in His blessed meekness and gentleness. Do not be afraid of Him; He is the Lamb of God. He is so patient with you, He is so kindly towards you, He is so tender and loving. Take courage to-day and trust Jesus to come into your heart and take possession of it. And when He has taken possession, there will be a life day by day of blessed fellowship with Him, and you will feel a necessity ever deeper for your quiet time with Him, and for worshiping and adoring Him, and for just sinking down before Him in helplessness and humility, and saying: "Jesus, I am nothing, and Thou art all." It will be a blessed life, because you will be conscious of being at the feet of Jesus. At this moment you can claim Jesus in His divine humility as the life of your soul. Will you? Will you not open your heart, and say: "Come in; come in?"

Come to-day, and take Him up afresh in this blessed power of His wonderful humility, and say to Him: "Oh, Thou who didst say, 'Learn of me, for I am meek and lowly in heart, and ye shall find rest unto your souls,' my Lord, I know why it is that I have not the perfect life; it is my pride, but to-day, come Thou and dwell in my heart. Thou who didst lead even Peter and John into the blessedness of Thy heavenly humility; Thou wilt not refuse me. Lord, here I am; do Thou, who by Thy wonderful humility alone canst save, come in. O Lamb of God, I believe in Thee; take possession of my heart, and dwell in me." When you have said that, go out in quiet, and retire, walking gently as holding the Lamb of God in your heart, and say: "I have received the Lamb of God; He makes my heart His care; He breathes His humility and dependence on God in me, and so brings me to God. His humility is my life and salvation."

The Complete Surrender

Genesis 39: 1-3.—Joseph was brought down to Egypt; and Potiphar, an officer of Pharaoh, captain of the guard, an Egyptian, bought him at the hands of the Ishmaelites, which had brought him down thither. And the Lord was with Joseph, and he was a prosperous man; and he was in the house of his master, the Egyptian, and his master saw that the Lord was with him.

We have in this passage an object lesson which teaches us what Christ is to us. Note: Joseph was a slave, but God was with him so distinctly that his master could see it. "And his master saw the Lord was with him, and that the Lord made all that he did prosper in his hands; and Joseph found grace in his sight, and he served him,"—that is to say, he was his slave about his person,—"and he made him overseer over his house,"—that was something new. Joseph had been a slave, but now he becomes a master. "And he made him overseer over his house, and all that he had he put into his hands. And it came to pass, from the time that he had made him overseer in his house, and over all that he had, that the Lord blessed the Egyptian's house for Joseph's sake, and the blessing of the Lord was upon all that he had in the house and in the field. And he left all that he had in Joseph's hand; and he knew not all he had, save the bread which he did eat."

We find Joseph in two characters in the house of Potiphar: first as a servant and a slave, one who is trusted and loved, but still entirely a servant; second, as master. Potiphar made him overseer over his house and his lands, and all that he had, so that we read afterward that he left everything in his hands, and he knew of nothing except the bread that came upon his table. I want to call your attention to Joseph as a type of Christ. We sometimes speak in the Christian life, of entire surrender, and rightly, and here we have a beautiful illustration of what it is. First, Joseph was in Potiphar's house to serve him and to help him, and he did that, and Potiphar learned to trust him, so that he said, "All that I have I will give into his hands." Now, that is exactly what is to take place with a great many Christians. They know Christ, they trust Him, they love Him, but He is not Master, He is a sort of helper. When there is trouble they come to Him, when they sin they ask Him for pardon in His precious blood, when they are in darkness they cry to Him; but often and often they live according to their own will, and they seek help from themselves. But how blessed is the man who comes and, like Potiphar, says, "I will give up everything to Jesus!" There are many who have accepted Christ as their Lord, but have never yet come to the final, absolute surrender of everything. Christians, if you want perfect rest, abiding joy, strength to work for God, oh, come and learn from that poor heathen Egyptian what you ought to do. He saw that God was with Joseph and he said, "I will give up my house to him." Oh, learn you to do that. There are some who have never yet accepted Christ, some who are seeking after Him, thirsting and hungering, but they do not know how to find Him.

Let me direct your attention to four thoughts regarding this surrender to Christ: First, its motives; second, its measures; third, its blessedness; lastly, its duration.

First of all, its motives. What moved Potiphar to do this? I think the answer is very easy: he was a trusted servant of the king and he had the king's work to take care of, and he very likely could not take care of his own house. All his time and attention were required at the court of Pharaoh. He had his duty there; he was in high honor; but his own house got neglected. Very likely he had had other overseers, one slave appointed to rule the others, and perhaps that one had been unfaithful, or dishonest, and somehow his house was not as he would have it. So he buys another slave, just as he had formerly done, but in this case he sees what he had never seen before. There is something unusual about the man. He walks so humbly, he serves so faithfully and so lovingly, and withal so successfully. Potiphar begins to look into the reason for this, and finally concludes that God is with him.

It is a grand thing to have a man with whom God is, to entrust one's business to. The heathen realized this, and between the need of his own house and what he saw in Joseph, he decided to make him overseer. I ask you, do not these two motives plead most urgently that you should say: "I will make Jesus master over my whole being?" Your house, Christian, your spiritual life, the dwelling, the temple of God in your heart,—in what state is that? Is it not often like the temple of old, in Jerusalem, that had been defiled and made a house of merchandise, and afterwards a den of thieves? Your heart, meant to be the home of Jesus, is it not often full of sin and darkness, full of sadness, full of vexation? You have done your very best to get it changed, and you have called in the help of man, and the help of means; you have used every method you could think of for getting it put right; but it will not come right until He whose it is, comes in to take charge.

If there is any trouble in your heart, if you are in darkness, or in the power of sin, I bring to you the Son of God, with the promise that He will come in and take charge. As Potiphar took Joseph, will you not take Jesus? Has He not proven Himself worthy to be trusted? Come and say, "Jesus shall have entire charge; He is worthy." Think not only of His Divine power, but think of His wonderful love; think of His coming from heaven to save you; think of His dying on Calvary and shedding His blood out of intense love for you. Oh, think of it; Christ in heaven loves every one who is given to Him, and whom He has made a child of God. "Having loved His own that were in the world, He loved them unto the end."

Must I plead in the name of the love of the crucified Jesus; must I plead with you Christians, and say, Look at Jesus, the Son of God, your Redeemer, and ask you to make Him overseer over all? Give Him charge of your temper, your heart's affections, your thoughts, your whole being, and He will prove Himself worthy of it. Joseph had been for a time just a common slave, and with the other slaves had served Pharaoh. Alas! many a Christian has used Christ for his own advancement and comfort, just as he uses everything in the world. He uses father and mother, minister, money, and all else the world will give, to comfort and make him happy; there is danger of his using Christ Jesus in the same way. But oh, brethren, this is not right. You are His house, and He has a right to dwell therein. Will you not come and surrender all, and say, "Lord Jesus, I have made Thee overseer over all?"

But now, secondly, the measure of that surrender. We read in the 4th verse: "All that he had he put into his hands." Then in verse 5: "And it came to pass from the time that he made him overseer over all that he had"—there you have it the second time—"the Lord blessed the Egyptian's house, and the blessing of the Lord was upon all that he had"—there the third time. Then in verse 6: "And he left all that he had"—there you have the words the fourth time—"in Joseph's hand, and he knew not all he had, save the bread which he did eat." What do I see here? That Potiphar actually gave everything into Joseph's hands. He made him master over his slaves. All the money was put into Joseph's hands, for we read that Potiphar had care of nothing. When dinner was brought upon the table, he ate of it, and that was all he knew of what was going on in his house. Is not this entire surrender?—he gives up everything into the hands of Joseph. Ah, beloved Christians, I want you to ask yourselves: "Have I done that?" You have offered more than one consecration prayer, and you have more than once said: "Jesus, all I have I give to Thee." You have said it, and meant it; but very probably you did not realize fully what it meant.

With the word surrender there seems always to be a larger and more comprehensive meaning. We do not succeed in carrying out our intentions, and afterward we take back one thing and another until we have lost sight of our original intention. Beloved Christians, let Christ Jesus have all. Let Him have your whole heart, with its affections; He Himself loves, with more than the love of Jonathan. Let Him have your whole heart, saying, "Jesus, every fiber of my being, ever power of my soul, shall be devoted to Thee." He will accept that surrender. He spoke a solemn word: "You must hate father and mother." Say you to-day: "Lord Jesus, the love to father and mother, to wife and child, to brother and sister, I give up to Thee. Teach Thou me how to love Thee. I have only one desire, which is to love Thee. I want to give my whole heart to be full of Thy love."

But when you have given your heart, there is yet more to give. There is the head—the brain with its thoughts. I believe Christians do not know how much they rob Christ of in reading so much of the literature of the world. They are often so occupied with their newspapers that the Bible gets a very small place. Oh, friends, I beseech you bring this noble power which God has given you, the power of a mind that can think heavenly, eternal, and infinite things, and lay it at the feet of Jesus, saying, "Lord Jesus, every faculty of my being I want to surrender to Thee, that Thou shouldst teach me what to think, and how to think, for Thee and Thy Kingdom." Bless God, there are men who have given their intellect to Jesus, and it has been accepted by Him. And in this connection there is my whole outer life. There is my relation to society, my position among men, my intercourse in my own home, with friends and family; there is my money, my time, my business; all these should be put in the hands of Jesus. One cannot know beforehand the blessedness of this surrender, but blessed it surely is. Come, because He is worthy; come because you know you can not keep things right yourself, and make Christ master over all you have. Give father and mother, wife and child, house and land, and money, all to Jesus, and you will find that in giving all you receive it back an hundred fold.

Thirdly, look at the blessing of the entire surrender. You have here the remarkable words: "And it came to pass from the time that Potiphar made Joseph overseer over all that he had, that the Lord blessed the Egyptian's house for Joseph's sake, and the blessing of the Lord was upon all that he had in the house, and in the field." I ask you Christians, If God did this to that heathen man, because he honored Joseph; if God, for Joseph's sake, blessed that Egyptian in this wonderful way, may a Christian not venture to say: "If I put my life into the hands of Jesus, I am sure God will bless all that I have?" Oh, dare to say it. Potiphar trusted Joseph implicitly and absolutely, and there was prosperity everywhere, because God was with Joseph. Beloved friends, if you but surrender everything, depend upon it, the blessing from that time will be yours. There will be a blessing within your own inner life, and a blessing in your outer life. He blessed Potiphar in the house, in the field, everywhere.

Oh, Christian, what is that blessing you will get? I can not tell all, but I can tell you this: if you will come to Christ Jesus and surrender all, the blessing of God will be on all that you have. There will be a blessing for your own soul. "Thou wilt keep him in perfect peace whose mind is stayed on Thee." Try that; trust Jesus for everything, and trust everything to Him, and the blessing of God will come upon you—the sweet rest, the rest of faith. It is all in the hands of Jesus; He will guide you; He will teach you; He will work in you; He will keep you; He will be everything to you. What a blessed rest and freedom from responsibility and from care, because it is all in the hands of Jesus! I do not say trouble and trial will never come; but in the midst of trial and trouble you will have the all-sufficiency of the presence of Jesus to be your comfort, your help, and your guide. Joseph was sold by his brethren, but he saw God in it, and he was quite content. Christ was betrayed by Judas, condemned by Caiaphas, and given over to execution by Pilate; but in all that, Christ saw God, and He was content. Give over your life, in all its phases, into the hands of Jesus; remembering that the very hairs of your head are numbered, and not a sparrow falls to earth without the Father's notice. Consent now and say: "I will give up everything into the hands of Jesus. Whatever happens is His will regarding me. Whether He comes in the light or in the dark, in the storm or on the troubled sea, I will rest in that blessed assurance. I give up my whole life entirely to Him."

In reading the Book of Jonah, we find God's hand in each step of Jonah's experience. It was God who sent the storm when Jonah went aboard the ship, who appointed a whale to swallow him, who ordered the whale to cast him out; and then afterwards it was God who caused the hot wind to blow when the sun was sending down its scorching rays, until the soul of Jonah was grieved, and made the gourd to grow, and sent the worm to kill the gourd, and set a sea-wind to dry the gourd up quickly. Do we not thus see that every circumstance of our living, every comfort and every trial, comes from God in Christ? There is nothing can touch a hair of my head. Not a sharp word comes against me; not an unexpected flurry surrounds me, but it is all Jesus.

With my life in His hands, I need care for nothing. I can be content with what Jesus gives.

God blessed Potiphar in the field; in the visible life outside of his house; and God will bless you, that, in your intercourse with men, you may be a blessing; that by your holy, humble, respectful, quiet walk, you may carry comfort; that by your loving readiness to be a servant and a helper to all, you may prove what the Spirit of God has done within you. Oh, my brother, my sister, you have no conception of it,—I have not—how God is willing to bless the soul utterly given up to Jesus. God can delight in nothing but Jesus. God delights infinitely in Jesus. God longs to see nothing in us but Jesus, and if I give up my heart and life to Jesus, and say, "My God, I want that Thou shouldst see in me nothing but Jesus," then I bring to the Father the sacrifice that is the most acceptable of all. Oh, believers, come to-day; come out of all your troubles, and all your self-efforts and your self-confidence, and let the blessed Son of God take possession.

Let me direct your thoughts, lastly, to the duration of this surrender. I want to emphasize this—because in many cases the surrender does not last. Some go away, and for a time have much gladness and joy, but it soon begins to decrease, and in a few weeks or perhaps months is all gone. Others who do not lose it entirely, complain sadly at times, that it goes away and comes again. They say: "My life has been very much blessed since that surrender I made to God, but it has not always been on the same level." What did Potiphar do? We read in the 4th verse: "He made him overseer over his house, and all that he had he left in Joseph's hands." What a simple word! He left it there.

And oh, children of God, if you will only get to that point and say, "For all eternity I leave it in the hands of Jesus," you will find what a blessing it is. Potiphar found now that he could do the king's business with two hands and an undivided heart. I might try to rescue a drowning man by holding fast somewhere with one hand, while I reached out the other hand to the man, but it is a grand thing for a person to be able to stretch out both hands, and that person is the one who has left all with Jesus—all his inner life, all his cares and troubles, and has given himself up entirely to do the will of God. Will you leave it there? I must press this, because I know temptations will come. One temptation will be that the feelings you had in your act of surrender will pass away; they will not be so bright; another, that circumstances will tempt you. Beloved, temptations will come; God means it for your good. Every temptation brings you a blessing. Do understand that. Learn the lesson of giving up everything to Jesus, and letting Jesus take charge of everything. Leave all with Jesus. Do not think that by a surrender to-day or on any day, however powerful, however mighty, things will keep right themselves. You need every morning afresh, when God wakes you up out of sleep, to put your heart, and your life, and your house, and your business, into the hands of Jesus. Wait on Him, if need be, in silence, or in prayer, until He gives you the assurance, "My child, for to-day all is safe; I take charge." And morning by morning He will renew to you the blessing, and morning by morning you will go out from your quiet time in the consciousness, "To-day I have had fellowship with my King, and it is all right." Jesus has taken charge. And so, day by day, you can have grace to leave all in the hands of Jesus.

In conclusion let me speak to two classes. There are times when your heart is restless; there are times when you are afraid to die.

There are some true believers who have perhaps never yet understood that it was their duty to give up everything to Christ. Beloved fellow Christians, I come with a message from your Father, to come and to-day take that word into your hearts and upon your lips, even though you do not understand it. "Jesus, I make Thee Master of everything and I will wait at Thy feet, that Thou wilt show me what Thou wouldst have me be and do." Do it now. And let me say to believers who have done it before, and who long with an unutterable longing to do it fully and perfectly,—Child of God, you can do it, for the Holy Spirit has been sent down from Heaven for this one purpose, to glorify Jesus; to glorify Jesus in your heart, by letting you see how perfectly Jesus can take possession of the whole heart; to glorify Jesus by bringing Him into your very life, that your whole life may shine out with the glory of Jesus. Depend upon it, the Father will give it to you by the Holy Spirit, if you are ready. Oh, come, and let your intercourse with God be summed up in a simple prayer and answer—"My God, as much as Thou wilt have of me to fill with Christ, Thou shalt have to-day." "My child, as much of Christ as thy heart longeth to have, thou shalt have; for it is My delight that My Son be in the hearts of My children."

Dead with Christ

Gal. 2: 20.—I am crucified with Christ.

The Revised Version properly has the above text "I have been crucified with Christ." In this connection, let us read the story of a man who was literally crucified with Christ. We may use all the narrative of Christ's work upon earth in the flesh as a type of His spiritual work. Let us take in this instance the story of the penitent thief, Luke 23: 39-43, for I think we may learn from him how to live as men who are crucified with Christ. Paul says: "I have been crucified with Christ." And again: "God forbid that I should glory, save in the cross of our Lord Jesus Christ, through whom I have been crucified to the world, and the world to me." We often ask earnestly: How can I be free from the self life? The answer is, "Get another life." We often speak about the power of the Holy Spirit coming upon us, but I doubt if we fully realize that the Holy Spirit is a heavenly life come to expel the selfish, and fleshly, and the earthly life. If we want, in very deed, to enjoy fully the rest that there is in Jesus, we can only have it as He comes in, in the power of His death, to slay what is in us of nature, and to take possession, and to live His own life in the fullness of the Holy Ghost. God's Word takes us to the cross of Christ, and it teaches us about that cross, two things. It tells us that Christ died for sin. We understand what that means, that in His atonement He died as I never die, as I never can die, as I never need die; He died for sin and for me. But what gave His death such power to atone? It was this: the spirit in which He died, not the physical suffering, not the external act of death, but the spirit in which He died. And what was that spirit? He died unto sin. Sin had tempted Him, and surrounded Him, and had brought Him very nigh to saying, "I cannot die." In Gethsemane He cried: "Father, is it not possible that the cup pass from me?" But God be praised, He gave up His life rather than yield to sin. He died to sin, and in dying He conquered. And now, I can not die for sin like Christ, but I can and I must die to sin like Christ. Christ died for me. In that He stands alone. Christ died to sin, and in that I have fellowship with Him. I have been crucified, I am dead.

And here is the great subject to which I want to lead you.—What it is to be dead with Christ, and how it is that I can practically enter into this death with Christ. We know that the great characteristic of Christ is His death. From eternity He came with the commandment of the Father that He should lay down His life on earth. He gave Himself up to it, and He set His face towards Jerusalem. He chose death, and He lived and walked upon earth to prepare Himself to die. His death is the power of redemption; death gave Him His victory over sin; death gave Him His resurrection, His new life, His exaltation, and His everlasting glory. The great mark of Christ is His death. Even in Heaven, upon the throne, He stands as the Lamb that was slain, and through eternity they ever sing, "Thou art worthy, for Thou wast slain." Beloved brother, your Boaz, your Christ, your all-sufficient Saviour, is a Man of whom the chief mark and the greatest glory is this: He died. And if the Bride is to live with her husband as His wife, then she must enter into His state, and into His spirit, and into His disposition, and ever be as He is. If we are to experience the full power of what Christ can do for us, we must learn to die with Christ. I ought not, perhaps, to use that expression, "We must learn to die with Christ;" I ought, rather, to say, "We must learn that we are dead with Christ." That is a glorious thought in the 6th chapter of Romans; to every believer in the Church of Rome—not to the select ones, or the advanced ones, but to every believer in the Church of Rome, however feeble, Paul writes, "You are dead with Christ." On the strength of that he says, "Reckon yourselves dead unto sin." What does that mean—You are dead to sin? We can not see it more clearly than by referring to Adam. Christ was the second Adam. What happened in the first Adam? I died, in the first Adam; I died to God; I died in sin. When I was born, I had in me the life of Adam, which had all the characteristics of the life of Adam after he had fallen. Adam died to God, and Adam died in sin, and I inherit the life of Adam, and so I am dead in sin as he was, and dead unto God. But at the very moment I begin to believe in Jesus, I become united to Christ, the second Adam, and as really as I am united by my birth to the first Adam, I am made partaker of the life of Christ. What life? That life which died unto sin on Calvary, and which rose again; therefore God by his apostle tells us: "Reckon yourselves indeed dead unto sin and alive unto God in Christ Jesus." You are to reckon it as true, because God says it—for your new nature is indeed, in virtue of your vital union to Christ, actually and utterly dead to sin.

If we want to have the real Christ that God has given us, the real Christ that died for us, in the power of His death and resurrection, we must take our stand here. But many Christians do not understand what the 6th chapter of the Epistle to the Romans teaches us. They do not know that they are dead to sin. They do not know it, and therefore Paul instructs them: "Know ye not that as many of you as are baptized into Christ Jesus, are baptized into His death." How can we who are dead to sin in Christ live any longer therein? We have indeed the death and the life of Christ working within us. But, alas! most Christians do not know this, and therefore do not experience or practice it. They need to be taught that their first need is to be brought to the recognition, to the knowledge, of what has taken place in Christ on Calvary, and what has taken place in their becoming united to Christ. The man must begin to say, even before he understands it, "In Christ I am dead to sin." It is a command: "Reckon ye yourselves indeed to be dead unto sin." Get hold of your union to Christ; believe in the new nature within you, that spiritual life which you have from Christ, a life that has died and been raised again. A man's acts are always in accordance with his idea of his state. A king acts like a king, otherwise we say, "That man has forgotten his kingship," but if a man is conscious of being a king, he behaves like a king. And so I cannot live the life of a true believer unless I am filled with a consciousness of this every day: "I thank God that I am dead in Christ. Christ died unto sin, and I am united with Christ, and Christ lives in me and I am dead to sin." What is the life Christ lives in me? Ask what is the life Adam lives in me? Adam lives in me the death life, a life that has fallen under the power of sin and death, death to God. That life Adam lives in me by nature as an unconverted man. And Christ, the second Adam, has come to me with a new life, and I now live in His life, the death-life of Christ. As long as I do not know it, I can not act according to it, though it be in me. Praise God, when a man begins to see what it is, and begins in obedience to say, "I will do what God's Word says; I am dead, I reckon myself dead," he enters upon a new life. On the strength of God's everlasting Word, and your union to Christ, and the great fact of Calvary, reckon, know yourself as dead indeed unto sin. A man must see this truth; this is the first step. The second is—he must accept it in faith. And what then? When he accepts it in faith, then there comes in him a struggle, and a painful experience, for that faith is still very feeble, and he begins to ask, "But why, if I am dead to sin, do I commit so much sin?" And the answer God's Word gives is simply this: You do not allow the power of that death to be applied by the Holy Spirit. What we need is to understand that the Holy Spirit came from Heaven, from the glorified Jesus, to bring His death and His life into us. The two are inseparably connected. That Christ died, He died unto sin, and that He liveth, He liveth unto God. The death and the life in Him are inseparable; and even so in us the life to God in Christ is inseparably connected with the death to sin. And that is what the Holy Ghost will teach us and work in us. If I have accepted Christ in faith by the Holy Ghost, and yield myself to Him, Christ every day keeps possession, and reveals the full power of my fellowship in His death and life in my heart. To some this comes undoubtedly in one moment of supreme power and blessing; all at once they see and accept it, and enter in, and there is death to sin as a Divine experience. It is not that the tendency to evil is rooted out. No; but the power of Christ's death keeps from sin, and destroys the power of sin; the power of Christ's death can be manifested in the Holy Spirit's unceasingly mortifying the deeds of the body.

Some one asks me if there is still growth needed. Undoubtedly. By the Holy Spirit a man can now begin to live and grow, deeper and deeper, into the fellowship of Christ's death. New things are discovered by him in spheres of which he never thought. A man may at times be filled with the Holy Ghost, and yet there may be great imperfections in him. Why? For this reason: because his heart, perhaps, had not been fully prepared by a complete discovery of sin. There may be pride, or self-consciousness, or forwardness, or other qualities of this nature which he has never noticed. The Holy Spirit does not always cast these out at once. No. There are different ways of entering into the blessed life. One man enters into the blessed life with the idea of power for service; another with the idea of rest from worry and weariness; another with the idea of deliverance from sin. In all these aspects there is something limited, and therefore every believer is to give himself up after he knows the power of Christ's death, and say continually: "Lord Jesus, let the power of Thy death work through, let it penetrate my whole being." As the man gives himself unreservedly up, he will begin to bear the marks of a crucified man. The apostle says: "I have been crucified," and he lives like a crucified man.

What are the marks of a crucified man? The first is, deep, absolute humility. Christ humbled Himself, and became obedient unto death, even the death of the cross. When the death to sin begins to work mightily, that is one of its chief and most blessed proofs. It breaks a man down, down, and the great longing of his heart is, "Oh, that I could get deeper down before my God, and be nothing at all, that the life of Christ might be exalted. I deserve nothing but the cursed cross; I give myself over to it." Humility is one of the great marks of a crucified man.

Another mark is impotence, helplessness. When a man hangs on the cross, he is utterly helpless, he can do nothing. As long as we Christians are strong, and can work, or struggle, we do not get into the blessed life of Christ; but when a man says, "I am a crucified man, I am utterly helpless, every breath of life and strength must come from my Jesus," then we learn what it is to sink into our own impotence, and say, "I am nothing."

Still another mark of crucifixion is restfulness. Yes. Christ was crucified, and went down into the grave, and we are crucified and buried with Him. There is no place of rest like the grave; a man can do nothing there, "My flesh shall rest in hope," said David, and said the Messiah. Yes, and when a man goes down into the grave of Jesus, it means this: that he just cries out, "I have nothing but God, I trust God; I am waiting upon God; my flesh rests in Him; I have given up everything, that I may rest, waiting upon what God is to do to me." Remember, the crucifixion, and the death, and the burial are inseparably one. And remember the grave is the place where the mighty resurrection power of God will be manifested. And remember those precious words in the 11th of John: "Said I not unto thee"—when did Christ say that? It was at the grave of Lazarus—"that if thou believest, thou shalt see the glory of God?" Where shall I see the glory of God most brightly? Beside the grave. Go down into death believing, and the glory of God will come upon thee, and fill thy heart.

Dear friends, we want to die. If we are to live in the rest, and the peace, and the blessedness of our great Boaz; if we are to live a life of joy and of fruitfulness, of strength and of victory, we must go down into the grave with Christ, and the language of our life must be: "I am a crucified man. God be praised, though I have nothing but sin in myself, I have an everlasting Jesus, with His death and His life, to be the life of my soul."

How can I enter into this fellowship of the cross? We find an illustration in the story of the penitent thief. Thomas said, before Christ's death, "Let us go and abide with Him." And Peter said, "Lord, I am ready to go with Thee to prison, or to death." But the disciples all failed, and our Lord took a man who was the offscouring of the earth, and he hung him upon the cross of Calvary beside Himself, and He said to Peter, and to all: "I will let you see what it is to die with Me." And He says that word to-day, to the weakest and the humblest; if you are longing to know what it is to enter into death with Jesus, come and look at the penitent thief. And what do we see there? First of all, we see there the state of a heart prepared to die with Christ. We see in that penitent thief, a humble, whole-hearted confession of sin. There he hung upon the cursed tree, and the multitudes were blaspheming that man beside him, but he was not ashamed publicly to make confession: "I am dying a death that I have deserved; I am suffering justly; this cross is what I have deserved." Here is one of the reasons why the Church of Christ enters so little into the death of Christ; men do not want to believe that the curse of God is upon everything in them that has not died with Christ. People talk about the curse of sin, but they do not understand that the whole nature has been infected by sin, and that the curse is on everything. My intellect, has that been defiled by sin? Terribly, and the curse of sin is on it, and therefore my intellect must go down into the death. Ah, I believe that the Church of Christ suffers more to-day from trusting in intellect, in sagacity, in culture, and in mental refinement, than from almost anything else. The Spirit of the world comes in, and men seek by their wisdom, and by their knowledge, to help the Gospel, and they rob it of its crucifixion mark. Christ directed Paul to go and preach the Gospel of the cross, but to do it not with wisdom of words. The curse of sin is on all that is of nature. If there be a minister who has delighted in preaching, who has done his very best, who has given his very best in the way of talent and of thought, and who asks, "Must that go down into the grave?" I say, "Yes, my brother, the whole man must be crucified." And so with the heart's affection. What is more beautiful than the love of a child to his mother? In that lovely nature there is something unsanctified, and it must be given up to die. God will raise it from the dead and give it back again, sanctified and made alive unto God. So I might go through the whole of our life. People often say to me: "But has God made all things so beautiful, and is it not right that we should enjoy them? Are not His gifts all good?" I answer, yes, but remember what it says; they are good, if sanctified by the Word of God and prayer. The curse of sin is on them; the blight of sin is on everything most beautiful, and it takes much of God's Word, and much of prayer to sanctify them. It is very hard to give up a thing to the death, and it is hardest of all to give up my life to the death, and I never will until I have learned that everything about that life is stamped by sin, and let it go down into the death as the only way to have it quickened and sanctified.

The penitent thief confessed his sin, and that he deserved death. Then, next, he had faith in the almighty power of Christ. A wonderful faith. It has no parallel in the Bible. There hangs the cursed malefactor with Jesus of Nazareth, and he dares speak, and say: "I am dying here, under the just curse of my sins, but I believe Thou canst take me into Thy heart, and remember me when Thou comest into Thy Kingdom." Oh, that we might learn to believe in the almighty power of Christ! That man believed that Christ was a King, and had a Kingdom, and that He would take him up in His arms, and in His heart, and remember him when He came into His Kingdom. He believed that, and believing that, he died. Brother, you and I need to take time to come to a much larger and deeper faith in the power of Christ, that the almighty Christ will indeed take us in His arms and carry us through this death life, revealing the power of His death in us. I cannot live it without personal contact with Christ every hour of the day. Christ must do it; Christ can do it. Come therefore and say: "Is He not the Almighty One; did He not come from the throne of God; did He not prove His omnipotence, and did the Father not prove it when He rose from the dead?" Would you be afraid, now that Christ is on the throne, of doing what the malefactor did when Christ was upon the cross, and entrusting yourself to Him to live as one dead with Him? Christ will carry you through the very process He went through; will make His death work in you every day of your life.

I note one thing more in the penitent thief—his prayer. There was his conviction of sin, and his faith, but there was, further, the utterance of his faith in prayer. He turned to Jesus. Remember that the whole world, with perhaps the exception of Mary and the women, was turned against Christ that day. Of the whole world of men as far as I know, there was but that one praying to Christ. Do not wait to see what others do; if you wait for that,—alas! I desire to say it in love and tenderness,—you will not find much company in the Church of Christ. Pray incessantly: "Lord Christ, let the power of Thy death come into me." For God's sake, pray the prayer. If you want to live the life of Heaven, there must be death to sin in the power of Jesus. There must be personal entrustment of the soul into His death to sin, personal acceptance of Jesus to do the mighty work.

We have seen what the preparation is on the part of this man; let us look, secondly, at how Christ met him. He met him, you know, with that wonderful promise, with its three wonderful parts: "To-day shalt thou be with me in Paradise." A promise of fellowship with Christ,—"Thou shalt be with me;" a promise of rest in eternity, in the Paradise from which sin had cast man out,—"With me in Paradise;" a promise of immediate blessing,—"To-day shalt thou be with Me." With that three-fold blessing Jesus comes to you and me, and He says: "Believer, are you longing to live the Paradise life, where I give souls to eat of the Tree of Life, in the Paradise of God, day by day? Are you longing for that uninterrupted communion with God that there was in Paradise before Adam fell? Are you longing for perfect fellowship with me, longing to live where I am living, in the love of the Father? To-day, to-day; even as the Holy Ghost says: 'To-day shalt thou be with me!' Longest thou for Me? I long more for thee. Longest thou for fellowship? I long unceasingly for thy fellowship, for I need thy love, my child, to satisfy my heart. Nothing can prevent My receiving thee into fellowship. I have taken possession of

Heaven for thee, as the Great High Priest, that thou mightest live the Heavenly life, that thou mightest have access into the holiest of all and an abiding dwelling place there. To-day, if thou wilt, thou shalt be with me in Paradise." Thank God, the Jesus of the penitent thief is my Jesus. Thank God, the cross of the penitent thief is my cross. I must confess my sinfulness if I want to come into the closest communion with my blessed Lord. There was not a man upon earth during the thirty-three years of Christ's life that had such wonderful fellowship with the Son of God, as the penitent thief, for with the Son of God he entered the glory. What made him so separate from others? He was on the cross with Jesus and entered Paradise with Him. And if I live upon the cross with Jesus, the Paradise life shall be mine every day.

And now, if Jesus gives me that promise, what have I to do? Let go. When a ship is moored alongside the dock, with everything ready for the start and all standing on the quay, the last bell is rung and the order is given, "Let go." Then the last rope is loosened, and the steamer moves. There are things that tie us to the earth, to the flesh-life, and to the self-life; but to-day the message comes: "If thou wouldst die with Jesus, let go." Thou needst not understand all. It may not be perfectly clear; the heart may appear dull, but never mind; Jesus carried that penitent thief through death to life. The thief did not know where he was going, he did not know what was to happen, but Jesus, the mighty conqueror, took him in His arms, and landed him, in his ignorance, in Paradise. Oh, I have sometimes said in my soul, bless God for the ignorance of that penitent thief. He knew nothing about what was going to happen, but he trusted Christ; and if I can not understand all about this crucifixion with Christ, and the death to sin, and the life to God, and the glory that comes into the heart, never mind, I trust my Lord's promise, I cast myself helpless into His arms, I maintain my position on the cross. Given up to Jesus, to die with Him, I can trust Him to carry me through.

Shall we not each one take the blessed opportunity of doing what Ruth did when she, in obedience to the advice of her mother, just cast herself at the feet of the great Boaz, the Redeemer, to be His? Shall we not come into personal contact with Jesus, and shall not each one of us just speak before the world these simple words: "Lord, here is this life; there is much in it still of self, and sinfulness, and self-will, but I come to Thee; I long to enter fully into Thy death; I long to know fully that I have been crucified with Thee; I long to live Thy life every day." Then say: "Lord Jesus, I have seen Thy glory, what Thou didst for the penitent one at Thy side on the cross; I am trusting Thee, that Thou wilt do it for me. Lord, I cast myself into Thy arms."

Joy in the Holy Ghost

Romans 14: 17.—For the Kingdom of God is not meat and drink, but righteousness, and peace, and joy in the Holy Ghost.

In this text we have the earthly revelation of the work of the Trinity. The Kingdom of God is righteousness; that represents the work of the Father. The foundations of His throne are justice and judgment. Then comes the work of the Son: He is our peace, our Shiloh, our rest. The Kingdom of God is peace; not only the peace of pardon for the past, but the peace of perfect assurance as to the future. Not only the work of atonement is finished, but the work of sanctification is finished in Christ, and I may receive and enjoy what is prepared for me. The new man has been created, and I may in Him live out my life; if a kingdom is established in righteousness, if the rule is perfect, there can be perfect rest. If there be peace, no war from without, and no civil dissension within, a nation can be happy and prosperous. And so there comes here, after righteousness and peace, the joy, the blessed happiness in which a man can live; "The Kingdom of God is righteousness and peace, and joy in the Holy Ghost." May we regard this joy of the Holy Ghost, not only as a beautiful thing to admire, not only as a thing to have beautiful thoughts about, but as a blessing that we are going to claim.

We often see a fruiterer's or confectioner's shop, with beautiful fruit or cake temptingly displayed in the window. There is a great pane of plate glass before it, and the hungry little boys stand there and look, and long, but they cannot reach it. If you were to say to one, "Now, little boy, take that fruit," he would look at you in surprise. He has learned that there is something between. If he had never known of glass he might attempt it. The plate glass is sometimes so clear that even a grown man might for a moment be deceived and stretch out his hand. But he soon finds there is something invisible between him and the fruit. This represents exactly the life of many Christians; they see, but they cannot take. And what now is this invisible pane of plate glass, that hinders my taking the beautiful things I see? It is nothing but the self-life; I see divine things but cannot reach them, the self-life is the invisible plate glass. We are willing, we are working, we are striving, and yet we are holding back something; we are afraid to give up everything to God. We do not know what the consequences may be. We have not yet comprehended that God and Christ Jesus are worth everything. Whatever is told us of the blessed life of peace and joy, we say, "Praise God; God's Word is true; I believe the Word;" and yet, day by day, we stand back. When some one says, "Take it," we say, "I can't take it; there is something between." Would we were willing to give up the self-life; would we had the courage to give up to-day, and let the joy of the Holy Ghost be our religion. That is the religion God has prepared for us; that is the religion we can claim; not only righteousness, not only peace, but the joy of the Holy Ghost. That is the Kingdom of God.

What is this joy? First of all, it is the joy of the presence of Jesus. We are often inclined to speak most of two other things, the power for sanctification, and the power for service. But I find there is a thing more important than either of those two, and that is that the Holy Ghost came from Heaven to be the abiding presence of Christ in His disciples, in the Church, and in the heart of every believer. The Lord Jesus was going away, and His disciples were very sad; their hearts was sorrowful; but He said to them, "I will come back again, and I will come to you. Your hearts shall rejoice, and your joy no man shall take from you." What took place with them, may take place with us too. The Holy Spirit is given to make the presence of Jesus an abiding reality, a continual experience. And what was that joy that no man could ever touch? It was the joy of Pentecost. And what was Pentecost? The coming of the Lord Jesus in the Holy Ghost to dwell with His disciples. While Jesus was with His disciples on earth, He could not get into their hearts in the right way. They loved Him, but they could not take in His teaching, they could not partake of His disposition, and they could not receive His very spirit into their being. But when He had ascended to Heaven, He came back in the Spirit to dwell in their hearts. It is this alone that will help us to go, the minister to his congregation with its difficulties, the business man to his counter, the mother to her large family with its care, the worker to her Bible class. It is this only that will help us to feel, "I can conquer, I can live in the rest of God." Why? "Because I have the almighty Jesus with me every day." With God's people, there seems to be one hindrance, they do not know their Saviour. They do not realize that this blessed Christ is an ever present, all-pervading, in-dwelling Christ, who wants to take charge of their entire lives. They do not know, they do not believe that He is an Almighty Christ, and ready in the midst of any difficulties and any circumstances to be their keeper and their

God. This is absolutely true. Many Christians are asked as to how one may have the joy unspeakable, the joy that nothing can take away, the joy of the friendship and nearness and love of Jesus filling his heart. We complain that the rush of competition is so terrible that we can not get time for private prayer. Brother, the Lord Jesus Christ, if He comes to you as a brother and a friend and an abiding guest, can give your heart the joy of the Holy Ghost, so that business will take its right place under your feet. Your heart is too holy to have it filled with business; let the business be in the head and under the feet, but let Christ have the whole heart, and He will keep the whole life. Our glorious, exalted, almighty, ever present Christ! why is it that you and I can not trust Him fully, perfectly to do His work? Shall we not say before God that we do trust Him, that we will trust Christ to be to us every moment all that we can desire? On the Cross of Calvary Christ was all alone, and you believe He did a perfect and a blessed work; and Christ in Heaven is all alone, as high priest and intercessor, and you trust Him for His work there. But, praise God! it is equally true, Christ in the heart is able all alone to keep it all the days. May it please God to reveal to His children the nearness of Christ standing and knocking at the door of every heart, ready to come in and rest forever there and to lead the soul into His rest.

We all know what the power of joy is; we know there is nothing so attractive as joy, there is nothing can help a man to bear and endure so much as joy; we know that the Lord Jesus Himself for the joy that was set before Him endured the cross. One is not living aright if he is living a sighing, trembling, doubting life. Come to-day and believe the joy of the Holy Ghost is meant for you. Does not the Scripture say, "Whom not having seen we love; in whom, though now ye see Him not, yet believing ye rejoice with joy unspeakable and full of glory." Do you not believe that this blessed, adorable, inconceivably beautiful Son of God, the delight of the Father,—do you not believe that this Son of God could fill your heart with delight day and night, if He were always present? And do you not believe that He loves you more than a bridegroom loves his bride? Do you not believe that, having bought you with His blood, Jesus is longing for you? He needs you to satisfy His heart of love. Begin to believe with your whole heart, "The joy of the Holy Ghost is my portion," for the Holy Ghost secures to me without interruption the presence and the love of Jesus.

But secondly, there is the joy of deliverance from sin. The Holy Ghost comes to sanctify us. Christ is our sanctification, and the Holy Ghost comes to communicate Him to us, to work out all that is in Christ and to reproduce it in us. Let us remember that in the sight of God there is something more than work. There is Christlikeness—the likeness and the life of Christ in us. That is what God wants; that will fit us for work. God asks not that Christ should live in us as separate persons; temples full of filthy, impure, foul creatures, with Christ hidden away somewhere there,—that is not the intention of God, but He wants Christ so formed in us that we are one with Christ, and that in our thinking, feeling and living, the image of His blessed Son is manifest before Him. The Holy Spirit is given to sanctify us. My brother, are you willing to be sanctified from every sin, be that sin great or small? I am not asking, do you feel that you have the power to conquer it? I am not even asking, do you feel the power to cast it out? It may be that you feel no power; that won't hinder if you are willing. I can not cast out sin, but I can get the Almighty Christ by the Holy Spirit to do it, and it is my work to say to Christ, "There is the sin, there is the evil thing, I lay it at Thy feet, I cast it there, I cast it into Thy very bosom. Lord, I am ready to cut off the right hand, anything, only deliver me from it." Then Christ will cast out the evil spirit and give deliverance. The Spirit of God is a holy spirit and His work is to make free from the power of sin and death. And if you want to live in the joy of the Holy Ghost, the question comes: "Are you willing to surrender everything that is sinful, even what appears good,—but has the stain of sin on it?" You may be involved in relationships that make your life very difficult. A pastor with his people maybe brought into very difficult relationships; or a business man with his partner or those with whom he has to associate, may be in an exceedingly trying position. But is not the blessed Lamb of God worth it all? What is the Christ worth to you? The question was once asked the disciples, "What think ye of Christ?" I ask, "What is Christ worth to you?" And I beseech you, whatever prospective difficulties there may be, and whatever perplexities surround you, take the whole world to-day and cast it at His feet. To have Him is worth any difficulty; to have Him will be the solution of every difficulty. There are not only such external, manifest difficulties and perplexities, there are a thousand little things that come in our life and that often disturb us, temptations to unloving feelings, and sharp words, and hasty judgments. Oh, come, and believe that the Holy Spirit, the sanctifier, can come in and rule, and give grace to pass through all without sinning, and you shall know what the joy of the Holy Ghost is. Our body, we read in 1st Corinthians, is the temple of the Holy Ghost. It is to be holy in things like eating and drinking. How often a Christian comes to the consciousness that he takes or seeks too much enjoyment in that eating, eating for pleasure, with no self-denial or self-sacrifice in his feeding the body! How often we tempt one another to eat, and how often the believer forgets that this body is the very secret temple of the Holy Ghost and that every mouthful we eat and drink must be for the glory of God in such a way as to be perfectly well pleasing to Him! Beloved, I bring you a message: There is access for you into the rest of God, and the Holy Spirit is given to bring you in, and the Holy Spirit will fill your heart with the unutterable joy of Christ's presence; and with the joy of deliverance from sin, of victory over sin; the unutterable joy of knowing that you are doing God's will and are pleasing in His sight; the unutterable joy of knowing that He is sanctifying and keeping the temple for Christ to dwell in. Believers, the joy of the Holy Ghost, the joy of that holiness of God, is His blessedness, His purity, His perfection, that nothing can mar or stain or disturb. The Holy Ghost waits to bring and to manifest it in our lives. He wants to come so into our hearts that we shall live, as Holy Ghost men, the sanctified life, with the sanctifying power of Jesus running through our whole beings.

My third thought is: the joy of the Holy Ghost is the joy of the love of the saints. The Holy Ghost was not given to any man on the day of Pentecost separate from the others; He came and filled the whole company. We know how much division and separation and pride there had been among them, but on that day the Holy Ghost so filled their hearts that we find it was afterward said: "Behold how these men love one another." There was a love in the primitive church that the very heathen noticed, and could not understand. Why was that? The Holy Spirit is the bond of union between the Father and Son; and that bond is love. The Holy Spirit is just the love of God come to dwell in the heart. When He dwells with me and my brother we learn to love each other. Though I be unloving naturally, and though I have very little grace, if the heart of my brother is full of the Holy Spirit he loves me through it all. You know love is a wonderful thing. As long as a man tries to love it is not real love, but when real love comes, the more opposition it meets the more it triumphs, for the more it can exercise itself and perfect itself, the more it rejoices. Take a mother with a son dishonoring her. How her love follows him! When she sees that he has fallen deeper than ever before, how the dear mother heart only loves him the more intensely through all the wretchedness! Does not the Scripture say, "If He gave His life for us, we are bound to give our life for the brethren?" The Holy Spirit comes as a spirit of love, and if you want to know the joy of the Holy Ghost, and want Him to lead you into the rest of God and keep you there, beware above everything on earth or in hell of being unloving. One sharp word to your brother or sister brings a cloud upon you without your knowing it. People are so accustomed to talk just as they like about each other that they say sharp and unkind and unloving things, and when a cloud comes in consequence they cannot understand it. If there is one thing that grieves God, if there is one thing that hinders the Spirit—the fruit of the Spirit is love—it is the want of lovingness. If you want to live in the joy of the Holy Ghost make your covenant with God. "But," you say, "there is a Christian man who makes me so impatient; he does trouble me and vex me so with his stupidity. And there are those worldly men; how they have tempted me in times past and done me harm! And there is that business man who is trying to ruin me." Take them all, and your own wife and children and every one around you and say, "I understand it, love is rest, and rest is love. God resteth in His love. Love is rest and rest is love, and where there is no love the rest must be disturbed." And let us say to-day, "I see what the joy is; it is the joy of always loving, it is the joy of losing my own life in love to others." In connection with humility, some one asks, "How about that text, 'In honor preferring one another?'" When a soul comes into perfect humility before God it becomes nothing, and God becomes all in all. I am nothing. There is no self to be affronted; I have said before God: "I am nothing; it is only Thy life and light that shines. The honor is Thine, and nothing may touch me but what is against the glory of my God."

Beloved, are you living in the joy of the Holy Ghost? Come and accept a blessing and give yourself up to live a life of humility in which you are nothing, and a life of love like Christ's in which you only live for your fellow-men, for the kingdom of God is the joy of the Holy Ghost.

My last thought is that the joy of the Holy Ghost is the joy of working for God. The joy of the presence of Jesus, the joy of deliverance from sin, the joy of love for the brethren, and then the joy of working for God. Some of us have at times felt what an incomprehensible thing it is that the everlasting God should work through us; and we have said, "Lord, what is this, that Thou the Almighty One dost work in me and through me, a vile worm by nature?" It is a mystery that passeth knowledge, and yet it is so true. The joy of the Holy Ghost comes when a man gives himself up to the Christlike work of carrying the love of God to men. Let us seek the perishing, let us live and die for souls, let us live and die that our fellow-men may be reclaimed and brought back to their God. There is no joy like hearing the joy-song of a new-born soul. But yes, there is another joy that may be as deep. Even if God does not give me the blessing of hearing the newborn soul sing its song, I may have the joy, the sympathy with Jesus in His rejected life, and the assurance that the Father looks with good pleasure on me. When I think of the thousands of believers in the Christian world and then think of the heathen world, the cry comes up in my heart: "What are we doing?" Ah, we need to be crying to God day and night, "Lord God, wake us up. Lord God, let the Holy Spirit burn within us." Are we the true successors of Jesus Christ? Are we indeed the followers and successors of Christ who went all the way to Calvary to give His blood for men? Do let us remember the joy of the Holy Ghost is the joy of working for God in Christ. I believe that God has new ways and new leadings and new power for His people, if they will only wait on Him. But what most of us do is this: we thank God for all He has given, we look at all the ways of working we have, and we say that we will try to do our work better. But oh, if we had a sense of the need, if we had any sense, by the vision of the Holy Ghost, of the state of the millions around us, I am sure we would fall on our faces before God and say, "God help me to something new. Oh that every fiber of my being may be taken possession of for this great work with God!" The great need is that all Christians should consecrate themselves wholly to God for His work. May God help us to know what is the joy of the Holy Ghost.

Concluding, I ask again: "Do you believe that it is possible for the Lord Jesus, our Shiloh, of whom Jacob prophesied, our Joshua, our glorious King and High Priest,—do you believe it is possible for Christ Jesus to bring you to-day into the rest of God?" Remember that word in Hebrews, "Even as the Holy Ghost saith, to-day." To-day, summon up courage and take up your ministry, and take up your business, and take up your surroundings, and take up your natural temperament, and take up your home, and take up your life for the days to come upon earth, and say, "I do not understand it, I know not what will come, but one thing I know, I do absolutely give everything into the hands of the crucified Lamb of God; He shall have me in my entirety." And oh, remember, beloved, that Christ will be to you more than you can think or understand, more than you can ask or desire.

Come, let us cast ourselves into those blessed, loving arms, and let us believe even now that our Joshua leads us into the rest of God, the rest in which we are saved from self-care and self-seeking and self-trusting and self-loving, the rest in which we do not think of ourselves, but where He who is almighty and omnipresent is always going to be with us and is always going to work within us. And let us when we have done that, claim the promise, that as we have sought first the kingdom and God's righteousness, all things shall be added unto us. Beloved, the kingdom of God is within you, and it is righteousness and peace and joy in the Holy Ghost. Come, let us claim it even now in simple, childlike, humble faith.

Triumph of Faith

John 4: 50.—And the man believed the word that Jesus had spoken unto him.

Let me quote from the Gospel according to St. John, the 4th chapter, beginning at the 46th verse: "So Jesus came again into Cana of Galilee, where He made the water wine. And there was a certain nobleman whose son was sick at Capernaum. When he heard that Jesus was come up out of Judea into Galilee, he went unto Him, and besought Him that He would come down and heal his son; for he was at the point of death. Then said Jesus unto him, Except ye see signs and wonders, ye will not believe." There you have the word "believe" the first time. "The nobleman saith unto Him, Sir, come down ere my child die. Jesus saith unto him, Go thy way; thy son liveth. And the man believed the word that Jesus had spoken unto him, and he went his way." There you have that word the second time. "And as he was now going down, his servants met him, and told him, saying, Thy son liveth. Then inquired he of them the hour when he began to amend. And they said unto him, Yesterday at the seventh hour the fever left him. So the father knew that it was at the same hour, in the which Jesus said unto him, Thy son liveth; and himself believed, and his whole house." There you have the word "faith".

This story has often been used to illustrate the different steps of faith in the spiritual life. It was this use made of it in an address that brought the sainted Canon Battersby into the full enjoyment of rest. He had been a most godly man, but had lived the life of failure. He saw in the story what it was to rest on the Word and trust the saving power of Jesus, and from that night he was a changed man. He went home to testify of it, and under God, he was allowed to originate the Keswick Convention.

Let me point out to you the three aspects of faith which we have here: first, faith seeking; then, faith finding; and then, faith enjoying. Or, still better: faith struggling; faith resting; faith triumphing. First of all, faith struggling. Here is a man, a heathen, a nobleman, who has heard about Christ. He has a dying son at Capernaum, and in his extremity leaves his home, and walks some six or seven hours away to Cana of Galilee. He has heard of the Prophet, possibly, as one who has made water wine; he has heard of His other miracles round Capernaum, and he has a certain trust that Jesus will be able to help him. He goes to Him, and his prayer is that the Lord will come down to Capernaum and heal his son. Christ said to him, "Except ye see signs and wonders, ye will not believe." He saw that the nobleman wanted Him to come and stand beside the child. This man had not the faith of the centurion—"Only speak a word." He had faith. It was faith that came from hearsay, and it was faith that did, to a certain extent, hope in Christ; but it was not the faith in Christ's power such as Christ desired. Still Christ accepted and met this faith. After the Lord had thus told him what He wished—a faith that could fully trust Him—the nobleman cried the second time, "Sir, come down ere my child die." Seeing his earnestness and his trust, Christ said, "Go thy way; thy son liveth." And then we read that the nobleman believed. He believed, and he went his way. He believed the word that Jesus had spoken. In that he rested and was content. And he went away without having any other pledge than the word of Jesus. As he was walking homeward, the servants met him, to tell him his son lived. He asked at what hour he began to amend. And when they told him, he knew it was at the very hour that Jesus had been speaking to him. He had at first a faith that was seeking, and struggling, and searching for blessing; then he had a faith that accepted the blessing simply as it was contained in the word of Jesus. When Christ said, "Thy son liveth," he was content, and went home, and found the blessing—the son restored.

Then came the third step in his faith. He believed with his whole house. That is to say, he did not only believe that Christ could do just this one thing, the healing of his son; but he believed in Christ as his Lord. He gave himself up entirely to be a disciple of Jesus. And that not only alone, but with his whole house. Many Christians are like the nobleman. They have heard about a better life. They have met certain individuals by whose Christian lives they have been impressed, and consequently have felt that Christ can do wonderful things for a man. Many Christians say in their heart, "I am sure there is a better life for me to live; how I wish I could be brought to that blessed state!" But they have not much hope about it. They have read, and prayed, but they have found everything so difficult, If you ask them, "Do you believe Jesus can help you to live this higher life?" they say, "Yes; He is omnipotent." If you ask, "Do you believe Jesus wishes to do it?" they say, "Yes, I know He is loving." And if you say, "Do you believe that He will do it for you?" they at once say, "I know He is willing, but whether He will actually do it for me I do not know. I am not sure that I am prepared. I do not know if I am advanced enough. I do not know if I have enough grace for that." And so they are hungering, struggling, wrestling, and often remain unblessed. This state of things sometimes goes on for years—they are expecting to see signs and wonders, and hoping that God, by a miracle, will put them all right. They are just like the Israelites; they limit the Holy One of Israel. Have you ever noticed that it is the very people whom God has blessed so wonderfully who do that? What did the Israelites say? "God hath provided water in the wilderness. But can He provide the table in the wilderness? We do not think He can." And so we find believers who say, "Yes, God has done wonders. The whole of redemption is a wonder, and God has done wonders for some whom I know. But will God take one so feeble as I, and put me entirely right?" The struggling and wrestling and seeking are the beginnings of faith in you—a faith that desires and hopes. But it must go on further. And how can that faith advance? Look at the second step. There is the nobleman, and Christ speaks to him this wonderful word: "Go thy way; thy son liveth;" and the nobleman simply rests upon that word of the living Jesus. He rests on it, and without any proof of what he is to get, and without one man in the world to encourage him. He goes away home with the thought, "I have received the blessing I sought; I have got life from the dead for my son. The living Christ promised it me, and on that I rest." The struggling, seeking faith has become a resting faith. The man has entered into rest about his son.

And now, dear believers, this is the one thing God asks you to do: God has said that in Christ you have eternal life, the more abundant life; Christ has said to you, "I live, and ye shall live also." The Word says to us that Christ is our Peace, our Victory over every enemy, who leads us into the rest of God. These are the words of God, and His message has come to us that Christ can do for us what Moses could not have done. Moses had no Christ to live in him. But it is told you that you can have what Moses had not; you can have a living Christ within you. And are you going to believe that, apart from any experience, and apart from any consciousness of strength? If the peace of God is to rule in your heart, it is the God of peace Himself must be there to do it. The peace is inseparable from the God. The light of the sun—can I separate that from the sun? Utterly impossible. As long as I have the sun I have the light. If I lose the sun; I lose the light. Take care! Do not seek the peace of God or the peace of Christ apart from God and Christ. But how does Christ come to me? He comes to me in this precious Word; and just as He said to the nobleman, "Go thy way home; thy son liveth," so Christ comes to me to-day, and He says, "Go thy way; thy Saviour liveth." "Lo, I am with you alway." "I live, and ye shall live also." "I wait to take charge of your whole life. Will you have me do this? Trust to me all that is evil and feeble; your whole sinful and perverse nature—give it up to Me; that dying, sin-sick soul—give it up to Me, and I will take care of it." Will you not listen and hear Him speak to your soul? "Child, go forward into all the circumstances of life that have tempted you; into all the difficulties that threaten you." Your soul lives with the life of God; your soul lives in the power of God; your soul lives in Christ Jesus. Will you not, like the nobleman, take the simple step of faith, and believe the word Jesus hath spoken? Will you not say, "Lord Jesus, Thou hast spoken: I can rest on Thy Word. I have seen that Christ is willing to be more to me than I ever knew; I have seen that Christ is willing to be my life in the most actual and intense meaning of the words." All that we know about the Holy Ghost sums itself up in this one thing: The Holy Ghost comes to make Christ an actual, indwelling, always-abiding Saviour.

Lastly, comes the triumphant faith. The man went home holding fast the promise. He had only one promise, but he held it fast. When God gives me a promise, He is just as near me as when He fulfills it. That is a great comfort. When I have the promise I have also the pledge of the fulfillment. But the whole heart of God is in His promise, just as much as in the fulfillment of it, and sometimes God, the promiser, is more precious because I am compelled to cling more to Him, and to come closer, and to live by simple faith, and to adore His love. Do not think this is a hard life, to be living upon a promise. It means living upon the everlasting God. Who is going to say that is hard? It means living upon the crucified, the loving Christ. Be ashamed to say that is a difficult thing. It is a blessed thing.

The nobleman went home and found the child living. And what happened then? Two things. First: he gave up his whole life to be a believer in Jesus. If there had been a division among the people of Capernaum, and thousands of them had hated Christ, this man would still have stood on His side. He believed in the Lord. This is what must take place with us. Let us go forward with our trust in the living Christ, knowing that He will keep us. Then we will get grace to carry the life of Christ into our whole conduct, into all our walk and conversation. The faith that rests in Jesus, is the faith that trusts all to Him, with all we have. Do we not read that when God had finished His work, and rested, it was only to begin new work? Yes; the great work was to be carried on—watching over and ruling His world and His church. And is it not so with the Lord Jesus? When He had finished His work, He sat upon the throne to do His work of perfecting the body, through the Holy Spirit. And now, the Holy Spirit is carrying on that blessed work, teaching us to rest in Christ, and in the strength of that rest to go on, and to cover our whole life with the power, and the obedience, and the will, and the likeness of the Lord Jesus. The nobleman gave up his whole life to be a believer in Christ; and from that day it was a believer in Jesus who walked about the streets of Capernaum; not only a man who could say, "Once He helped me," but, "I believe in Him with my whole life." Let that be so with us everywhere; let Christ be the one object of our trust.

One thought more,—he believed with his whole house. That was triumphant faith. He took up his position as a believer in Christ; and his wife, his children, his servants—he gathered them all together, and laid them at the feet of Christ. And if you want power in your own house, if you want power in your Bible-class, if you want power in your social circle, if you want power to influence the nation and if you want power to influence the Church of Christ, see where it begins. Come into contact with Jesus in this rest of faith that accepts His life fully, that trusts Him fully, and the power will come by faith to overcome the world; by faith to bless others; by faith to live a life to the glory of God. Go thy way, thy soul liveth; for it is Jesus Christ who liveth within you. Go thy way; be not trembling and fearful, but rest in the word and the power of the Son of God. "Lo, I am with you alway." Go thy way, with the heart open to welcome Him, and the heart believing He has come in. Surely we have not prayed in vain. Christ has listened to the yearnings of our hearts and has entered in. Let us go our way quietly, restfully, full of praise, and joy, and trust; ever hearing the words of our Master, "Go thy way, thy soul liveth;" and ever saying, "I have trusted Christ to reveal His abundant life in my soul; by His grace I will wait upon Him to fulfill His promise." Amen.

The Source of Power in Prayer

Romans 8: 26-27.—Likewise the Spirit also helpeth our infirmities: for we know not what we should pray for as we ought: but the Spirit itself maketh intercession for us with groanings which cannot be uttered. And he that searcheth the hearts knoweth what is the mind of the Spirit, because he maketh intercession for the saints according to the will of God.

Here we have the teaching of God regarding the help the Holy Spirit will give us in prayer. The first half of this chapter is of much importance in connection with the teaching of God's word regarding the Spirit. In Romans vi. we read about being dead to sin and alive to God, and in Romans vii., about being dead to the law and married to Christ, and also about the impotency of the unregenerate man to do God's will. This is only a preparation to show us how helpless we are; and then in the eighth chapter comes the blessed work of the Spirit, expressed chiefly in the following words: "The Spirit hath made us free from the law of sin and death." The Spirit makes us free from the power of sin, and teaches and leads us so that we walk after the Spirit. In our inner disposition we may become spiritually minded, and enabled to mortify the deeds of the body. The Holy Spirit helps our infirmities. Prayer is the most necessary thing in the spiritual life. Yet we do not know how to pray nor what to pray for as we ought. The Spirit, Paul tells us, prays with groanings unutterable. And again he tells us that we ourselves often do not know what the Spirit is doing within us, but there is one, God, who searches the hearts. Words often reveal my thought and my wishes, but not what is deep in my heart, and God comes and searches my heart, and deep down, hidden, what I can not see and what was to me an unutterable longing, God finds.

Powerful prayer! The confession of ignorance! Ah, friends, I am often afraid for myself as a minister that I pray too easily. I have been praying for these forty or fifty years and it becomes, as far as man is concerned, an easy thing to pray. We all have been taught to pray, and when we are called upon we can pray, but it gets far too easy, and I am afraid we think we are praying often when there is little real prayer. Now if we are to have the praying of the Holy Ghost in us one thing is needed; we must begin by feeling, "I can not pray." When a man breaks down and can not pray, and there is a fire burning in his heart, and a burden resting upon him, there is something drawing him to God. "I know not what to pray,"—oh, blessed ignorance! We are not ignorant enough. Abraham went out not knowing whither he went; in that was an element of ignorance and also an element of faith. Jesus said to His disciples when they came with their prayer for the throne, "You know not what you ask." Paul says, "No man knoweth the things of God but the Spirit of God." You say, "If I am not to pray the old prayers I learned from my mother or from my professor in college or from my experience yesterday and the day before, what am I to pray?" I answer, pray new prayers, rise higher into the riches of God. You must begin to feel your ignorance. You know what we think of a student who goes to college fancying he knows everything. He will not learn much. Sir Isaac Newton said, "I do not know what I may appear to the world; but to myself I seem to have been only like a boy playing on the seashore and diverting myself in now and then finding a smoother pebble or a prettier shell than ordinary, whilst the great ocean of truth lay all undiscovered before me." When I see a man who can not pray glibly and smoothly and readily, I say that is a mark of the Holy Spirit. When he begins in his prayers to say, "Oh, God, I want more, I want to be led deeper in. I have prayed for the heathen, but I want to feel the burden of the heathen in a new way," it is an indication of the presence of the Holy Spirit. I tell you, beloved, if you will take time and let God lay the burden of the heathen heavier upon you until you begin to feel, "I have never prayed," it will be the most blessed thing in your life. And so with regard to the church: We want to take up our position as members of the church of Christ in this land; and as belonging to that great body, to say, "Lord God, is there nothing that can be done to bless the church of this land and to revive it and bring it out of its worldliness and out of its feebleness?" We may confer together and conclude faithlessly, "No, we do not know what is to be done; we have no influence and power over all these ministers and their churches." But on the other hand, how blessed to come to God and say, "Lord, we know not what to ask. Thou knowest what to grant." The Holy Spirit could pray a hundred fold more in us if we were only conscious of our ignorance, because we would then feel our dependence upon Him. May God teach us our ignorance in prayer and our impotence, and may God bring us to say, "Lord, we can not pray; we do not know what prayer is." Of course some of us do know in a measure what prayer is, many of us, and we thank God for what he has been to us in answer to prayer, but oh, it is only a little beginning compared to what the Holy Spirit of God teaches.

There is the first thought: our ignorance. "We know not what we should pray for as we ought;" but "the Spirit itself maketh intercession for us with groanings which cannot be uttered." We often hear about the work of God the Father and the Son and the Holy Ghost in working out and completing the great redemption, and we know that when God worked in the creation of the world, He was not weary, and yet we read that wonderful expression in the book of Exodus about the Sabbath day, "God rested and was refreshed." He was refreshed, the Sabbath day was a refreshment to Him. God had to work and Christ had to work, and now the Holy Spirit works, and His secret working place, the place where all work must begin, is in the heart where He comes to teach a man how to pray. When a man begins to get an insight into that which is needed and that which is promised and that which God waits to perform, he feels it to be beyond his conception; then is the time he will be ready to say, "I can not limit the holy one of Israel by my thoughts; I give myself up in the faith that the Holy Spirit can be praying for me with groanings, with longings, that can not be expressed." Apply that to your prayers.

There are different phases of prayer. There is worship, when a man just bows down to adore the great God. We do not take time to worship. We need to worship in secret, just to get ourselves face to face with the everlasting God, that He may overshadow us and cover us and fill us with His love and His glory. It is the Holy Spirit that can work in us such a yearning that we will give up our pleasures and even part of our business, that we may the oftener meet our God.

The next phase of prayer is fellowship. In prayer there is not only the worship of a king, but fellowship as of a child with God. Christians take far too little time in fellowship. They think prayer is just coming with their petitions. If Christ is to make me what I am to be, I must tarry in fellowship with God. If God is to let his love enter in and shine and burn through my heart, I must take time to be with Him. The smith puts his rod of iron into the fire. If he leaves it there but a short time it does not become red hot. He may take it out to do something with it and after a time put it back again for a few minutes, but this time it does not become red hot. In the course of the day he may put the rod into the fire a great many times and leave it there two or three minutes each time, but it never becomes thoroughly heated. If he takes time and leaves the rod ten or fifteen minutes in the fire the whole iron will become red hot with the heat that is in the fire. So if we are to get the fire of God's holiness and love and power we must take more time with God in fellowship. That was what gave men like Abraham and Moses their strength. They were men who were separated to a fellowship with God, and the living God made them strong. Oh, if we did but realize what prayer can do!

Another, and a most important phase of prayer is intercession. What a work God has set open for those who are His priests—intercessors! We find a wonderful expression in the prophecy of Isaiah; God says, "Let him take hold of me;" and again, "There is none that stirreth up himself to take hold of thee." In other passages God refers to the intercessors for Israel. Have you ever taken hold of God? Thank God, some of us have; but oh, friends, representatives of the church of Christ in the United States, if God were to show us how much there is of intense prayer for a revival through the church, how much of sincere confession of the sins of the church, how much of pleading with God and giving Him no rest till He make Jerusalem a glory in the earth, I think we should all be ashamed. We need to give up our hearts to the Holy Spirit, that He may pray for us and in us with groanings that can not be uttered.

What am I to do if I am to have this Holy Spirit within me? The Spirit wants time and room in the heart; He wants the whole being. He wants all my interest and influence going out for the honor and the glory of God; He wants me to give myself up. Beloved friend, you do not know what you could do if you would give yourself up to intercession. It is a work that a sick one lying on a bed year by year may do in power. It is a work that a poor one who has hardly a penny to give to a missionary society can do day by day. It is a work that a young girl who is in her father's house and has to help in the housekeeping can do by the Holy Spirit. People often ask: What does the Church of our day do to reach the masses? They ask, though they ask it tremblingly, for they feel so helpless: What can we do against the materialism and infidelity in places like London and Berlin and New York and Paris? We have given it up as hopeless. Ah, if men and women could be called out to band themselves together to take hold upon God! I am not speaking of any prayer union or any prayer time statedly set apart, but if the Spirit could find men and women who would give up their lives to cry to God, the Spirit would most surely come. It is not selfishness and it is not mere happiness that we seek when we talk about the peace and the rest and the blessing Christ can give. God wants us, Christ wants us, because He has to do a work; the work of Calvary is to be done in our hearts, we are to sacrifice our lives to pleading with God for men. Oh, let us yield ourselves day by day and ask God that it may please Him to let His Holy Spirit work in us.

Then comes the last thought, that God Himself comes to look with complacency upon the attitude of His child. Perhaps that poor man does not know that he is praying; perhaps he is ashamed of his prayers. So much the better. Perhaps he feels burdened and restless, but God hears, God discovers what is the mind of the Spirit, and will answer. Oh, think of this wonderful mystery, God the Father on the throne ready to grant unto us His blessings according to the riches of His glory; Christ the almighty high priest pleading day and night. His whole person is one intercession, and there goes up from Him without ceasing the pleading to the Father, "Bless thy church," and the answer comes from the Father to the Son, and from the Son down to the church, and if it does not reach us, it is because our hearts are closed. Let us open and enlarge our hearts and say to God, "Oh that I might be a priest, to enter God's presence continually and to take hold of God and to bring down a blessing to my perishing fellowmen!" God longs to find the intercession of Jesus reflected in the hearts of His children, and where He finds it, it is a delight. And He that searcheth the hearts knoweth the mind of the Spirit, because he prayeth for the saints, according to the will of God. Some one has spoken of that word, "for the saints," as meaning the spirit of praise in the believer for the saints throughout the world. God's word continually comes to us to pray for all not to be content with ourselves. Think upon the hundreds of church members in this land, multitudes unconverted, multitudes just converted, but yet worldly and careless. Think of the thousands of nominal Christians—Christians in name, but robbing God! and can we be happy? If we bear the burden of souls, can we have this peace and joy? God gives you peace and joy with no other object than that you should be strong to bear the burden of souls in the joy of Christ's salvation.

We do not wish to say, "I am trying to be as holy as I can; what have I to do with those worldly people about me?" If there is a terrible disease in my hand, my body can not say, "I have nothing to do with it." When the people had sinned Ezra rent his garments and bowed in the dust and made confession. He repented on the part of the people. And Nehemiah, when the nation sinned, made confession, and cast himself before God, deploring their disobedience to the God of their fathers. Daniel did the very same. And think you that we as believers have not a great work to do? Suppose we were each, persons without a single sin; just suppose it; could we then make confession? Look at Christ, without sin! He went down into the waters of baptism with sinners; He made Himself one with them. God has spoken to us to ask us if we realize what we are. He now asks us whether we belong to the church of this land, whether we have borne the burden of sin around us. Let us go to

God and may He by the Holy Spirit fill our hearts with unutterable sorrow at the state of the church, and may God give us grace to mourn before Him. And when we begin to confess the sins of the church, we will begin to feel our own sins as never before. In five of the epistles to the seven churches in Asia the keynote was "Repent;" there was to be no idea of overcoming and getting a blessing unless they repented. Let us on behalf of the church of Christ repent, and God will give us courage to feel that He will revive His work.

That God May Be All in All

1 Corinthians 15: 24-28.—*"Then cometh the end, when He shall have delivered up the kingdom to God, even the Father; when He shall have put down all rule, and all authority and power. For He must reign till He hath put all enemies under His feet. The last enemy that shall be destroyed is death. For He hath put all things under His feet. But when He saith, All things are put under Him, it is manifest that He is excepted, which did put all things under Him. And when all things shall be subdued unto him, then shall the Son also Himself be subject unto Him, that God may be all in all."*

This will be the grand conclusion of the great drama of the world's history, and of Christ's redemption. There will come a day—the glory is such we can form no conception of it, the mystery is so deep we can not realize it, but there is a day coming, when the Son shall deliver up the Kingdom that the Father gave Him, and that He won with His blood, and that He hath established and perfected from the throne of His glory. "He shall deliver up the Kingdom unto the Father." The Son Himself shall be subject also unto the Father, "that God may be all in all." I cannot understand it—the ever blessed Son equal with God, from eternity, and through eternity; the ever blessed Son on the throne shall be subject unto the Father; and in some way utterly beyond our comprehension, it shall then be made manifest, as never before, that God is all in all. It is this that Christ has been working for; it is this that He is working for to-day in us; it is this that He thought it worth while to give His blood for; it is this that His heart is longing for in each of us; this is the very essence and glory of Christianity, "that God may be all in all." And now, if this is what fills the heart of Christ; if this expresses the one end of the work of Christ, then, if I want to have the spirit of Christ in me, the motto of my life must be: Everything made subject, and swallowed up in Him, "that God may be all in all." What a triumph it would be if the Church were fighting really with that banner floating over her! What a life ours could be if that were really our banner! To serve God fully, wholly, only, to have Him all in all! How it would ennoble, and enlarge, and stimulate our whole being!

I am working, I am fighting, "that God may be all in all;" that the day of glory may be hastened. I am praying, and the Holy Spirit makes His wrestling in me with unutterable longing, "that God may be all in all." Would that we Christians realized in connection with what a grand cause we are working and praying; that we had some conception of what a Kingdom we are partakers of, and what a manifestation of God we are preparing for. To illustrate what a grand thing it is to belong to the Kingdom of God, and to the glorious Church of Christ on earth, John McNeill tells how when he was a boy twelve years of age, working on a railway line and earning the grand wages of six shillings a week, he used to go home to his mother and sisters, who thought no end of their little Johnnie, and delight them by telling of the position he had. He would say with great pride, "Oh, our company—it has so many thousands of pounds passing through its hands every year; it carries so many hundreds of thousands of passengers every year; and it has so many miles of railway, and so many engines and carriages; and so many thousands in its employ!" And the mother and the sisters had great pride in him, because he was a partner in such an important business. Christians, if we would only rouse ourselves to believe that we belong to the Kingdom that Christ is preparing to deliver up to the Father, that God may be all in all, how the glory would fill our hearts, and expel everything mean, and low, and earthly! How we should be borne along in this blessed faith! I am living for this: that Christ may have the Kingdom to deliver to the Father. I am living for this, and I will one day see Him made subject to the Father, and then God all in all. I am living for Him, and I shall be there not only as a witness, but I will have a part in it all. The Kingdom delivered up, the Son made subject, and God all in all! I shall have a part in it, and in adoring worship share the glory and the blessedness.

Let us take this home to our hearts, that it may rule in our lives—this one thought, this one faith, this one aim, this one joy: Christ lived, and died, and reigns; I live and die and in His power I reign; only for this one thing, "that God may be all in all." Let it possess our whole heart, and life. How can we do this? It is a serious question, to which I wish to give you a few simple answers. And I say, first of all: Allow God to take His place in your heart and life. Luther often said to people, when they came troubling him about difficulties, "Do let God be God." Oh, give God His place. And what is that place? "That God may be all in all." Let God be all in all every day, from morning to evening. God to rule and I to obey. Ah, the blessedness of saying, "God and I!" What a privilege that I have such a partner! God first, and then I! And yet there might be secret self-exaltation in associating God with myself. And I find in the Bible a more precious word still. It is, "God and not I." It is not, "God first, and I second;" God is all, and I am nothing. Paul said, "I labored more abundantly than they all; though I be nothing." Let us try to give God His place—begin in our closet, in our worship, in our prayer. The power of prayer depends almost entirely upon our apprehension of who it is with whom I speak. It is of the greatest consequence, if we have but half an hour in which to pray, that we take time to get a sight of this great God, in His power, in His love, in His nearness, just waiting to bless us. This is of far more consequence than spending the whole half hour in pouring out numberless petitions, and pleading numberless promises. The great thing is to feel that we are putting our supplications into the bosom of omnipotent Love. Before and above everything, let us take time ere we pray to realize the glory and presence of God. Give God His place in every prayer. I say, allow God to have His place. I can not give God His place upon the throne—in a certain sense I can, and I ought to try. The great thing, however, is for me to feel that I can not realize what that place is, but God will increasingly reveal Himself and the place He holds. How do I know anything about the sun? Because the sun shines, and in its light I see what the sun is. The sun is its own evidence. No philosopher could have told me about the sun if the sun did not shine. No power of meditation and thought can grasp the presence of God. Be quiet, and trusting, and resting, and the everlasting God will shine into your heart, and will reveal Himself. And then, just as naturally as I enjoy the light of the sun, and as naturally as I look upon the pages of a book knowing that I can see the letters because the light shines; just as naturally will God reveal Himself to the waiting soul, and make His presence a reality. God will take His place as God in the presence of His child, so that absolutely and actually the chief thing in the child's heart shall be: "God is here, God makes Himself known." Beloved, is not this what you long for—that God shall take a place that He has never had; and that God shall come to you in a nearness that you have never felt yet; and, above all, that God shall come to you in an abiding and unbroken fellowship? God is able to take His place before you all the day. I repeat what I have referred to before, because God has taught me a lesson by it: As God made the light of the sun so soft, and sweet, and bright, and universal, and unceasing, that it never costs me a minute's trouble to enjoy it; even so, and far more real than the light shining upon me, the nearness of my God can be revealed to me as my abiding portion. Let us all pray "that God may be all in all," in our everyday life.

"That God may be all in all," I must not only allow Him to take His place, but secondly, I must accept His will in everything. I must accept His will in every providence. Whether it be a Judas that betrays, or whether it be a Pilate in his indifference, who gives me up to the enemy; whatever the trouble, or temptation, or vexation, or worry, that comes, I must see God in it, and accept it as God's will to me. Trouble of any sort that comes to me is God's will for me. It is not God's will that men should do the wrong, but it is God's will that they should be in circumstances of trial. There is never a trial that comes to us but it is God's will for us, and if we learn to see God in it, then we bid it welcome.

Suppose away in South Africa there is a woman whose husband has gone on a long journey into the interior. He is to be away for months from all posts. The wife is anxious to receive news. In weeks she has had no letter or tidings from him. One day, as she stands in her door, there comes a great, savage Kafir. He is frightful in appearance, and carries his spears and shield. The woman is alarmed and rushes into the house and closes the door. He comes and knocks at the door, and she is in terror. She sends her servant, who comes back and says, "The man says he must see you." She goes, all affrighted. He takes out an old newspaper. He has come a month's journey on foot from her husband, and inside the dirty newspaper is a letter from her husband, telling her of his welfare. How that wife delights in that letter! She forgets the face that has terrified her. And now as weeks are passing away again, how she begins to long for that ugly Kafir messenger! After long waiting he comes again, and this time she rushes out to meet him because he is the messenger that comes from her beloved husband, and she knows that with all his repelling exterior, he is the bearer of a message of love. Beloved, have you learned to look at tribulation, and vexation, and disappointment, as the dark, savage-looking messenger with a spear in his hand, that comes straight from Jesus? Have you learned to say, "There is never a trouble, and never a hurt by which my heart is touched or even pierced, but it comes from Jesus, and brings a message of love?" Will you not learn to say from to-day, "Welcome every trial, for it comes from God?" If you want God to be all in all, you must see and meet God in every providence. Oh, learn to accept God's will in everything! Come learn to say of every trial, without exception, "It is my Father who sent it. I accept it as His messenger," and nothing in earth or hell can separate you from God.

If God is to be all in all in your heart and life, I say not only, Allow Him to take His place, and accept all His will, but, thirdly, Trust in His power. Dear friends, it is "God who worketh to will and to do according to His good pleasure." It is "the God of peace," according to another passage, "who perfects you in every good thing to do His will, working in you what is well-pleasing in His sight." You complain of weakness, of feebleness, of emptiness. Never mind; that is what you are made for—to be an emptied vessel, in which God can put His fullness and His strength. Do learn the lesson. I know it is not easy. Long after Paul had been an apostle, the Lord Jesus had to come in a very special way to teach him to say, "I do gladly glory in my infirmities." Paul was in danger of being exalted, owing to the revelations from Heaven, and Jesus sent him a thorn in the flesh—yes, Jesus sent it—a messenger of Satan—to buffet him. Paul prayed, and struggled, and wanted to get rid of it. And Jesus came to him, and said, "It is my doing that you may not be free from that. You need it. I will bless you wonderfully in it." Paul's life was changed from that moment in this one respect, and he said, "I never knew it so before, from henceforth I glory in my infirmities; for when I am weak, then am I strong." Do you indeed desire God to be all in all? Learn to glory in your weakness. Take time to say every day as you bow before God, "The almighty power of God that works in the sun, and the moon, and the stars, and the flowers, is working in me. It is as sure as that I live. The almighty power of God is working in me. I only need to get down, and be quiet; I need to be more submissive, and surrendered to His will; I need to be more trustful, and to allow God to do with me what He will." Give God His way with you, and let God work, and He will work mightily. The deepest quietness has often been proved to be the inspiration for the highest action. It has been seen in the experience of many of God's saints, and it is just the experience we need,—that in the quietness of surrender and faith, God's working has been made manifest.

Fourthly: If God is to be all in all, sacrifice everything for His kingdom and glory. "That God may be all in all." This is such a noble, glorious, holy aim that Christ said, "For this I will give my life. For this I will give my all, even to the death of the cross. For this I will give myself." If it was worth that to Christ, is it worth less to you? If one had asked Jesus of Nazareth, "What is it Thou hast a body for; what is to Thee the highest use of the body?" He would have said, "The use and the glory of my body is that I can give it a sacrifice to God. That is every thing." What is the use of having a mind; and what is the use of having money; and what is the use of having children? That I can give them to God; for God must be all in all in everything. I pray God that He may give us such a sight of His kingdom, and His glory, that everything else may disappear. Then, if you had ten thousand lives, you would say, "This is the beauty and the worth of life, 'that God may be all in all' to me, and that I may prove to men that God is more than everything, that life is only worth living as it is given to God to fill." Do let us sacrifice everything for His kingdom and glory. Begin to live day by day with the prayer, "My God, I am given up to Thee. Be Thou my all in all." You say, "Am I able to realize that?" Yes, in this way: Let the Holy Spirit dwell in you; let the Holy Spirit burn in you as a fire, and burn in you with unutterable groanings, crying unto God, Himself to reveal His presence and His will in you. In the eighth of Romans, Paul spoke about the groanings of the whole creation. And what is the whole creation groaning for? For the redemption, the glorious liberty of the children of God. And I am persuaded that was what Paul meant when he spoke of the groanings of the Holy Spirit—the unutterable groanings for the coming time of glory when God should be all in all. Christians, sacrifice your time; sacrifice your interests; sacrifice your heart's best powers in praying, and desiring, and crying that "God may be all in all."

And lastly: if God is to be all in all, wait continually on Him all the day. My first point had reference to giving God His place; but I want to bring this out more pointedly in conclusion. Wait continually on God all the day. If you are to do that, you must live always in His presence. That is what we have been redeemed for. Do we not read in the Epistle to the Hebrews, "Let us draw near within the veil, through the blood, where the high priest is?" The holy place in which we are to live in the heavens is the immediate presence of God. The abiding presence of God is certainly the heritage of every child of God, as that the sun shines. The Father never hides His face from His child. Sin hides it, and unbelief hides it, but the Father lets His love shine all the day on the face of His children. The sun is shining day and night. Your sun shall never go down. Begin to seek for this. Come and live in the presence of God. There is indeed an abiding place in His presence, in the secret of His pavilion, of which some one has sung very beautifully:

With me, wheresoe'er I wander,   That great Presence goes;   That unutterable gladness,   Undisturbed repose.

Everywhere, the blessed stillness   Of that Holy Place;   Stillness of the love that worships,   Dumb before His face.

This is the portion of those to whom the prayer is granted—"One thing have I desired of the Lord, and that will I seek after; that I may dwell all my days in the house of the Lord, to behold the beauty of the Lord, and to inquire in His temple." "In the secret of His pavilion He hideth me." God Himself will take you up, and will keep you there, so that all your work shall be done in God. Beloved, wait continually upon God. You can not do this unless you are in His presence. You must live in His presence. Then the blessed habit of waiting upon God will be learned. The real difficulty of getting to the point of real waiting upon God, is because most Christians have not sought to realize the nearness of God, and to give God the first place. But let us strive after this, let us trust God to give it to us by His grace, let us wait on God all the day. "My eyes," says one, "are ever towards Thee." Wait upon God for guidance, and God, if you wait much upon Him, will lead you up into new power for His service, into new gladness in His fellowship. He will lead you out into a larger trust in Him; He will prepare you to expect new things from Him. Beloved, there is no knowing what God will do for a man who is utterly given up to Him. Praise His name! Let each one of us say, "May my life be to live and die, to labor and to pray continually for this one thing: that in me, and around me, and in the church; that throughout the world 'God may be all in all.'" A little seed is the beginning of a great tree. A mustard seed becomes a tree in which the birds of the air can nestle. That great day of which the text speaks, when Christ Himself shall be subject to the Father, and deliver up the Kingdom to the Father, and God shall be all in all—that is the great tree of the Kingdom of God reaching its perfect consummation and glory. Oh, let us take the seed of that glory into our hearts, and let us bow in lowly surrender and submission, and say, "Amen, Lord; this be my one thought. This be my life—to speak and to work, to pray and to exist only that others may be brought to know Him too. This be my life—to yield myself to the unutterable yearnings of the Holy Spirit, that I may not rest, but ever keep my eye on that day—the day of glory, when in very deed God shall be all in all."

God help every one of us. God help us all to yield ourselves to Him, and to Christ, and to make it our every-day life; for His name's sake. Amen.

The Prayer Life

Chapter 1

If conscience is to do its work, and the contrite heart is to feel its misery, it is necessary that each individual should mention his sin by name. The confession must be severely personal. In a meeting of ministers there is probably no single sin which each one of us ought to acknowledge with deeper shame—'Guilty, verily guilty'—than the sin of prayerlessness.

What is it, then, that makes prayerlessness such a great sin? At first it is looked upon merely as a weakness. There is so much talk about lack of time and all sorts of distractions that the deep guilt of the situation is not recognized. Let it be our honest desire that, for the future, the sin of prayerlessness may be to us truly sinful. Consider

1. What a reproach it is to God

There is the holy and most glorious God who invites us to come to him, to hold converse with him, to ask from him such things as we need, and to experience what a blessing there is in fellowship with him. He has created him we might find our highest glory and salvation.

What use do we make of this heavenly privilege? How many there are who take only five minutes for prayer! They say that they have no time and that the heart desire for prayer is lacking; they do not know how to spend half an hour with God! It is not that they absolutely do not pray; they pray every day—but they have no joy in prayer, as a token of communion with God which shows that God is everything to them.

If a friend comes to visit them, they have time, they make time, even at the cost of sacrifice, for the sake of enjoying converse with him. Yes, they have time for everything that really interests them, but no time to practice fellowship with God and delight themselves in him! They find time for a creature who can be of service to them; but day after day, month after month passes, and there is no time to spend one hour with God.

Do not our hearts begin to acknowledge what a dishonor, what a despite of God this is, that I dare to say I cannot find time for fellowship with him? If this sin begins to appear plain to us, shall we not with deep shame cry out:

'Woe is me, for I am undone, O God; be merciful to me, and forgive this awful sin of prayerlessness.' Consider further

2. It is the cause of a deficient spiritual life

It is a proof that, for the most part, our life is still under the power of 'the flesh'. Prayer is the pulse of life; by it the doctor can tell what is the condition of the heart. The sin of prayerlessness is a proof for the ordinary Christian or minister that the life of God in the soul is in deadly sickness and weakness.

Much is said and many complaints are made about the feebleness of the Church to fulfill her calling, to exercise an influence over her members, to deliver them from the power of the world, and to bring them to a life of holy consecration to God. Much is also spoken about her indifference to the millions of heathen whom Christ entrusted to her that she might make known to them his love and salvation. What is the reason that many thousands of Christian workers in the world have not a greater influence? Nothing save this—the prayerlessness of their service. In the midst of all their zeal in the study and in the work of the Church, of all their faithfulness in preaching and conversation with the people, they lack that ceaseless prayer which has attached to it the sure promise of the Spirit and the power from on high. It is nothing but the sin of prayerlessness which is the cause of the lack of a powerful spiritual life! Consider further

3. The dreadful loss which the Church suffers as a result of the prayerlessness of the minister

It is the business of a minister to train believers up to a life of prayer; but how can a leader do this if he himself understands little the art of conversing with God and of receiving from the Holy Spirit, every day, out of heaven, abundant grace for himself and for his work? A minister cannot lead a congregation higher than he is himself. He cannot with enthusiasm point out a way, or explain a work, in which he is not himself walking or living.

How many thousands of Christians there are who know next to nothing of the blessedness of prayer fellowship with God! How many there are who know something of it and long for a further increase of this knowledge, but in the preaching of the Word they are not persistently urged to keep on till they obtain the blessing! The reason is simply and only that the minister understands so little about the secret of powerful prayer and does not give prayer the place in his service which, in the nature of the case and in the will of God, is indispensably necessary. Oh, what a difference we should notice in our congregations if ministers could be brought to see in its right light the sin of prayerlessness and were delivered from it! Once more consider

4. The impossibility of preaching the gospel to all men—as we are commanded by Christ to do—so long as this sin is not overcome and cast out.

Many feel that the great need of missions is the obtaining of men and women who will give themselves to the Lord to strive in prayer for the salvation of souls. It has also been said that God is eager and able to deliver and bless the world he has redeemed, if his people were but willing, if they were but ready, to cry to him day and night But how can congregations be brought to that unless there comes first an entire change in ministers and that they begin to see that the indispensable thing is not preaching, not pastoral visitation, not church work, but fellowship with God in prayer till they are clothed with power from on high?

Oh, that all thought and work and expectation concerning the kingdom might drive us to the acknowledgment of the sin of prayerlessness! God help us to root it out! God deliver us from it through the blood and power of Christ Jesus! God teach every minister of the Word to see what a glorious place he may occupy if he first of all is delivered from this root of evils; so that with courage and joy, in faith and perseverance, he can go on with his God!

The sin of prayerlessness! The Lord lay the burden of it so heavy on our hearts that we may not rest till it is taken far from us through the name and power of Jesus He will make this possible for us.

A witness from America

In 1898, there were two members of the Presbytery in New York who attended the Northfield Conference for the deepening of the spiritual life. They returned to their work with the fire of a new enthusiasm. They endeavored to bring about a revival in the entire Presbytery. In a meeting which they held, the chairman was guided to ask the brethren a question concerning their prayer life: 'Brethren,' said he, 'let us today make confession before God and each other. It will do us good. Will everyone who spends half an hour every day with God in connection with his work hold up a hand?' One hand was held up. He made a further request: 'All who thus spend fifteen minutes hold up a hand.' Not half of the hands were held up. Then he said: 'Prayer, the working power of the Church of Christ, and half of the workers make hardly any use of it! All who spend five minutes hold up hands.' All hands went up. But one man came later with the confession that he was not quite sure if he spent five minutes in prayer every day. 'It is,' said he, 'a terrible revelation of how little time I spend with God.'

The cause of prayerlessness.

In an elder's prayer meeting, a brother put the question: 'What, then, is the cause of so much prayerlessness? Is it not unbelief?'

The answer was: 'Certainly; but then comes the question what is the cause of that unbelief?' When the disciples asked the Lord Jesus: 'Why could not we cast the devil out?' His answer was: 'Because of your unbelief.' He went further and said: 'Howbeit this kind goeth not out but by prayer and fasting' (Matt. 17:19-21). If the life is not one of self-denial—of fasting—that is, letting the world go; of prayer—that is, laying hold of heaven, faith cannot be exercised. A life lived according to the flesh and not according to the Spirit—it is in this that we find the origin of the prayerlessness of which we complain. As we came out of the meeting a brother said to me: 'That is the whole difficulty; we wish to pray in the Spirit and at the same time walk after the flesh, and this is impossible.'

If one is sick and desires healing, it is of prime importance that the true cause of the sickness be discovered. This is always the first step toward recovery. If the particular cause is not recognized, and attention is directed to subordinate causes, or to supposed but not real causes, healing is out of the question. In like manner, it is of the utmost importance for us to obtain a correct insight into the cause of the sad condition of deadness and failure in prayer in the inner chamber, which should be such a blessed place for us. Let us seek to realize fully what is the root of this evil.

Scripture teaches us that there are but two conditions possible for the Christian. One is a walk according to the Spirit, the other a walk according to 'the flesh'. These two powers are in irreconcilable conflict with each other. So it comes to pass, in the case of the majority of Christians, that, while we thank God that they are born again through the Spirit and have received the life of God—yet their ordinary daily life is not lived according to the Spirit but according to 'the flesh'. Paul writes to the Galatians: 'Are ye so foolish? having begun in the Spirit, are ye now made perfect by the flesh?' (Gal. 3:3). Their service lay in fleshly outward performances. They did not understand that where 'the flesh' is permitted to influence their service of God, it soon results in open sin.

So he mentions not only grave sins as the work of 'the flesh', such as adultery, murder, drunkenness; but also the more ordinary sins of daily life—wrath, strife, variance; and he gives the exhortation: 'Walk in the Spirit, and ye shall not fulfill the lust of the flesh... If we live in the Spirit, let us also walk in the Spirit' (Gal. 5:16, 25). The Spirit must be honored not only as the author of a new life but also as the leader and director of our entire walk. Otherwise we are what the apostle calls 'carnal'.

The majority of Christians have little understanding of this matter. They have no real knowledge of the deep sinfulness and godlessness of that carnal nature which belongs to them and to which unconsciously they yield. 'God... condemned sin in the flesh' (Rom. 8:3)—in the cross of Christ. 'They that are Christ's have crucified the flesh with the affections and lusts' (Gal. 5:24). 'The flesh' cannot be improved or sanctified. 'The carnal mind is enmity against God; for it is not subject to the law of God, neither indeed can be' (Rom. 8:7). There is no means of dealing with 'the flesh' save as Christ dealt with it, bearing it to the cross. 'Our old man is crucified with him' (Rom. 6:6); so we by faith also crucify it, and regard and treat it daily as an accursed thing that finds its rightful place on the accursed cross.

It is saddening to consider how many Christians there are who seldom think or speak earnestly about the deep and immeasurable sinfulness of 'the flesh'—'In me (that is, in my flesh) dwelleth no good thing'(Rom. 7:18). The man who truly believes this may well cry out: 'I see another law in my members ... bringing me into captivity to the law of sin... O wretched man that I am! who shall deliver me from the body of this death?' (Rom. 7:23, 24). Happy is he who can go further and say: 'I thank God, through Jesus Christ our Lord... For the law of the Spirit of life in Christ Jesus hath made me free from the law of sin and death' (Rom. 7:25; 8:2).

Would that we might understand God's counsels of grace for us! 'The flesh' on the cross—the Spirit in the heart and controlling the life.

This spiritual life is too little understood or sought after; yet it is literally what God has promised and will accomplish in those who unconditionally surrender themselves to him for this purpose.

Here then we have the deep root of evil as the cause of a prayerless life. 'The flesh' can say prayers well enough, calling itself religious for so doing and thus satisfying conscience. But 'the flesh' has no desire or strength for the prayer that strives after an intimate knowledge of God; that rejoices in fellowship with him; and that continues to lay hold of his strength. So, finally, it comes to this, 'the flesh' must be denied and crucified.

The Christian who is still carnal has neither disposition nor strength to follow after God. He rests satisfied with the prayer of habit or custom; but the glory, the blessedness of secret prayer is a hidden thing to him, till some day his eyes are opened, and he begins to see that 'the flesh', in its disposition to turn away from God, is the archenemy which makes powerful prayer impossible for him.

I had once, at a conference, spoken on the subject of prayer and made use of strong expressions about the enmity of 'the flesh' as a cause of prayerlessness. After the address, the minister's wife said that she thought I had spoken too strongly. She also had to mourn over too little desire for prayer, but she knew her heart was sincerely set on seeking God. I showed her what the word of God said about 'the flesh', and that everything which prevents the reception of the Spirit is nothing else than a secret work of 'the flesh'. Adam was created to have fellowship with God and enjoyed it before his fall. After the fall, however, there came immediately, a deep-seated aversion to God, and he fled from him. This incurable aversion is the characteristic of the unregenerate nature and the chief cause of our unwillingness to surrender ourselves to fellowship with God in prayer. The following day she told me that God had opened her eyes; she confessed that the enmity and unwillingness of 'the flesh' was the hidden hindrance in her defective prayer life.

O my brethren, do not seek to find in circumstances the explanation of this prayerlessness over which we mourn; seek it where God's word declares it to be, in the hidden aversion of the heart to a holy God.

When a Christian does not yield entirely to the leading of the Spirit—and this is certainly the will of God and the work of his grace—he lives, without knowing it, under the power of 'the flesh'. This life of 'the flesh' manifests itself in many different ways. It appears in the hastiness of spirit, or the anger which so unexpectedly arises in you, in the lack of love for which you have so often blamed yourself; in the pleasure found in eating and drinking, about which at times your conscience has chidden you; in that seeking for your own will and honor, that confidence in your own wisdom and power, that pleasure in the world, of which you are sometimes ashamed before God. All this is life 'after the flesh'. 'Ye are yet carnal' (1 Con 3:3) that text, perhaps, disturbs you at times; you have not full peace and joy in God.

I pray you take time and give an answer to the question: Have I not found here the cause of my prayerlessness, of my powerlessness to effect any change in the matter? I live in the Spirit, I have been born again, but I do not walk after the Spirit—'the flesh' lords it over me. The carnal life cannot possibly pray in the spirit and power. God forgive me. The carnal life is evidently the cause of my sad and shameful prayerlessness.

The storm center on the battlefield

Mention was made in conference of the expression 'strategic position' used so often in reference to the great strife between the kingdom of heaven and the powers of darkness.

When a general chooses the place from which he intends to strike the enemy, he pays most attention to those points which he thinks most important in the fight. Thus there was on the battlefield of Waterloo a farmhouse which Wellington immediately saw was the key to the situation.

He did not spare his troops in his endeavors to hold that point: the victory depended on it. So it actually happened. It is the same in the conflict between the believer and the powers of darkness. The inner chamber is the place where the decisive victory is obtained.

The enemy uses all his power to lead the Christian and above all the minister, to neglect prayer. He knows that however admirable the sermon may be, however attractive the service, however faithful the pastoral visitation, none of these things can damage him or his kingdom if prayer is neglected. When the Church shuts herself up to the power of the inner chamber, and the soldiers of the Lord have received on their knees 'power from on high', then the powers of darkness will be shaken and souls will be delivered. In the Church, on the mission field, with the minister and his congregation, everything depends on the faithful exercise of the power of prayer.

In the week of conference I found the following in The Christian:

Two persons quarrel over a certain point. We call them Christian and Apollyon. Apollyon notices that Christian has a certain weapon which would give him a sure victory. They meet in deadly strife, and Apollyon resolves to take away the weapon from his opponent and destroy it. For the moment the main cause of the strife has become subordinate; the great point now is who shall get possession of the weapon on which everything depends? It is of vital importance to get hold of that.

So it is in the conflict between Satan and the believer. God's child can conquer everything by prayer. Is it any wonder that Satan does his utmost to snatch that weapon from the Christian, or to hinder him in the use of it?

How now does Satan hinder prayer? By temptation to postpone or curtail it, by bringing in wandering thoughts and all sorts of distractions; through unbelief and hopelessness. Happy is the prayer hero who, through it all, takes care to hold fast and use his weapon. Like our Lord in Gethsemane, the more violently the enemy attacked the more earnestly he prayed and ceased not till he had obtained the victory. After all the other parts of the armor had been named, Paul adds: 'with all prayer and supplication in the Spirit' (Eph. 6:18). Without prayer, the helmet of salvation, and the shield of faith, and the sword of the Spirit which is God's word, have no power. All depends on prayer. God teach us to believe and hold this fast!

Chapter 2

As soon as the Christian becomes convinced of his sin in this matter, his first thought is that he must begin to strive, with God's help, to gain the victory over it. But alas, he soon experiences that his striving is worth little, and the discouraging thought comes over him, like a wave, that such a life is not for him—he cannot continue faithful! At conferences on the subject of prayer, held during the past years, many a minister has openly said that it seemed impossible for him to attain such a strict life.

Recently I received a letter from a minister, well known for his ability and devotion, in which he writes, 'As far as I am concerned, it does not seem to help me to hear too much about the life of prayer, about the strenuous exertion for which we must prepare ourselves, and about all the time and trouble and endless effort it will cost us. These things discourage me—I have so often heard them. I have time after time put them to the test, and the result has always been sadly disappointing. It does not help me to be told: "You must pray more, and hold a closer watch over yourself, and become altogether a more earnest Christian.

My reply to him was as follows: 'I think in all I spoke at the conference or elsewhere, I have never mentioned exertion or struggle, because I am so entirely convinced that our efforts are futile unless we first learn how to abide in Christ by a simple faith.'

My correspondent said further: 'The message I need is this: "See that your relationship to your living Savior is what it ought to be. Live in his presence, rejoice in his love, rest in him." A better message could not be given, if it is only rightly understood. 'See that your relationship to the living Savior is what it ought to be.' But this is just what will certainly make it possible for one to live the life of prayer.

We must not comfort ourselves with the thought of standing in a right relationship to the Lord Jesus while the sin of prayerlessness has power over us, and while we, along with the whole Church, have to complain about our feeble life which makes us unfit to pray for ourselves, for the Church, or for missions, as we ought. But if we recognize, in the first place, that a right relationship to the Lord Jesus, above all else, includes prayer, with both the desire and power to pray according to God's will, then we have something which gives us the right to rejoice in him and to rest in him.

I have related this incident to point out how naturally discouragement will be the result of self-effort and will so shut out all hope of improvement or victory. And this indeed is the condition of many Christians when called on to persevere in prayer as intercessors. They feel it is certainly something entirely beyond their reach—they have not the power for the self-sacrifice and consecration necessary for such prayer; they shrink from the effort and struggle which will, as they suppose, make them unhappy. They have tried in the power of the flesh to conquer the flesh—a wholly impossible thing. They have endeavored by Beelzebub to cast out Beelzebub and this can never happen. It is Jesus alone who can subdue the flesh and the devil.

We have spoken of a struggle which will certainly result in disappointment and discouragement. This is the effort made in our own strength. But there is another struggle which will certainly lead to victory. The Scripture speaks of 'the good fight of faith', that is to say, a fight which springs from and is carried on by faith. We must get right conceptions about faith and stand fast in our faith. Jesus Christ is ever the author and finisher of faith. It is when we come into right relationship with him that we can be sure of the help and power he bestows. Just, then, as earnestly as we must, in the first place. say: 'Do not strive in your own strength; cast yourself at the feet of the Lord Jesus, and wait upon him in the sure confidence that he is with you, and works in you'; so do we, in the second place, say: 'Strive in prayer; let faith fill your heart—so will you be strong in the Lord, and in the power of his might.'

An illustration will help us to understand this. A devoted Christian woman who conducted a large Bible class with zeal and success once came in trouble to her minister. In her earlier years she had enjoyed much blessing in the inner chamber, in fellowship with the Lord and his word. But this had gradually been lost and, do what she would, she could not get right. The Lord had blessed her work, but the joy had gone out of her life. The minister asked what she had done to regain the lost blessedness. 'I have done everything,' said she, 'that I can think of, but all in vain.'

He then questioned her about her experience in connection with her conversion. She gave an immediate and clear answer: 'At first I spared no pains in my attempt to become better, and to free myself from sin, but it was all useless. At last I began to understand that I must lay aside all my efforts, and simply trust the Lord Jesus to bestow on me his life and peace, and he did it.'

'Why then,' said the minister, 'do you not try this again? As you go to your inner chamber, however cold and dark your heart may be, do not try in your own might to force yourself into the right attitude. Bow before him, and tell him that he sees in what a sad state you are that your only hope is in him. Trust him with a childlike trust to have mercy upon you, and wait upon him. In such a trust you are in a right relationship to him. You have nothing he has everything.' Some time later she told the minister that his advice had helped her; she had learned that faith in the love of the Lord Jesus is the only method of getting into fellowship with God in prayer.

Do you not begin to see, my reader, that there are two kinds of warfare—the first when we seek to conquer prayerlessness in our own strength. In that case, my advice to you is: 'Give over your restlessness and effort; fall helpless at the feet of the Lord Jesus; he will speak the word, and your soul will live.' If you have done this, then, second, comes the message: 'This is but the beginning of everything. It will require deep earnestness, and the exercise of all your power, and a watchfulness of the entire heart—eager to detect the least backsliding. Above all, it will require a surrender to a life of self-sacrifice that God really desires to see in us and which he will work out for us.'

Chapter 3

The greatest stumbling-block in the way of victory over prayerlessness is the secret feeling that we shall never obtain the blessing of being delivered from it. Often have we put forth effort in this direction, but in vain. Old habit and the power of the flesh, our surroundings with their attractions, have been too strong for us. What good is it to attempt that which our heart assures us is out of our reach? The change needed in the entire life is too great and too difficult. If the question is put: 'Is a change possible?' our sighing heart says: 'Alas, for me it is entirely impossible!' Do you know why that reply comes? It is simply because you have received the call to prayer as the voice of Moses and as a command of the law. Moses and his law have never yet given anyone the power to obey.

Do you really long for the courage to believe that deliverance from a prayerless life is possible for you and may become a reality? Then you must learn the great lesson that such a deliverance is included in the redemption that is in Christ Jesus, that it is one of the blessings of the New Covenant which God himself will impart to you through Christ Jesus. As you begin to understand this you will find that the exhortation, 'Pray without ceasing', conveys a new meaning. Hope begins to spring up in your heart that the Spirit—who has been bestowed on you to cry constantly, 'Abba, Father'—will make a true life of prayer possible for you. Then you will hearken, not in the spirit of discouragement, but in the gladness of hope, to the voice that calls you to repentance.

Many a one has turned to his inner chamber, under bitter self-accusation that he has prayed so little, and has resolved for the future to live in a different manner. Yet no blessing has come—there was not the strength to continue faithful, and the call to repentance had no power, because his eyes had not been fixed on the Lord Jesus, If he had only understood, he would have said: 'Lord, thou seest how cold and dark my heart is: I know that I must pray, but I feel I cannot do so; I lack the urgency and desire to pray.'

He did not know that at that moment the Lord Jesus in his tender love was looking down upon him and saying: 'You cannot pray; you feel that all is cold and dark: why not give yourself over into my hands? Only believe that I am ready to help you in prayer; I long greatly to shed abroad my love in your heart, so that you, in the consciousness of weakness, may confidently rely on me to bestow the grace of prayer. Just as I will cleanse you from all other sins, so also will I deliver from the sin o prayerlessness—only do not seek the victory in your own strength. Bow before me as one who expects everything from his Savior. Let your soul keep silence before me however sad you feel your state to be. Be assured of this—I will teach you how to pray.'

Many a one will acknowledge: 'I see my mistake; I had not thought that the Lord Jesus must deliver and cleans me from this sin also. I had not understood that he was with me every day in the inner chamber, in his great love ready to keep and bless me, however sinful and guilty felt myself to be. I had not supposed that just as he will give all other grace in answer to prayer, so, above all and before all, he will bestow the grace of a praying heart. What folly to think that all other blessings must come from him, but that prayer, whereon everything else depends, must be obtained by personal effort! Thank God I begin to comprehend—the Lord Jesus is himself in the inner chamber watching over me, and holding himself responsible to teach me how to approach the Father. This only he demands—that I, with childlike confidence, wait upon him and glorify him.'

Brethren, have we not seriously forgotten this truth? From a defective spiritual life nothing better can be expected than a defective prayer life. It is vain for us, with our defective spiritual life, to endeavor to pray more or better. It is an impossibility. Nothing less is necessary than that we should experience that he who is in Christ Jesus is a new creature: old things have passed away; behold, all things are become new.' This is literally true for the man who understands and experiences what it is to be in Jesus Christ.

Our whole relationship to the Lord Jesus must be a new thing. I must believe in his infinite love, which really longs to have communion with me every moment and to keep me in the enjoyment of his fellowship. I must believe in his divine power, which has conquered sin and will truly keep me from it. I must believe in him who, as the great intercessor, through the Spirit, will inspire each member of his body with joy and power for communion with God in prayer. My prayer life must be brought entirely under the control of Christ and his love. Then, for the first time, will prayer become what it really is, the natural and joyous breathing of the spiritual life, by which the heavenly atmosphere is inhaled and then exhaled in prayer.

Do you not see that, just as this faith possesses us, the call to a life of prayer which pleases God will be a welcome call? The cry, 'Repent of the sin of prayerlessness', will not be responded to by a sigh of helplessness, or by the unwillingness of the flesh. The voice of the Father will be heard as he sets before us a widely opened door and receives us into blessed fellowship with himself. Prayer for the help of the Spirit to pray will no longer be in fear of an effort too great for our power; it will be but falling down in utter weakness at the feet of the Lord Jesus, to find there that victory comes through the might and love which stream from his countenance.

If the question arises in our mind: 'will this continue?' and the fear comes: 'You know how often you have tried and been disappointed', faith will find its strength, not in the thought of what you will, or do, but in the changeless faithfulness and love of Christ, who afresh has succored you and assured you that those who wait on him shall not be ashamed.

If fear and hesitation still remain, I pray you by the mercies of God in Jesus Christ, and by the unspeakable faithfulness of his tender love, dare to cast yourselves at his feet. Only believe with your whole heart that there is deliverance from the sin of prayerlessness. `If we confess our sins, he is faithful and just to forgive us our sins, and to cleanse us from all unrighteousness' (1 John 1:9). In his blood and grace there is complete deliverance from all unrighteousness and from all prayerlessness, Praised be his name for ever!

How deliverance from prayerlessness may continue

What we have said about deliverance from the sin of prayerlessness has also application as answer to the question: `How may the experience of deliverance be maintained?' Redemption is not granted to us piecemeal, or as something of which we may make use from time to time. It is bestowed as a fullness of grace stored up in the Lord Jesus, which may be enjoyed in a new fellowship with him every day. It is so necessary that this great truth should be driven home and fastened in our minds that I will once more mention it. Nothing can preserve you from carelessness, or make it possible for you to persevere in living, powerful prayer, but a daily close fellowship with Jesus our Lord.

He said to his disciples: 'Ye believe in God, believe also in me... Believe me that I am in the Father, and the Father in me ...He that believeth on me, the works that I do shall he do also; and greater works than these shall he do' (John 14:1, 11, 12).

The Lord wished to teach his disciples that all they had learned from the Old Testament concerning the power and holiness and love of God must now be transferred to him. They must not believe merely in certain written documents but in him personally. They must believe that he was in the

Father, and the Father in him, in such a sense that they had one life, one glory. All that they knew about Christ they would find in God. He laid much emphasis on this because it was only through such a faith in him and his divine glory that they could do the works which he did, or even greater works. This faith would lead them to know that just as Christ and the Father are one, so also they were in Christ and Christ was in them.

It is this intimate, spiritual, personal, uninterrupted relationship to the Lord Jesus which manifests itself powerfully in our lives, and especially in our prayer lives. Let us consider this and see what it means: that all the glorious attributes of God are in our Lord Jesus Christ. Think of—

1. God's omnipresence

God fills the world and every moment is present in everything. Just as it is with the Father, so now our Lord Jesus is everywhere present, above all with each of his redeemed ones. This is one of the greatest and most important lessons which our faith must learn. We can clearly understand this from the example of our Lord's disciples. What was the peculiar privilege of the disciples, who were always in fellowship with him? It was uninterrupted enjoyment of the presence of the Lord Jesus. It was because of this they were so sorrowful at the thought of his death. They would be deprived of that presence. He would be no longer with them. How, under these circumstances, did the Lord Jesus comfort them? He promised that the Holy Spirit from heaven should so work in them a sense of the fullness of his life and of his personal presence that he would be even more intimately near and have more unbroken fellowship with them than ever they experienced while he was upon earth.

This great promise is now the inheritance of every believer, although so many of them know little about it. Jesus Christ, in his divine personality, in that eternal love which led him to the cross, longs to have fellowship with us every moment of the day and to keep us in the enjoyment of that fellowship. This ought to be explained to every new convert: 'The Lord loves you so that he would have you near him without a break, that you may have experience of his love.' This is what every believer must learn who has felt his powerlessness for a life of prayer, of obedience, and of holiness. This alone will give us power as intercessors to conquer the world and to win souls out of it for our Lord.

2. The omnipotence of God

How wonderful is God's power! We see it in creation; we see it in the wonders of redemption recorded in the Old Testament. We see it in the wonderful works of Christ which the Father wrought in him, and above all in his resurrection from the dead. We are called on to believe in the Son, just as we believe in the Father. Yes, the Lord Jesus who, in his love, is so unspeakably near us, is the almighty one with whom nothing is impossible. Whatever may be in our hearts or flesh, which will not submit to us, he can and will conquer. Everything that is promised in God's word, all that is our inheritance as children of the New Covenant, the almighty Jesus can bestow upon us. If I bow before him in my inner chamber, then I am in contact with the eternal, unchanging power of God. If I commit myself for the day to the Lord Jesus, then I may rest assured that it is his eternal almighty power which has taken me under its protection and which will accomplish everything for me.

Oh, if we would only take time for the inner chamber so that we might experience in full reality the presence of this almighty Jesus! What a blessedness would be ours through faith! An unbroken fellowship with an omnipresent and almighty Lord.

3. The holy love of God

This means that he, with his whole heart, offers all his divine attributes for our service and is prepared to impart himself to us. Christ is the revelation of his love. He is the Son of his love—the gift of his love—the power of his love; and this Jesus, who has sought on the cross to give an overwhelming proof of his love in his death and blood-shedding, so as to make it impossible for us not to believe in that love—this Jesus is he who comes to meet us in the inner chamber, and gives the positive assurance that unbroken fellowship with him is our inheritance, and will, through him, become our experience. The holy love of God which sacrificed everything to conquer sin and bring it to naught, comes to us in Christ to save us from every sin.

Brethren, take time to think over that word of our Lord: 'Ye believe in God, believe also in me'...Believe me that I am in the Father ... and ye in me, and I in you' (John 14: 1, 11, 20). That is the secret of the life of prayer. Take time in the inner chamber to bow down and worship; and wait on him till he unveils himself, and takes possession of you, and goes out with you to show how a man may live and walk in abiding fellowship with an unseen Lord.

Do you long to know how you may always experience deliverance from the sin of prayerlessness? Here you have the secret. Believe in the Son of God, give him time in the inner chamber to reveal himself in his ever present nearness, as the eternal and almighty one, the eternal love who watches over you. You will experience what, up till now, you have perhaps not known—that it has not entered into the heart of man what God can do for those who love him.

Chapter 4

If now we are delivered from the sin of prayerlessness, and understand how this deliverance may continue to be experienced, what will be the fruit of our liberty? He who sees this aright will, with renewed earnestness and perseverance, seek after this liberty. His life and experience will indeed be an evidence that he has obtained something of unspeakable worth. He will be a living witness of the blessing which victory has brought.

Consider—

1. The blessedness of unbroken fellowship with God

Think of the confidence in the Father which will take the place of the reproach and self-condemnation which was the earlier characteristic of our lives. Think of the deep consciousness that God's almighty grace has effected something in us, to prove that we really bear his image and are fitted for a life of communion with him and prepared to glorify him. Think how we, notwithstanding our conviction of our nothingness, may live as true children of a King, in communion with their Father, and may manifest something of the character of our Lord Jesus in the holy fellowship with his Father which he had when on earth. Think how in the inner chamber the hour of prayer may become the happiest time in the whole do for us, and how God may use us to take a share in the carrying out of his plans, and make us fountains of blessing for the world around us.

2. The power which we may have for the work to which we are called

The preacher will learn to receive his message really from God, through the power of the Holy Spirit, and t deliver it in that power to the congregation. He will know where he can be filled with the love and zeal which will enable him, in his rounds of pastoral visiting, t meet and help each individual in a spirit of tender com passion. He will be able to say with Paul: 'I can do all things through Christ which strengtheneth me' (Ph 4:13). 'We are more than conquerors through him that loved us' (Rom. 8:37). 'We are ambassadors for Christ ... we pray you in Christ's stead, be ye reconciled to God' (2 Cor. 5:20). These are no vain dreams or p tures of a foolish imagination. God has given us Paul an illustration, so that, however we may differ from him in gifts or calling, yet in inner experience we may know the all-sufficiency of grace which can do all things for as it did for him.

3. The prospect which opens before us for the future

This is to be consecrated to take part as intercessors in great work of bearing on our hearts the need of the en Church and world. Paul sought to arouse men to pray all saints, and he tells us what a conflict he had for them who had not yet seen his face. In his personal presence he was subject to conditions of time and place, but in Spirit he had power in the name of Christ to pray blessing on those who had not yet heard of the Savior.

In addition to his life in connection with men here on earth, far or near, he lived another, a heavenly life—one of love and of a wonderful power in prayer which he continually exercised. We can hardly form a conception of the power God will bestow, if only we get freed from the sin of prayerlessness and pray with the daring which reaches heaven and brings down blessing in the almighty name of Christ.

What a prospect! Minister and missionaries brought by God's grace to pray, let us say twice as much as formerly, with twofold faith and joy! What a difference it would make in the preaching, in the prayer meeting, in the fellowship with others! What a gentle power would come down in an inner chamber, sanctified by communion with God and his love in Christ! What an influence would be exercised on believers, in urging them forward to the work of intercession! How greatly would this influence be felt in the Church and among the heathen! What power might be exercised over ministers of other churches, and who knows how God might use us for his Church through the whole world! Is it not worth while to sacrifice everything, and to beseech God without ceasing to give us real and full victory over the prayerlessness which has covered us with such shame?

Why do I now write these things and extol so highly the blessedness of victory over'the sin which doth so easily beset us' and which has so terribly robbed us of the power which God has intended for us? I can give an answer. I know all too well what low thoughts we have concerning the promises and the power of God and how prone we are always to backslide, to limit God's power, and to deem it impossible for him to do greater things than we have seen. It is a glorious thing to get to know God in a new way in the inner chamber. That, however, is but the beginning. It is something still greater and more glorious to know God as the allsufficient One and to wait on his Spirit to open our hearts and minds wide to receive the great things, the new things which he really longs to bestow on those who wait for him.

God's object is to encourage faith and to make his children and servants see that they must take trouble to understand and rely upon the unspeakable greatness and omnipotence of God, so that they may take literally and in a childlike spirit this word: 'Unto him that is able to do exceeding abundantly above all that we ask or think ... be glory ... throughout all ages' (Eph. 3:20, 21). Oh, that we knew what a great and glorious God we have!

Someone may ask: 'May not this note of certain victory become a snare and lead to levity and pride?' Undoubtedly. That which is the highest and best on earth is always liable to abuse. How, then, can we be saved from this? Through nothing so surely as through true prayer, which brings us really into contact with God. The holiness of God, sought for in persistent prayer, will cover our sinfulness. The omnipotence an greatness of God will make us feel our nothingness. Fellowship with God in Jesus Christ will lead us to the experience that there is in us no good thing, and that we can have fellowship with God only as our faith become a humbling of ourselves as Christ humbled himself, an we truly live in him as he is in the Father.

Prayer is not merely coming to God to ask something from him. It is above all fellowship with God and being brought under the power of his holiness and love, till he takes possession of us and stamps our entire nature with the lowliness of Christ, which is the secret of all true worship.

Yes, it is in Christ Jesus that we draw near to the Father, as those who have died with Christ and have entirely done with their own life, as those in whom lives and whom he enables to say: 'Christ liveth in m What we have said about the work that the Lord Jesus does in us to deliver us from prayerlessness is true not only of the beginning of the life of prayer, and of the joy which a new experience of power to pray causes us, it true for the whole life of prayer all the day lot 'Through him' we have access to the Father. In this always, as in the whole spiritual life, 'Christ is all. ''They saw no man save Jesus only' (Matt. 17.8).

May God strengthen us to a belief that there is certain victory prepared for us, and that the blessing will be what the heart of man has not conceived! God will do this for those who love him.

This does not come to us all at once. God has great patience with his children. He bears with us in our slow progress with fatherly patience. Let each child of God rejoice in all that God's word promises. The stronger our faith, the more earnestly will we persevere to the end.

The more abundant life

Our Lord spoke this word concerning the more abundant life when he said that he had come to give his life for his sheep: 'I am come that they might have life, and that they might have it more abundantly' (John 10:10). A man may have life, and yet, through lack of nourishment, or through illness, there may be no abundance of life or power. This was the distinction between the Old Testament and the New. In the former there was indeed life, under the law, but not the abundance of grace of the New Testament. Christ had given life to his disciples, but they could receive the abundant life only through his resurrection and the gift of the Holy Spirit.

All true Christians have received life from Christ. The greater portion of them, however, know nothing about the more abundant life which he is willing to bestow. Paul speaks constantly of this. He says about himself that the grace of God was 'exceeding abundant' (1 Tim. 1:14). 'I can do all things through Christ which strengtheneth me' (Phil. 4:13). 'Thanks be unto God, which always causeth us to triumph in Christ' (2 Cor. 2:14). 'We are more than conquerors through him that loved us' (Rom. 8:37).

We have spoken of the sin of prayerlessness, and the means of deliverance, and how to be kept free from that sin. What has been said on these points is all included in that expression of Christ: 'I am come that they might have life, and that they might have it more abundantly.' It is of the utmost importance for us so to understand this more abundant life, that we may clearly see that for a true life of prayer nothing less is necessary than that we should walk in an ever increasing experience of that overflowing life.

It is possible for us to commence this conflict against prayerlessness in dependence on Christ, and looking to him to be assisted and kept in it, and yet to be disappointed. This is the case when prayerlessness is looked upon as the one sin against which we must strive. It must be recognized as part of the whole life of the flesh and as closely connected with other sins which spring from the same source. We forget that the entire flesh with all its affections, whether manifested in the body or soul, must be regarded as crucified, and be handed over to death. We must not be satisfied with a feeble life, but must seek for an abundant life. We must surrender ourselves entirely, that the Spirit may take full possession of us, so manifesting that life in us that there may come an entire transformation in our spiritual being, by which the complete mastery of Christ and the Spirit is recognized.

What is it, then, which peculiarly constitutes this abundant life? We cannot too often repeat, or in different ways too often set it forth—the abundant life is nothing less than the full Jesus having the full mastery over our entire being, through the power of the Holy Spirit. As the Spirit makes known in us the fullness of Christ, and the abundant life which he gives, it will be chiefly in three aspects:

1. As the crucified one

Not merely as the one who died for us, to atone for our sins; but as he who has taken us up with himself on the cross to die with him, and who now works out in us the power of his cross and death. You have the true fellowship with Christ when you can say: 'I have been crucified with Christ—he, the crucified one, lives in me.' The feelings and the disposition which were in him, his lowliness and obedience even to the death of the cross—these were what he referred to when he said of the Holy Spirit: 'He shall take of mine, and shall shew it unto you' (John 16:15)—not as an instruction, but as childlike participation of the same life which was in him.

Do you desire that the Holy Spirit should take full possession of you, so as to cause the crucified Christ to dwell in you? Understand then, that this is just the end for which he has been given, and this he will surely accomplish in all who yield themselves to him.

2. As the risen one

The Scripture frequently mentions the resurrection in connection with the wonder-working power of God, by which Christ was raised from the dead; and from which comes the assurance of 'the exceeding greatness of his power to us who believe, according to the working of his mighty power, which he wrought in Christ, when he raised him from the dead' (Eph- 1:19, 20). Do not pass hastily from these words. Turn back and read them once more, and learn the great lesson that, however powerless and weak you feel, the omnipotence of God is working in you; and, if you only believe, will give you in daily life a share in the resurrection of his Son.

Yes, the Holy Spirit can fill you with the joy and victory of the resurrection of Christ, as the power of your daily life, here in the midst of the trials and temptations of this world. Let the cross humble you to death. God will work out the heavenly life in you through his Spirit. Ah, how little have we understood that it is entirely the work of the Holy Spirit to make us partakers of the crucified and risen Christ, and to conform us to his life and death!

3. As the glorified one

The glorified Christ is he who baptizes with the Holy Spirit. When the Lord Jesus himself was baptized with the Spirit, it was because he had humbled himself and offered himself to take part in John's baptism of repentance—a baptism for sinners—in Jordan. Even so, when he took upon himself the work of redemption, he received the Holy Spirit to fit him for his work from that hour till on the cross he 'offered himself without spot to God' (Heb. 9:14). Do you desire that this glorified Christ should baptize you with the Holy Spirit? Offer yourself then to him for his service, to further his great work of making known to sinners the love of the Father.

God help us to understand what a great thing it is to receive the Holy Spirit with power from the glorified Jesus! It means a willingness—a longing of the soul—to work for him, and, if need be, to suffer for him. You have known and loved your Lord, and have worked for him, and have had blessing in that work; but the Lord has more than that to bestow. He can so work in us, and in our brethren around us, and in the ministers of the church, by the power of the Holy Spirit, as to fill our hearts with adoring wonder.

Have you laid hold of it, my reader? The abundant life is neither more nor less than the full life of Christ as the crucified, the risen, the glorified one, who baptizes with the Holy Ghost and reveals himself in our hearts and lives as Lord of all within us.

I read not long since an expression—'Live in what must be.' Do not live in your human imagination of what is possible. Live in the word—in the love and infinite faithfulness of the Lord Jesus. Even though it is slow, and with many a stumble, the faith that always thanks him not for experiences, but for the promises on which it can rely—goes on from strength to strength, still increasing in the blessed assurance that God himself will perfect his work in us.

Chapter 5

The connection between the prayer life and the Spirit life is close and indissoluble. It is not merely that we receive the Spirit through prayer, but the Spirit life requires, as an indispensable thing, a continuous prayer life. I can be led continually by the Spirit only as I continually give myself to prayer.

This was very evident in the life of our Lord. A study of his life will give us a wonderful view of the power and holiness of prayer. Consider his baptism. It was when he was baptized and prayed that heaven was opened and the Holy Spirit came down upon him. God desired to crown Christ's surrender of himself to the sinner's baptism in Jordan (which was also a surrender of himself to the sinner's death), with the gift of the Spirit for the work that he must accomplish. But this could not have taken place had he not prayed. In the fellowship of worship the Spirit was bestowed on him to lead him out into the desert to spend forty days there in prayer and fasting. Turn to Mark 1:32-35: 'And at even, when the sun did set, they brought unto him all that were diseased, and them that were possessed with devils. And all the city was gathered together at the door... And in the morning, rising up a great while before day, he went out, and departed into a solitary place, and there prayed.'

The work of the day and evening had exhausted him. In his healing of the sick and casting out devils, power had gone out of him. While others still slept, he went away to pray and to renew his strength in communion with his Father, He had need of this, otherwise he would not have been ready for the new day. The holy work of delivering souls demands constant renewal through fellowship with God.

Think again of the calling of the apostles as given in Luke 6:12,13. 'And it came to pass in those days, that he went out into a mountain to pray, and continued all night in prayer to God. And when it was day, he called unto him his disciples: and of them he chose twelve, whom also he named apostles.' Is it not clear that if anyone wishes to do God's work, he must take time for fellowship with him, to receive his wisdom and power? The dependence and helplessness of which this is an evidence, open the way and give God the opportunity of revealing his power. How great was the importance of the choosing of the apostles for Christ's own work, for the early Church, and for all time! It had God's blessing and seal; the stamp of prayer was on it.

Read Luke 9:18, 20: 'And it came to pass, as he was alone praying, his disciples were with him: and he asked them saying, Whom say the people that I am? ... Peter answering said, The Christ of God.' The Lord had prayed that the Father might reveal to them who he was. It was in answer to prayer that 'he chose twelve, whom also he named apostles'. And when Peter said: 'The Christ of God' the Lord said to him, 'Flesh and blood hath not revealed it unto thee, but my Father which is in heaven' (Matt. 16:17). This great confession was the fruit of prayer.

Read further Luke 9:28-35: 'He took Peter and John and James, and went up into a mountain to pray. And as he prayed, the fashion of his countenance was altered ... And there came a voice out of the cloud, saying, This is my beloved Son: hear him.' Christ had desired that, for the strengthening of their faith, God might give them an assurance from heaven that he was the Son of God. Prayer obtained for our Lord Jesus himself, as well as for his disciples, what happened on the Mount of Transfiguration.

Does it not become still more clear that what God wills to accomplish on earth needs prayer as its indispensable condition? And there is but one way for Christ and believers. A heart and mouth open toward heaven in believing prayer will certainly not be put to shame.

Read Luke 11:1-13: 'As he was praying in a certain plain, when he ceased, one of his disciples said unto him, Lord, teach us to pray...' And then he gave them that inexhaustible prayer: 'Our Father who art in heaven'. In this he showed what was going on in his heart, when he prayed that God's name might be hallowed, and his kingdom come, and his will be done, and all of this 'on earth as it is in heaven'. How will this ever come to pass? Through prayer. This prayer has been uttered through the ages by countless millions, to their unspeakable comfort. But forget not this—it was born out of the prayer of our Lord Jesus. He had been praying, and therefore was able to give that glorious answer.

Read John 14:16: 'I will pray the Father, and he shall give you another Comforter. 'The entire dispensation of the New Testament, with the wonderful outpouring of the Holy Spirit, is the outcome of the prayer of the Lord Jesus. It is as though God had impressed on the gift of the Holy Spirit this seal—in answer to the prayer of the Lord Jesus, and later of his disciples, the Holy Spirit will surely come. But it will be in answer to prayer like that of our Lord, in which he took time to be alone with God and in that prayer offered himself wholly to God.

Read John 17, the high priestly, most holy prayer! Here the Son prays first for himself, that the Father will glorify him by giving him power for the cross, by raising him from the dead, by setting him at his right hand. These great things could not take place save through prayer. Prayer had power to obtain them.

Afterward he prayed for his disciples, that the Father might preserve them from the evil one, might keep them from the world, and might sanctify them. And then, further, he prayed for all those who through their word might believe on him, that all might be one in love, even as the Father and the Son were one. This prayer gives us a glimpse into the wonderful relationship between the Father and the Son, and teaches us, that all the blessings of heaven come continually through the prayer of him who is at God's fight hand and ever prays for us. But it teaches us, also, that all these blessings must in the same manner be desired and asked for by us. The whole nature and glory of God's blessings consist in this—they must be obtained in answer to prayer, by hearts entirely surrendered to him, and hearts that believe in the power of prayer.

Now we come to the most remarkable instance of all. In Gethsemane we see that our Lord, according to his constant habit, consulted and arranged with the Father the work he had to do on earth. First he besought him in agony and bloody sweat to let the cup pass from him; when he understood that this could not be, then he prayed for strength to drink it, and surrendered himself with the words: 'Thy will be done.' He was able to meet the enemy full of courage and in the power of God gave himself over to the death of the cross. He had prayed.

Oh, why is it that God's children have so little faith in the glory of prayer, as the great power for subjecting our own wills to that of God, as well as for the confident carrying out of the work of God in spite of our great weakness? Would that we might learn from our Lord Jesus how impossible it is to walk with God, to obtain God's blessing or leading, or to do his work joyously and fruitfully, apart from close unbroken fellowship with him who is ever a living fountain of spiritual life and power!

Let every Christian think over this simple study of the prayer life of our Lord Jesus and endeavor from God's word, with prayer for the leading of the Holy Spirit, to learn what the life is which the Lord Jesus Christ bestows upon him and supports in him. It is nothing else than a life of daily prayer. Let each minister especially recognize how entirely vain it is to attempt to do the work of our Lord in any other way than that in which he did it. Let us, as workers, begin to believe that we are set free from the ordinary business of the world, that we may, above everything, have time, in our Savior's name, and with his Spirit, and in oneness with him, to ask for and obtain blessing for the world.

Chapter 6

Is it not sad that our thoughts about the Holy Spirit are so often coupled with grief and self-reproach? Yet he bears the name of Comforter, and is given to lead us to find in Christ our chief delight and joy. But there is something still more sad: he who dwells within us to comfort us is often grieved by us because we will not permit him to accomplish his work of love. What a cause of inexpressible pain to the Holy Spirit is all this prayerlessness in the Church! It is the cause also of the low vitality and utter impotence which are so often found in us, because we are not prepared to permit the Holy Spirit to lead us.

God grant that our meditation on the work of the Holy Spirit may be matter for rejoicing and for the strengthening of our faith!

The Holy Spirit is 'the Spirit of prayer'. He is definitely called by this name in Zechariah 12, 10: 'The spirit of grace and of supplications. 'Twice in Paul's epistles there is a remarkable reference to him in the matter of prayer. 'Ye have received the Spirit of adoption, whereby we cry, Abba, Father' (Rom. 8:15). 'God hath sent forth the Spirit of his Son into your hearts, crying, Abba, Father' (Gal. 4:6). Have you ever meditated on these words: 'Abba, Father'? In that name our Savior offered his greatest prayer to the Father, accompanied by the entire surrender and sacrifice of his life and love. The Holy Spirit is given for the express purpose of teaching us, from the very beginning of our Christian life onward, to utter that word in childlike trust and surrender. In one of these passages we read: 'We cry'; in the other: 'He cries.' What a wonderful blending of the divine and human cooperation in prayer. What a proof that God—if I may say so—has done his utmost to make prayer as natural and effectual as though it were the cry of a child to an earthly Father, as he says: 'Abba, Father'.

Is it not a proof that the Holy Spirit is to a great extent a stranger in the Church, when prayer, for which God has made such provisions, is regarded as a task and a burden? And does not this teach us to seek for the deep root of prayerlessness in our ignorance of, and disobedience to, the divine instructor whom the Father has commissioned to teach us to pray?

If we desire to understand this truth still more clearly we must notice what is written in Romans 8:26, 27: 'Likewise the Spirit also helpeth our infirmities: for we know not what we should pray for as we ought: but the Spirit himself maketh intercession for us with groanings which cannot be uttered. And he that searcheth the hearts knoweth what is the mind of the Spirit, because he maketh intercession for the saints according to the will of God.' Is it not clear from this that the Christian if left to himself does not know how to pray; or how he ought to pray; and that God has stooped to meet us in this helplessness of ours by giving us the Holy Spirit himself to pray for us; and that his operation is deeper than our thought or feeling, but is noticed and answered by God?

Our first work, therefore, ought to be to come into God's presence not with our ignorant prayers, not with many words and thoughts, but in the confidence that the divine work of the Holy Spirit is being carried on within us. This confidence will encourage reverence and quietness, and will also enable us, in dependence on the help which the Spirit gives, to lay our desires and heart-needs before God. The great lesson for every prayer is—see to it, first of all, that you commit yourself to the leading of the Holy Spirit, and with entire dependence on him, give him the first place; for through him your prayer will have a value you cannot imagine, and through him also you will learn to speak out your desires in the name of Christ.

What a protection this faith would be against deadness and despondency in the inner chamber! Only think of it! In every prayer the triune God takes a part—the Father who hears: the Son in whose name we pray; the Spirit who prays for us and in us. How important it is that we should be in right relationship to the Holy Spirit and understand his work!

The following points demand serious consideration.

1. Let us firmly believe, as a divine reality, that the Spirit of God's Son, the Holy Spirit, is in us. Do not imagine that you know this and have no need to consider it. It is a thought so great and divine that it can gain an entrance to our hearts and be retained there only by the Holy Spirit himself. 'The Spirit itself beareth witness with our spirit' (Rom. 8:16). Our position ought to be that of reckoning with full assurance of faith that our heart is his temple, yes, that he dwells within us and rules soul and body. Let us thank God heartily as often as we pray, that we have his Spirit in us to teach us to pray. Thanksgiving will draw our hearts out to God and keep us engaged with him; it will take our attention from ourselves and give the Spirit room in our hearts.

Oh, it is no wonder that we have been prayerless, and have felt this work too heavy for us, if we have sought to hold fellowship with the eternal God apart from his Spirit, who reveals the Father and the Son.

2. In the practice of this faith in the certainty that the Spirit dwells and works in us, there must also be the understanding of all that he desires to accomplish in us. His work in prayer is closely connected with his other work. We have seen in an earlier chapter that his first and greatest work is to reveal Christ in his omnipresent love and power. So the Holy Spirit will in prayer constantly remind us of Christ, of his blood and name, as the sure ground of our being heard.

He will, further, as 'the Spirit of holiness', teach us to recognize, and hate, and have done with sin. He is 'the Spirit of light and wisdom' who leads us into the heavenly secret of God's overflowing grace. He is 'the Spirit of love and power' who teaches us to witness for Christ and to labor for souls with tender pity. The more closely I associate all these blessings with the Spirit, the more shall I be convinced of his deity and shall be the more ready to commit myself to his guidance, as I give myself to prayer. What a different life mine would be if I knew the Spirit as the Spirit of prayer! There is still another thing which I need constantly to learn afresh, that—

3. The Spirit desires to have full possession of my life.

We pray for more of the Spirit, and we pray well, if alongside this prayer we set the truth that the Spirit wants more of me. The Spirit would possess me entirely. Just as my soul has my whole body for its dwelling-place and service, so the Holy Spirit would have my body and soul as his dwelling-place, entirely under his control. No one can continue long and earnestly in prayer without beginning to perceive that the Spirit is gently leading to an entirely new consecration, of which previously he knew nothing. 'I seek Thee with my whole heart.' The Spirit will make such words more and more the motto of our lives. He will cause us to recognize that what remains in us of double-mindedness is truly sinful. He will reveal Christ as the almighty deliverer from all sin, who is always near to defend us. He will lead us in this way in prayer, to forget ourselves and make us willing to offer ourselves for training as intercessors, to whom God can entrust the carrying out of his plans, and who day and night cry to him to avenge his church of her adversary.

God help us to know the Spirit and to reverence him as the Spirit of prayer!

Chapter 7

To understand grace, to understand Christ aright, we must understand what sin is. And how otherwise can we come to this understanding than through the light of God and his word?

Come with me to the beginning of the Bible. See there man created by God, after his image, and pronounced by his creator to be very good. Then sin entered, as rebellion against God. Adam was driven out of paradise and was brought along with the untold millions of following generations under curse and ruin. That was the work of sin. Here we learn its nature and power.

Come further on and see the ark of Noah on Ararat. So terrible had godlessness become among men, God saw nothing for it but to destroy man from off the earth. That was the work of sin.

Come once more with me to Sinai. God wished to establish his covenant with a new nation—with the people of Israel. But because of man's sinfulness, he could do this only by appearing in darkness and lightning so terrible that Moses said: 'I exceedingly fear and quake' (Heb. 12:21). And before the end of the giving of the law that awful message came: 'Cursed is every one that continueth not in all things which are written in the book of the law to do them' (Gal. 3:10) It was sin which made that necessary.

Come once more with me, and this time to Calvary There see what sin is, and the hatred and enmity with which the world cast out and crucified the Son of God. There sin reached its climax. There Christ was, by God himself, made sin, and became a curse, as the only way to destroy sin. In the agony in which he prayed in Gethsemane, that he might not drink the terrible cup, and in the agony in which on the cross, in the deep darkness of desertion, he cried out: 'My God, my God, why hast thou forsaken me?' we obtain at least some faint idea of the curse and indescribable suffering which sin brings. If anything can make us hate and detest sin, it is Christ on the cross.

Come once again with me to the judgment seat of the Great Day, and see the bottomless pit of darkness wherein countless souls will be plunged under the sentence: 'Depart from me, ye cursed, into everlasting fire' (Matt. 25:41). Oh, will not these words soften our hearts and fill us with a never-to-be-forgotten horror of sin, so that we may hate it with a perfect hatred?

And now is there anything else that can help us to understand what sin is? Yes, there is. Turn your eyes inward, and behold your own heart, and see sin there. Remember that all you have already seen of the hatefulness and godlessness of sin should teach you what sin in your own heart means—all the enmity against God, all the ruin of men, all of its inner nature of hatefulness, lie hidden in the sin you have committed, guilt of every transgression against God. And when you remember that you are a child of God, and yet commit sin and allow it sometimes to fulfill its lusts, is it not fitting that you should cry out with shame: 'Woe is me, because of my sin'? 'Depart from me; for I am a sinful man, O Lord' (Luke 5:8).

One great power of sin is that it blinds men so that they do not recognize its true character. Even the Christian himself finds an excuse in the thought that he can never be perfect and that daily sin is a necessity. He is so accustomed to the thought of sinning that he has almost lost the power and ability of mourning over sin. And yet there can be no real progress in grace apart from an increased consciousness of the sin and guilt of every transgression against God. And there cannot be a more important question than this: 'How can I regain the lost tenderness of conscience and become prepared really to offer to God the sacrifice of a broken heart?'

Scripture teaches us the way. Let the Christian remember what God thinks about sin—the hatred with which his holiness bums against it, the solemn sacrifice which he made to conquer sin, and deliver us from it. Let him tarry in God's presence till his holiness shines upon him, and he cries out with Isaiah: 'Woe is me! for I am undone' (Isa. 6:5).

Let him remember the cross, and what the love of Christ had to endure there, through the unspeakable pain which sin caused him; and let him ask if this will not teach him to hearken to the voice which says: 'Oh, do not this abominable thing which I hate' (Jer. 44:4). Let him take time, so that the blood and love of the cross may exercise their full influence on him, and let him think of sin as nothing less than giving his hand to Satan and to his power. Is not this a terrible result of our prayerlessness, and of our short and hasty tarrying before God—that the true knowledge of sin is almost lost?

Let the believer think not only of what redemption has cost Christ, but also of the fact that Christ is offered to him, by the Holy Spirit, as a gift of inconceivable grace, through whom divine forgiveness and purification and renewing have taken possession of him; and let him ask himself with what return such love should be repaid. If only time were taken to tarry in God's presence and ask such questions, the Spirit of God would accomplish his work of conviction of sin in us and would teach us to take an entirely new standpoint, and would give us a new view of sin. The thought would begin to arise in our hearts that we have in very deed been redeemed, so that in the power of Christ we may live every day as partners in the great victory which Christ obtained over sin on the cross, and manifest it in our walk.

What think you? Do you not begin to see that the sin of prayerlessness has had a more terrible effect than you at first supposed? It is because of this hasty and superficial converse with God that the sense of sin is so weak and that no motives have power to help you to hate and flee from sin as you ought. Nothing, nothing except the hidden, humble, constant fellowship with God can teach you, as a child of God, to hate sin as God wants you to hate it. Nothing, nothing but the constant nearness and unceasing power of the living Christ can make it possible for you rightly to understand what sin is and to detest it. And without this deeper understanding of sin, there will be no thought of appropriating the victory which is made possible for you in Christ Jesus, and will be wrought in you by the Spirit.

O my God, cause me to know my sin and teaching me to tarry before thee and to wait on thee till thy Spirit causes something of thy holiness to rest upon me! O my God, cause me to know my sin, and let this drive me to listen to the promise: 'He that abideth in him sinneth not,' and to expect the fulfillment from Thee!

The Holiness of God

It has often been said that the conception of sin and of the holiness of God has been lost in the Church. In the inner chamber we have the place where we may team again how to give God's holiness the position it should have in our faith and life. If you do not know how to spend half an hour in prayer, take up the subject of God's holiness. Bow before him. Give yourself time, and give God also time, that he and you may come into touch with one another. It is a great work, but one fraught with great blessing.

If you wish to strengthen yourself in the practice of this holy presence, take up the holy word. Take, for instance, the book of Leviticus and notice how God seven times gives the command: 'Ye shall be holy, for I am holy' (11:44, 45; 19:2; 20:7, 26; 21:8; 22:32). Still more frequent is the expression: 'I am the Lord that doth sanctify you.' This great thought is taken over into the New Testament. Peter says (1 Pet. 1:15,16): 'Be ye holy in all manner of conversation; because it is written, Be ye holy; for I am holy.' Paul writes in his first epistle (1 Thess. 3:13; 4:7; 5:24): 'he may stablish your hearts unblamable in holiness.... God hath not called us unto uncleanness, but unto holiness... Faithful is he that calleth you, who also will do it.'

Nothing but the knowledge of God, as the holy one, will make us holy. And how are we to obtain that knowledge of God, save in the inner chamber? It is a thing utterly impossible unless we take time and allow the holiness of God to shine on us. How can any man on earth obtain intimate knowledge of another man of remarkable wisdom, if he does not associate with him, and place himself under his influence? And how can God himself sanctify us, if we do not take time to be brought under the power of the glory of his holiness? Nowhere can we get to know the holiness of God, and come under its influence and power, save in the inner chamber. It has been well said: 'No man can expect to make progress in holiness who is not often and long alone with God.'

And what now is this holiness of God? It is the highest and most glorious and most all-embracing of all the attributes of God. Holiness is the most profound word in the Bible. It is a word that is at home in heaven. Both the Old and New Testaments tell us this. Isaiah heard the seraphs with veiled faces cry out: 'Holy, holy, holy, is the Lord of hosts' (6:3). John heard the four living creatures say: 'Holy, holy, holy, Lord God Almighty' (Rev. 4: 8). This is the highest expression of God's glory in heaven, by beings who live in his immediate presence and bow low before him. And dare we imagine that we, by thinking, and reading, and bearing, can understand or become partakers of the holiness of God? What folly! Oh, that we might begin to thank God that we have a place in the inner chamber, a place where we can be alone with him, and take time for the prayer: 'Let thy holiness, O Lord, shine more and more into our hearts, that they may become holy.'

And let our hearts be deeply ashamed of our prayerlessness, through which we have made it impossible for God to impart his holiness to us. Let us beseech God fervently to forgive us this sin, and to allure us by his heavenly grace, and to strengthen us to have fellowship with him, the holy God.

I have said that the meaning of the words, 'The holiness of God', is not easily expressed. But we may begin by saying that they imply the unspeakable aversion and hatred with which God regards sin. And if you wish to understand what that means, remember that he preferred to see his Son die, rather than that sin should reign. Think of the Son of God, who gave up his life rather than act in the least matter against the will of the Father. Still further, he had such a hatred of sin that he preferred to die rather than that men should be held in its power. That is something of the holiness of God, which is a pledge that he will do everything for us—for you and me—to deliver us from sin. Holiness is the fire of God that will consume sin in us and make us holy sacrifices, pure and acceptable before him. It was for this reason that the Spirit came down as fire. He is the Spirit of God's holiness, the Spirit of sanctification in us.

Oh, think over the holiness of God, and bow in lowliness before him, till your heart is filled with the assurance of what the holy one will do for you. Take a week, if necessary, to read and re-read the words of God on this great truth, till your heart is brought under the conviction: 'This is the glory of the inner chamber, to converse with God the holy one; to bow down in deep humility and shame before him, because we have so despised him and his love through our prayerlessness.' There we shall receive the assurance that he will again take us into-fellowship with himself. No one can expect to understand and receive the holiness of God who is not often and long alone with God.

Someone has said that the holiness of God is the expression of the unspeakable distance by which he in his righteousness is separated from us, and yet also of the unspeakable nearness in which he in his love longs to hold fellowship with us and dwell in us. Bow in humble reverence, as you think of the immeasurable distance between you and God. Bow in childlike confidence in the unspeakable desire of his love to be united with you in the deepest intimacy; and reckon most confidently on him to reveal something of his holiness to the soul which thirst after him and waits upon him and is quiet before him.

Notice how the two sides of the holiness of God are united in the cross. So terrible was the aversion and anger of God against our sin that Christ was left in the thick darkness, because God, when sin was laid upon him, had to hide his face from him. And yet so deep was the love of God toward us and he so desired to be united to us that he spared not his Son but gave him over to unutterable sufferings, that so he might receive us, in union with Christ, into his holiness, and press us to his heart as his beloved children. It was of this suffering that our Lord Jesus said: 'I sanctify myself, that they also might be sanctified through the truth' (John 17:19). Thus he is become of God our sanctification, and we are holy in him.

I beseech you, think not little of the grace that you have a holy God who longs to make you holy. Think not little of the voice of God which calls you to give time to him in the stillness of the inner chamber, so that he may cause his holiness to rest on you. Let it be your business every day, in the secrecy of the inner chamber, to meet the holy God. You will be repaid for the trouble it may cost you. The reward will be sure and rich. You will learn to hate sin, and to regard it as accursed and conquered. 'Me new nature will give you a horror of sin. The living Jesus, the holy God, will, as conqueror, be your power and strength; and you will begin to believe the great promise contained in 1 Thessalonians 5:23, 24: 'The very God of peace sanctify you wholly... Faithful is he that calleth you, who also will do it.'

Chapter 8

In opposition to sin stands obedience. 'For as by one man's disobedience many were made sinners, so by the obedience of one shall many be made righteous... Ye became the servants of righteousness' (Rom. 5:19; 6:18). In connection with all that has been said about sin, and the new life, and the reception of the Holy Spirit, we must always give to obedience the place assigned to it by God.

It was because Christ humbled himself and became obedient unto death, yea, the death of the cross, that God so highly exalted him. And Paul, in this connection, exhorts us: 'Let this mind be in you, which was also in Christ Jesus' (Phil. 2:5). We see, above everything else, that the obedience of Christ, which was so pleasing to God, must become really the characteristic of our disposition and of our entire walk. Just as a servant knows that he must first obey his master in all things, so the surrender to an implicit and unquestioning obedience must become the essential characteristic of our lives.

How little this is understood by Christians! How many there are who allow themselves to be misled, and rest satisfied with the thought that sin is a necessity, that one must sin every day! It would be difficult to say how great the harm is which has been done by this mistake. It is one of the chief causes why the sin of disobedience is so little recognized. I have myself heard Christians, speaking about the cause of darkness and weakness, say, half laughingly: 'Yes, it is just disobedience again.' We try to get rid of a servant as speedily as possible who is habitually disobedient, but it is not regarded as anything extraordinary that a child of God should be disobedient every day. Disobedience is daily acknowledged, and yet there is no turning away from it.

Have we not here the reason why so much prayer for the power of the Holy Spirit is offered, and yet so few answers come? Do we not see from Acts 5:32 that God has given his Holy Spirit to them that obey him? Every child of God has received the Holy Spirit— If he uses the measure of the Holy Spirit which he has, with the definite purpose of being obedient to the utmost, then God can and will favor him with further manifestations of the Spirit's power. But if he permits disobedience to get the upper hand, day by day, he need not wonder if his prayer for more of the Spirit remains unanswered.

We have already said that we must not forget that the Spirit desires to possess more of us. How can we wholly surrender ourselves to him otherwise than by being obedient? The Scripture says that we must be led by the Spirit, that we must walk by the Spirit. My right relationship to the Holy Spirit is that I allow myself to be guided and ruled by him. Obedience is the great factor in our whole relationship to God. 'Obey my voice, and I will be your God' (Jer. 7:23; 11:4).

Mark how the Lord Jesus, on the last night, when giving his great promise about the Holy Spirit, lays emphasis on this point. 'If ye love me, keep my commandments. And I will pray the Father, and he shall give you another Comforter' (John 14:15,16). Obedience was essential as a preparation for the reception of the Spirit. And this thought is often repeated by him. 'He that hath my commandments, and keepeth them, he it is that loveth me: and he that loveth me shall be loved of my Father, and I will love him, and will manifest myself to him' (John 14:21). So also in verse 23: 'If a man love me, he will keep my words: and my Father will love him, and we will come unto him, and make our abode with him.' 'If ye abide in me, and my words abide in you, ye shall ask what ye will, and it shall be done unto you' (15:7). 'If ye keep my commandments, ye shall abide in my love' (verse 10). 'Ye are my friends, if ye do whatsoever I command you' (verse 14).

Can words more plainly or impressively declare that the whole life, in the new dispensation, following the resurrection of Christ, depends on obedience? That is the Spirit of Christ. He lived to do not his own will, but the will of the Father. And he cannot with his Spirit make an abiding home in the heart of one who does not surrender himself utterly to a life of obedience.

Alas, how few there are who are truly concerned because of this disobedience! How little it is believed that Christ really asks for and expects this from us because he has undertaken to make it possible for us. How much is it manifested in prayer, or walk, or in the depths of the soul-life, that we really endeavour to be well—pleasing to the Lord in all things? We say too little in regard to our disobedience. 'I will be sorry for my sin.'

But is obedience really possible? It is certain for the man who believes that Christ Jesus is his sanctification and relies on him.

Just as it is impossible for a man whose eyes have not yet been opened to see that Christ can at once forgive his sin, so is it also with faith in the assurance that there is in Christ a sure promise of power to accomplish all that God desires from his child. Just as, through faith, we found the fullness of forgiveness; so through a new act of faith, a real deliverance from the dominion of the sin which has so easily beset us is obtained, and the abiding blessing of the continuous experience of the keeping power of Christ becomes ours. This faith obtains a new insight into promises the meaning of which was not previously understood: 'The God of peace ... make you perfect in every good work to do his will, working in you that which is well pleasing in his sight, through Jesus Christ' (Heb. 13:20, 21). 'Unto him that is able to keep you from falling ... be glory and majesty' (Jude 24, 25). 'Give diligence to make your calling and election sure: for if ye do these things, ye shall never fall' (2 Pet. 1:10). 'To the end he may stablish your hearts unblamable in holiness' (1 Thess. 3:13). 'But the Lord is faithful, who shall stablish you, and keep you from evil' (2 Thess. 3:3).

When the soul understands that the fulfilment of these and other promises is secured for us in Christ, and that, as certainly as the forgiveness of sin is assured to us in him, so also is power against new or fresh attacks of sin assured to us. Then for the first time is the lesson learned aright that faith can confidently rely upon a full Christ and his abiding protection.

This faith sheds a wholly new light on the life of obedience. Christ holds himself responsible to work this out in me every moment if I only trust him for it. Then I begin to understand the important phrase with which Paul begins and closes his epistle to the Romans (Rom. 1:5; 16:26): 'The obedience of faith.' Faith brings me to the Lord Jesus, not only to obtain the forgiveness of sin, but also that I may every moment enjoy the power which will make it possible for me, as a child of God, to abide in him and to be numbered among his obedient children of whom it is written that, as he who has called them is holy, as they also may be holy in all manner of conversation. Everything depends on whether or not I believe on the whole Christ, with the fullness of his grace, that he will, not now and then but every moment, be the strength of my life. Such faith will lead to an obedience which will enable me to 'walk worthy of the Lord unto all pleasing, being fruitful in every good work... strengthened with all might, according to his glorious power' (Col. 1:10,11).

The soul which feeds on such promises will experience now, instead of the disobedience of self-effort, what the obedience of faith means. All such promises have their measure, their certainty, and their strength in the living Christ.

The victorious life

In the chapter on 'The More Abundant Life', we viewed the matter chiefly from the side of our Lord Jesus. We saw that there is to be found in him—the crucified, and the risen, and the glorified one who baptizes with the Holy Spirit—all that is needful for a life of abundant grace. In speaking of the victorious life, we shall now look at the matter from another standpoint. We want to see how a Christian can live really as a victor. We have already often said that the prayer life is not something which can be improved by itself. It is so intimately bound up with the entire spiritual life that it is only when that whole life (previously marked by lack of prayer) becomes renewed and sanctified that prayer can have its rightful place of power. We must not be satisfied with less than the victorious life to which God calls his children.

You remember how our Lord, in the seven epistles in the Revelation of John, concludes with a promise to those who overcome. Take the trouble of going over that seven-times repeated 'him that overcometh'; and notice what unspeakably glorious promises are there given. And they were given even to churches like Ephesus, that had lost its first love; and Sardis, to whom it was said, 'thou hast a name that thou livest, and art dead' (Rev. 3:1); and Laodicea, with her lukewarmness and self-satisfaction—as proof that, if only they would repent, they might win the crown of victory. The call comes to every Christian to strive for the crown. It is impossible to be a healthy Christian, still more impossible to be a preacher in the power of God, if everything is not sacrificed to gain the victory.

The answer to the question, of how we attain to it, is simple. All is in Christ. 'Thanks be unto God, which always causeth us to triumph in Christ' (2 Cor. 2:14). 'In all these things we are more than conquerors through him that loved us' (Rom. 8:37). All depends on our right relationship to Christ, our entire surrender, perfect faith, and unbroken fellowship with him. But you wish to know how to attain to all this. Listen once more to the simple directions as to the way by which the full enjoyment of what is prepared for you in Christ may be yours. These are—a new discovery of sin; a new surrender to Christ; a new faith in the power which will make it possible for you to persevere.

1. A new discovery of sin

In Romans 3, you find described the knowledge of sin which is necessary, in repentance, for forgiveness 'That every mouth may be stopped, and all the world may become guilty before God' (verse 19). There you took your stand, you recognized your sin more or less consciously, and confessed it, and you obtained mercy. But if you would lead the victorious life, something more is needful. This comes with the experience that in you, that is, in your flesh, there 'dwelleth no good thing' (Rom. 7:18). You have a delight in the law of God after the inner man, but you see another law in your members bringing you into captivity to the law of sin and compelling you to cry out: 'O wretched man that I am! who shall deliver me from the body of this death?' (verse 24). It is not, as it was at conversion, when you thought over your few or many sins. This work goes much deeper. You find that, as a Christian, you have no power to do the good that you wish to do. You must be brought to a new and deeper insight into the sin of your nature and into your utter weakness, even though you are a Christian, to live as you ought. And you will learn to cry out: 'Who shall deliver me; I, wretched man, a prisoner bound under the law of sin?'

The answer to this question is: 'I thank God through Jesus Christ our Lord' (Rom. 7:25). Then follows the revelation of what there is in Christ. It is not just as given in Romans 3. It is more: I am in Christ Jesus, and 'the law of the Spirit of life in Christ Jesus hath made me free from the law of sin and death', (Rom. 8:2) under which I was bound. It is the experience that the law or power of the life of the Spirit in Christ has made me free and now calls on me, in a new sense and by a new surrender, to acknowledge Christ as the bestower of the victory.

2. A new surrender to Christ

You may have used these words 'surrender' and 'consecration' many times, but without rightly understanding what they mean. As you have been brought by the teaching of Romans 7 to a complete sense of the hopelessness of leading a true Christian life, or a true prayer life, by your own efforts, so you feel that the Lord Jesus must take you up, by his own power, in an entirely new way; and must take possession of you, by his Spirit, in an entirely new measure. This alone can preserve you from constantly sinning afresh. This only can make you really victorious. This leads you to look away from yourself, really to get free from yourself, and to expect everything from the Lord Jesus.

If we begin to understand this, we are prepared to admit that in our nature there is nothing good, that it is under a curse, and is nailed with Christ to his cross. We come to see what Paul means when he says that we are dead to sin by the death of Christ. Thus do we obtain a share of the glorious resurrection life there is in him. By such an insight we are encouraged to believe that Christ, through his life in us, through his continual indwelling, can keep us. Just as, at our conversion, we had no rest till we knew he had received us so now we feel the need of coming to him, to receive from him the assurance that he has really undertaken to keep us by the power of his resurrection life.

And we feel then that there must be an act as definite as his reception of us at conversion, by which he gives us the assurance of victory. And although it appears to us to be too great and too much, yet the man who casts himself, without plea, into the arms of Christ will experience that he does indeed receive us into such a fellowship as will make us, from the beginning onwards, 'more than conquerors'.

3. A new faith in the power which will make it possible for you to persevere in your surrender

You have heard of Keswick, and the truth for which it stands. It is that Christ is prepared to take upon himself the care and preservation of our lives every day, and all the day long, if we trust him to do it. In the testimony given by many, this thought is emphasized. They have told us that they felt themselves called to a new surrender, to an entire consecration of life to Christ, reaching to the smallest things, but they were hindered by the fear of failure. The thirst after holiness, after an unbroken fellowship with Jesus, after a life of persevering childlike obedience, drew them one way. But the question arose: 'Shall I continue faithful?' And to this question there came no answer, till they believed that the surrender must be made, not in their own strength, but in a power which was bestowed by a glorified Lord. He would not only keep them for the future, but he must first make possible for them the surrender of faith which expects that future grace. It was in the power of Christ himself that they were able to present themselves to him.

O Christian, only believe that there is a victorious life! Christ, the victor, is your Lord, who will undertake for you in everything and will enable you to do all that the Father expects from you. Be of good courage. Will you not trust him to do this great work for you who has given his life for you and has forgiven your sins? Only dare, in his power, to surrender yourself to the life of those who are kept from sin by the power of God. Along with the deepest conviction that there is no good in you, confess that you see in the Lord Jesus all the goodness of which you have need, for the life of a child of God; and begin literally to live 'by the faith of the Son of God, who loved me, and gave himself for me' (Gal. 2:20).

Let me, for your encouragement, give the testimony of Bishop Monte, a man of deep humility and tender piety. When he first heard of Keswick he was afraid of 'perfectionism' and would have nothing to do with it. Unexpectedly, during a vacation in Scotland, he came in contact with some friends at a small convention. There he heard an address by which he was convinced how entirely the teaching was according to Scripture. There was no word about sinlessness in the flesh or in man. It was a setting forth of how

Jesus can keep from sin a man with a sinful nature. The light shone into his heart. He who had always been counted a tender Christian came into touch now with a new experience of what Christ is willing to do for one who gives himself entirely to him Listen to what he says on the text: 'I can do all things through Christ which strengtheneth me' (Phil. 4:13). I dare to say that it is possible for those who really are willing to reckon on the power of the Lord, for keeping and victory, to lead a life in which his promises are taken as they stand, and are found to be true. It is possible to cast all our care on him daily, and to enjoy deep peace in doing it. It is possible to have the thoughts and imaginations of our hearts purified in the deepest meaning of the word, through faith. It is possible to see the will of God in everything, and to receive it, not with sighing, but with singing. It is possible, in the inner life of desire and feeling, to lay aside all bitterness, and wrath, and anger, and evil-speaking, every day and every hour. It is possible, by taking complete refuge in divine power, to become strong through and through; and where previously our greatest weakness lay, to find that the things which formerly upset all our resolves to be patient, or pure, or humble, furnish today an opportunity—through him who loved us, and works in us an agreement with his will, and a blessed sense of his presence and his power to make sin powerless. These things are divine possibilities, and because they are his work, the true experience of them will always cause us to bow lower at his feet and to learn to thirst and long for more. We cannot possibly be satisfied with anything less than—each day, each hour, each moment, in Christ, through the power of the Holy Spirit—to walk with God.'

Thank God, a life of victory is sure for those who have a knowledge of their inward ruin and are hopeless in themselves, but who, in 'the confidence of despair', have looked to Jesus, and, in faith in his power to make the act of surrender possible for them, they have done it, in his might, and now rely on him alone every day and every hour.

Chapter 9

At the conference, a brother who had earnestly confessed his neglect of prayer, but who was able, later, to declare that his eyes had been opened to see that the Lord really supplied grace for all that he required from us, asked if some hints could not be given as to the best way of spending time profitably in the inner chamber. There was no opportunity then for giving an answer. Perhaps the following thoughts may be of help:

1. As you enter the inner chamber let your first work be to thank God for the unspeakable love which invites you to come to him and to converse freely with him. If your heart is cold and head, remember that religion is not a matter of feeling, but has to do first with the will. Raise your heart to God and thank him for the assurance you have that he looks down on you and will bless you. Through such an act of faith you honor God and draw your soul away from being occupied with itself. Think also of the glorious grace of the Lord Jesus, who is willing to teach you to pray and to give you the disposition to do so. Think, too, of the Holy Spirit who was purposely given to cry, 'Abba, Father', in your heart, and to help your weakness in prayer. Five minutes spent thus will strengthen your faith for your work in the inner chamber. Once more I say, begin with an act of thanksgiving and praise God for the inner chamber and the promise of blessing there.

2. You must prepare yourself for prayer by prayerful Bible study. The great reason why the inner chamber is not attractive is that people do not know how to pray. Their stock of words is soon exhausted and they do not know what further to say, because they forget that prayer is not a soliloquy, where everything comes from one side; but it is a dialogue, where God's child listens to what the Father says, and replies to it, and then asks for the things he needs.

Read a few verses from the Bible. Do not concern yourself with the difficulties contained in them. You can consider these later; but take what you understand, apply it to yourself, and ask the Father to make his word light and power in your heart. Thus you will have material enough for prayer from the word which the Father speaks to you; you will also have the liberty to ask for things you need. Keep on in this way, and the inner chamber will become at length, not a place where you sigh and struggle only, but one of living fellowship with the Father in heaven. Prayerful study of the Bible is indispensable for powerful prayer.

3. When you have thus received the word into your heart, turn to prayer. But do not attempt it hastily or thoughtlessly, as though you knew well enough how to pray. Prayer in our own strength brings no blessing. Take time to present yourself reverently and in quietness before God. Remember his greatness and holiness and love. Think over what you wish to ask from him. Do not be satisfied with going over the same things every day. No child goes on saying the same thing day after day to his earthly father .

Converse with the Father is colored by the needs of the day. Let your prayer be something definite, arising either out of the word which you have read, or out of the real soul—needs which you long to have satisfied. Let your prayer be so definite that you can say as you go out, 'I know what I have asked from my Father, and I expect an answer.' It is a good plan sometimes to take a piece of paper and write down what you wish to pray for. You might keep such a paper for a week or more, and repeat the prayers till some new need arises.

4. What has been said is in reference to your own needs. But you know that we are allowed to Pray that we may help also in the needs of others. One great reason why prayer in the inner chamber does not bring more joy and blessing is that it is too selfish, and selfishness is the death of prayer.

Remember your family; your congregation, with its interests; your own neighbourhood; and the church to which you belong. Let your heart be enlarged and take up the interests of missions and of the church through the whole world. Become an intercessor, and you will experience for the first time the blessedness of prayer, as you find out that God will make use of you to share his blessing with others through prayer. You will begin to feel that there is something worth living for, as you find that you have something to say to God, and that he from heaven will do things in answer to your prayers which otherwise would not have been done.

A child can ask his father for bread. A full-grown son converses with him about all the interests of his business, and about his further purposes. A weak child of God prays only for himself, but a full-grown man in Christ understands how to consult with God over what must take place in the kingdom. Let your prayer list bear the names of those for whom you pray—your minister, and all other ministers, and the different missionary affairs with which you are connected. Thus the inner chamber will really become a wonder of God's goodness and a fountain of great joy. It will become the most blessed place on earth. It is a great thing to say, but it is the simple truth, that God will make it a Bethel, where his angels shall ascend and descend, and where you will cry out: 'The Lord shall be my God.' He will make it also Peniel, where you will see the face of God, as a prince of God, as one who wrestled with the angel and overcame him.

5. Do not forget the close bond between the inner chamber and the outer world. The attitude of the inner chamber must remain with us all the day. The object of the inner chamber is so to unite us to God that we may have him always abiding with us. Sin, thoughtlessness, and yielding to the flesh, or to the world unfit us for the inner chamber and bring a cloud over the soul. If you have stumbled, or fallen, return to the inner chamber; let your first work be to invoke the blood of Jesus and to claim cleansing by it. Rest not till by confession you have repented of and put away your sin. Let the precious blood really give you a fresh freedom of approach to God. Remember that the roots of your life in the inner chamber strike far out in body and soul so as to manifest themselves in business life. Let 'the obedience of faith', in which you pray in secret, rule you constantly. The inner chamber is intended to bind man to God, to supply him with power from God, to enable him to live for God alone. God be thanked for the inner chamber and for the blessed life which he will enable us there to experience and nourish.

Time

Before the creation of the world time did not exist. God lived in eternity in a way which we little understand. With creation, time began, and everything was placed under its power. God has placed all living creatures under a law of slow growth. Think of the length of time it takes for a child to become a man in body and mind. In learning, in wisdom, in business, in handicraft, and in politics, everything somehow depends on patience and perseverance. Everything needs time.

It is just the same in religion. There can be no converse with a holy God, no fellowship between heaven and earth, no power for the salvation of the souls of others, unless much time is set apart for it. Just as it is necessary for a child for long years to eat and learn every day, so the life of grace entirely depends on the time men are willing to give to it day by day.

The minister is appointed by God to teach and help those who are engaged in the ordinary avocations of life to find time and to use it aright for the preservation of the spiritual life. The minister cannot do this unless he himself has a living experience of a life of prayer. His highest calling is not preaching, or speaking, or parochial visitation, but it is to cultivate the life of

God daily, and to be a witness of what the Lord teaches him and accomplishes in him.

Was it not so with the Lord Jesus? Why must he, who had no sin to confess, sometimes spend all night in prayer to God? Because the divine life had to be strengthened in intercourse with his Father. His experience of a life in which he took time for fellowship with God has enabled him to share that life with us.

Oh, that each minister might understand that he has received his time from God with a servitude on it! God must have for fellowship with himself the first and the best of your time. Without this, your preaching and labor have little power. Here on earth I may spend my time for the money or the learning which I receive in exchange. The minister can exchange his time for the divine power and the spiritual blessings to be obtained from heaven. That, and nothing else, makes him a man of God and ensures that his preaching will be in the demonstration of the Spirit and power.

Chapter 10

'Be Ye followers of me, even as I also am of Christ.' I Corinthians 11:1

1. Paul was a minister who prayed much for his congregation

Let us read his words prayerfully and calmly so that we may hear the voice of the Spirit.

'Night and day praying exceedingly that we ... might perfect that which is lacking in your faith... The Lord make you to increase ... to the end he may stablish your hearts unblamable in holiness' (1 Thess. 3:10-13). 'The very God of peace sanctify you wholly' (I Thess. 5:23).

What food for meditation!

'Now our Lord Jesus Christ himself ... comfort your hearts, and stablish you in every good word and work' (2 Thess. 2:16,17).

'Without ceasing, I make mention of you always in my prayers; Making request...that I may impart unto you some spiritual gift, to the end ye may be established' (Rom. 1:9-11).

'My heart's desire and prayer to God for Israel is, that they might be saved' (Rom. 10:1).

'I ... cease not ... making mention of you in my prayers; that God ... may give unto you the spirit of wisdom and revelation in the knowledge of him ... that ye may know ... what is the exceeding greatness of his power to us who believe' (Eph. 1:16-19).

'For this cause I bow my knees unto the Father ... that he would grant you ... to be strengthened with might by his Spirit in the inner man; that Christ may dwell in your hearts by faith; that ye, being rooted ... in love ... might be filled with all the fullness of God' (Eph. 3:14-19).

'Always in every prayer of mine for you all making request with joy ... I pray, that your love may abound yet more and more ... that ye may be sincere ... filled with the fruits of righteousness' (Phil. 1:4, 9-11).

'But my God shall supply all your need according to his riches in glory by Christ Jesus' (Phil. 4:19).

'We ... do not cease to pray for you, and to desire that ye might be filled with the knowledge of his will ... that ye might walk worthy of the Lord ...

strengthened with all might according to his glorious power' (Col. 1:9-11). 'I would that ye knew what great conflict I have for you ... as many as have not seen my face in the flesh; that their hearts might be comforted, being knit together in love' (Col. 2:1,2).

What a study for the inner chamber! These passages teach us that unceasing prayer formed a large part of Paul's service in the gospel; we see the high spiritual aim which he set before himself, in his work on behalf of believers; and the tender and self-sacrificing love with which he ever continued to think of the Church and its needs. Let us ask God to bring each one of us, and all the ministers of his word, to a life of which such prayer is the healthy and natural outflow. We shall need to turn again and again to these pages if we would really be brought by the Spirit to the apostolic life which God has given us as an example.

2. Paul was a minister who asked his congregation to pray much

Read again with prayerful attention:

'I beseech you, brethren, for the Lord Jesus Christ's sake, and for the love of the Spirit, that ye strive together with me in your prayers to God for me; that I may be delivered from them that do not believe in Judea' (Rom. 15:30,31). 'We ... trust ... in God ... that he will yet deliver us; Ye also helping together by prayer for us' (2 Cor. 1:9-11).

'Praying always, with all prayer and supplication in the Spirit, and watching thereunto with all perseverance and supplication for all saints; and for me, that utterance may be given unto me, that I may open my mouth boldly to make known the mystery of the gospel ... as I ought to speak' (Eph. 6:18-20).

'For I know that this shall turn to my salvation, through your prayer, and the supply of the Spirit of Jesus Christ' (Phil. 1:19).

'Continue in prayer, and watch in the same with thanksgiving; withal praying also for us, that God would open unto us a door of utterance, to speak ... as I ought to speak' (Col. 4:2-4).

'Finally, brethren, pray for us, that the word of the Lord may have free course, and be glorified, even as it is with you' (2 Thess. 3:1).

What a deep insight Paul had as to the unity of the body of Christ and the relation of the members one to another! It is as we permit the Holy Spirit to work powerfully in us that he will reveal this truth to us, and we too shall have this insight. What a glimpse he gives us of the power of the spiritual life among these Christians, by the way in which he reckoned that at Rome, and Corinth, and Ephesus, and Colossae, and Philippi, there were men and women on whom he could rely for prayer that would reach heaven and have power with God! And what a lesson for all ministers, to lead them to inquire if they truly appreciate the unity of the body at its right value; if they are endeavoring to train up Christians as intercessors; and if they indeed understand that Paul had that confidence because he was himself so strong in prayer for the congregation! Let us learn the lesson and beseech God that ministers and congregations together may grow in the grace of prayer, so that their entire service and Christian life may witness that the Spirit of prayer rules them. Then we may be confident that God will avenge his own elect which cry out day and night unto him.

Ministers of the Spirit

What is the meaning of the expression: the minister of the gospel is a minister of the Spirit (see 2 Cor. 3:6, 8)? It means:

1. That the preacher is entirely under the power and control of the Spirit, so that he may be led and used by the Spirit as he wills.

2. Many pray for the Spirit, that they may make use of him and his power for their work. This is certainly wrong. It is he who must use you. Your relationship toward him must be one of deep dependence and utter submission. The Spirit must have you entirely, and always, and in all things under his power.

3. There are many who think they must preach the word only, and that the Spirit will make the word fruitful. They do not understand that it is the Spirit in and through the preacher who will bring the word to the heart. I must not be satisfied with praying to God to bless, through the operation of his Spirit, the word that I preach. The Lord wants me to be filled with the Spirit: then I shall speak aright and my preaching will be in the manifestation of the Spirit and power.

4. We see this on the day of Pentecost. They were filled with the Spirit and began to speak, and spoke with power through the Spirit who was in them.

5. Thus we learn what the relationship of the minister toward the Spirit should be. He must have a strong belief that the Spirit is in him, that the Spirit will teach him in his daily life and will strengthen him to bear witness to the Lord Jesus in his preaching and visiting; he must live in ceaseless prayer that he may be kept and strengthened by the power of the Spirit.

6. When the Lord promised the apostles that they should receive power when the Holy Spirit had come upon them and commanded them to wait for him, it was as though he had said: 'Do not dare to preach without this power. It is the indispensable preparation for your work. Everything depends on it.'

7. What then is the lesson we may learn from the phrase 'ministers of the Spirit'? Alas, how little we have understood this! How little have we lived in it! How little have we experienced of the power of the Holy Spirit! What

must we do then? There must be deep confession of guilt, that we have so constantly grieved the Spirit, because we have not lived daily as his ministers; and simple childlike surrender to his leading in sure confidence that the Lord will work a change in us; and further, daily fellowship with the Lord Jesus in ceaseless prayer. He will bestow on us the Holy Spirit as rivers of living water.

Chapter 11

Little of the word with little prayer is death to the spiritual life. Much of the word with little prayer gives a sickly life. Much prayer with little of the word gives more life, but without steadfastness. A full measure of the word and prayer each day gives a healthy and powerful life. Think of the Lord Jesus. In his youth and manhood he treasured the word in his heart. In the temptation in the wilderness, and on every opportunity that presented itself—till he cried out on the cross in death, 'My God, my God, why hast thou forsaken me?' (Matt. 27:46). He showed that the word of God filled his heart. And in his prayer life he manifested two things: first, that the word supplies us with material for prayer and encourages us in expecting everything from God. The second is that it is only by prayer that we can live such a life that every word of God can be fulfilled in us. And how then can we come to this, so that the word and prayer may each have its undivided right over us? There is only one answer. Our lives must be wholly transformed. We must get a new, a healthy, a heavenly life, in which the hunger after God's word and the thirst after God express themselves in prayer as naturally as do the needs of our earthly life. Every manifestation of the power of the flesh in us and the weakness of our spiritual life must drive us to the conviction that God will, through the powerful operation of his Holy Spirit, work out a new and strong life in US.

Oh, that we but understood that the Holy Spirit is essentially the Spirit of the word and the Spirit of prayer! He will cause the word to become a joy and a light in our souls, and he will also most surely help us in prayer to know the mind and will of God, and find in it our delight. If we as ministers wish to explain these things and to train God's people for the inheritance which is prepared for them, then we must commit ourselves from this moment forward to the leading of the Holy Spirit; must, in faith in what he will do in us, appropriate the heavenly life of Christ as he lived it here on earth, with certain expectation that the Spirit, who filled him with the word and prayer, will also accomplish that work in us,

Yes, let us believe that the Spirit who is in us is the Spirit of the Lord Jesus, and that he is in us to make us truly partakers of his life. If we firmly believe this and set our hearts upon it, then there will come a change in our intercourse with the word and prayer such as we could not have thought possible. Believe it firmly; expect it surely.

We are familiar with the vision of the valley of dry bones. We know that the Lord said to the prophet: 'Prophesy upon these bones ... Behold, I will cause breath to enter into you, and ye shall live' (Ezek. 37:4,5). And we know how, when he had done this, there was a noise, and bone came together to its bone, and flesh came up, and skin covered them—but there was no breath in them. The prophesying to the bones—the preaching of the word of God—had a powerful influence. It was the beginning of the great miracle which was about to happen, and there lay an entire army of men newly made. It was the beginning of the work of life in them, but there was no spirit there.

How then the Lord said to the prophet: 'Prophesy unto the wind ... Thus saith the Lord God; Come from the four winds, O breath, and breathe upon these slain, that they may live' (verse 9). And when the prophet had done this, the Spirit came upon them, and they lived, and stood on their feet, a very great army. Prophesying to the bones, that is, preaching, has accomplished a great work. There lay the beautiful new bodies. But the prophesying to the Spirit, 'Come, O Spirit', that is, prayer, accomplished a far more wonderful thing. The power of the Spirit was revealed through prayer.

Is not the work of our ministers mostly this prophesying to dry bones in making known the promises of God? This is followed sometimes by great results. Everything which belongs to the form of godliness has been brought to perfection; a careless congregation becomes regular and devout, but it remains true for the most part: 'There is no life in them. 'Preaching must be followed by prayer. The preacher must come to see that his preaching is comparatively powerless to bring in a new life till he begins to take time for prayer and, according to the teaching of God's word, strives and labors and continues in prayer, and takes no rest, and gives God no rest, till he bestows the Spirit in overflowing power.

Do you not feel that a change must come in our work? We must learn from Peter to continue in prayer in our ministry of the word. Just as we are zealous preachers, we must be zealous in prayer. We must, with all our power, constantly like Paul, pray unceasingly. For the prayer: 'Come, breathe on these slain' (Ezek. 37:9), the answer is sure.

Wholeheartedness

Experience teaches us that if anyone is engaged in a work in which he is not wholehearted, he will seldom succeed. Just think of a student, or his teacher, a man of business, or a warrior. He who does not give himself wholeheartedly to his calling is not likely to succeed. And that is still more true of religion, and above all of the high and holy task of intercourse in prayer with a holy God and of being always well pleasing to him. It is because of this that God has said so impressively: 'Ye shall seek me, and find me, when ye shall search for me with all your heart' (Jer. 29:13).

As also more than one of God's servants has said: 'I seek thee with my whole heart.' Have you ever thought how many Christians there are of whom it is all too plain that they do not seek God with the whole heart? When they were in trouble over their sins, they seemed to seek God with the whole heart. But when they knew that they had been pardoned one could see by their lives that they were religious, it is true but no one would think: 'This man has surrendered himself with his whole heart to follow God, and to serve him as the supreme work of his life.'

How is it with you? What does your heart say? While you, as minister, for instance, have given yourself up with wholehearted devotion to fulfil your office faithfully and zealously, will you not perhaps acknowledge: 'I fear, or rather I am convinced, that my unsatisfactory prayer life is to be attributed to nothing else than that I have not lived with a wholehearted surrender of all on earth that could hinder me in fellowship with God.' What a deeply important question to consider in the inner chamber and to give the answer to God! How important to arrive at a plain answer and to utter it all before God! Prayerlessness cannot be overcome as an isolated thing. It is in the closest relationship to the state of the heart. True prayer depends on an undivided heart.

But I cannot give myself that undivided heart which can enable me to say: 'I seek God with my whole heart.' No, that is impossible for you, but God will do it. 'I will give them an heart to know me' (Jer. 24:7). 'I will ... write it [my law] [as a power of life] in their hearts' (Jer. 31:33; Heb. 8:10). Such promises serve to awaken desire. How ever weak the desire may be, if there is but the sincere determination to strive after what God holds out to us, then he will himself work in our hearts both to will and to do. It is the great work of the Holy Spirit in us to make us willing and to enable us to seek God with the whole heart. May there not be found in us confusion of face because, while we have given ourselves to so many earthly things with all our heart and strength, yet if anything is said about fellowship with our glorious God it so little affects us that we have not sought him with the whole heart.

Chapter 12

The Lord did not speak these words to all who believed on him, or who hoped to be blessed by him, but to those whom he would make fishers of men. He said this not only at the first calling of the apostles, but also later on to Peter: 'Henceforth thou shalt catch men' (Luke 5:10). The holy art of winning souls, of loving and saving them, can be learned only in close and persistent intercourse with Christ. What a lesson for ministers and for Christian workers and others! This intercourse was the great and peculiar privilege of his disciples. The Lord chose them that they might be always with and near him. We read of the choice of the twelve apostles in Mark 3:14: 'And he ordained twelve, that they should be with him, and that he might send them forth to preach. 'So also our Lord said on the last night (John 15:27): 'And ye also shall bear witness, because ye have been with me from the beginning.'

This fact was noticed by outsiders. Thus, for instance, the woman who spoke to Peter: 'This fellow was also with Jesus' (Matt. 26:71). So in the Sanhedrin: 'They took knowledge of them, that they had been with Jesus' (Acts 4:13). The chief characteristic and indispensable qualification for the man who will bear witness to Christ is that he has been with him. Continuous fellowship with Christ is the only school for the training of ministers of the Holy Spirit. What a lesson for all ministers! It is only he who, like Caleb, follows the Lord fully, who will have power to teach other souls the art of following Jesus. But what an unspeakable grace that the Lord Jesus himself would train us after his own likeness, so that others may learn from us! Then we might say with Paul to our converts: 'Ye became followers of us, and of the Lord...' (I Thess. 1:6), 'Be ye followers of me, even as I also am of Christ' (1 Cor. 11:1).

Never was there a teacher who took such trouble with his scholars as Jesus Christ will with us who preach his word. He will spare no pains; no time will be too precious or too long for him. In the love which brought him to the cross, he would hold intercourse, converse with us, fashion us, sanctify us, and make us fit for his holy service. Dare we still complain that it is too much for us to spend so much time in prayer? Shall we not commit ourselves entirely to the love which gave up all for us, and look upon it as our greatest happiness now to hold fellowship with him daily? Oh, all you who long for blessing in your ministry, he calls you to be with him. Let this be the greatest joy of your life; it will be the surest preparation for blessing in your service. O my Lord, draw me, help me, hold me fast, and teach me how daily to live in thy fellowship by faith.

The Holy Trinity

1. God is an ever flowing fountain of pure love and blessedness.

2. Christ is the reservoir wherein the fullness of God was made visible as grace, and has been opened for us.

3. The Holy Spirit is the stream of living water that flows from under the throne of God and of the Lamb.

4. The redeemed, God's believing children, are the channels through which the love of the Father, the grace of Christ, and the powerful operation of the Spirit are brought to the earth, there to be imparted to others.

5. What an impression we gain here of the wonderful partnership into which God takes us up, as dispensers of the grace of God! Prayer, when we chiefly pray for ourselves, is but the beginning of the life of prayer. The glory of prayer is that we have power as intercessors to bring the grace of Christ, and the energising power of the Spirit, upon those souls which are still in darkness.

6. The more surely the channel is connected with the reservoir, the more certainly will the water flow unhindered through it. The more we are occupied in prayer with the fullness of Christ, and with the Spirit who proceeds from him, and the more firmly we abide in fellowship with him, the more surely will our lives be happy and strong. This, however, is still only a preparation for the reality. The more we give ourselves up to fellowship and converse with the triune God, the sooner shall we receive the courage and ability to pray down blessing on souls, on ministers, and on the Church around us.

7. Are you truly a channel which is always open, so that the water may flow through you to the thirsty ones in the dry land? Have you offered yourself unreservedly to God, to become a bearer of the energising operations of the Holy Spirit?

8. Is it not, perhaps, because you have thought only of yourself in prayer that you have experienced so little of the power of prayer? Do understand that the new prayer life into which you have entered in the Lord Jesus can be sustained and strengthened only by the intercession in which you labour for

the souls around you, to bring them to know the Lord? Oh, meditate on this—God an ever flowing fountain of love and blessing, and I his child, a living channel through which every day the Spirit and life can be brought to the earth!

Life and Prayer

Our life has a great influence on our prayer, just as our prayer influences our life. The entire life of man is a continuous prayer, to nature or to the world, to provide for his wants and make him happy. This natural prayer and desire can be so strong in a man who also prays to God that the words of prayer which his mouth utters cannot be heard. God cannot at times hear the prayer of your lips because the desires of your heart after the world cry out to him much more strongly and loudly.

The life exercises a mighty influence over prayer. A worldly life, a self-seeking life, makes prayer powerless and an answer impossible. With many Christians there is a conflict between the life and prayer, and the life holds the upper hand. But prayer can also exercise a mighty influence over the life. If I give myself entirely to God in prayer, then prayer can conquer the life of the flesh and sin. The entire life may be brought under the control of prayer. Prayer can change and renew the whole life, because prayer calls in and receives the Lord Jesus and the Holy Spirit to purify and sanctify the life.

Many think that they must, with their defective spiritual life, work themselves up to pray more. They do not understand that only in proportion as the spiritual life is strengthened can the prayer life increase. Prayer and life are inseparably connected. What do you think? Which has the stronger influence over you, prayer for five or ten minutes, or the whole day spent in the desires of the world? Let it not surprise you if your prayers are not answered. The reason may easily lie here; your life and your prayer are at strife with each other; your heart is more wholly devoted to living than to prayer. Learn this great lesson: my prayer must rule my whole life. What I request from God in prayer is not decided in five or ten minutes. I must learn to say: 'I have prayed with my whole heart. 'What I desire from God must really fill my heart the whole day; then the way is open for a certain answer.

Oh, the sacredness and power of prayer, if it takes possession of the heart and life! It keeps one constantly in fellowship with God. We can then literally say, 'On thee do I wait all the day' (Ps. 25:5). Let us be careful to consider not only the length of the time we spend with God in prayer, but the power with which our prayer takes possession of our whole life.

Perseverance in Prayer

'It is not reason,' said Peter, 'that we should leave the word of God, and serve tables' (Acts 6:2). For that work deacons were chosen. And this word of Peter serves for all time and for all who are set apart as ministers. 'But we will give ourselves continually to prayer, and to the ministry of the word' (Acts 6:4). Dr Alexander Whyte, in an address, once said: 'I think sometimes, when my salary is paid to me so faithfully and punctually: the deacons have performed faithfully their part of the agreement; have I been so faithful in my part, in persevering in prayer and the ministry of the word?' Another minister has said: 'How surprised people would be if I proposed to divide my time between these two equally—one-half given to prayer, the other to the ministry of the word!'

Notice, in the case of Peter, what perseverance in prayer meant. He went up on the roof to pray. There, in prayer, he received heavenly instruction as to his work among the heathen. There, the message from Cornelius came to him. There, the Holy Spirit said to him: 'Behold, three men seek thee. Arise therefore, and get thee down, and go with them' (Acts 10:19-20). And from there he went to Caesarea, where the Spirit was so unexpectedly outpoured on the heathen. All this is to teach us that it is through prayer God will give the instruction of his Spirit to make us understand his will, to let us know with whom we are to speak, to give us the assurance that his Spirit will make his word powerful through us.

Have you ever earnestly thought over why it is that you have a salary and a parsonage, and are set free from the need of following earthly business? It is for nothing else than that you should continue in prayer and the ministry of the word. That will be your wisdom and power. That will be the secret of a blessed service of the gospel.

No wonder that there is complaint about the ineffective spiritual life in minister and congregation, while that which is of prime importance, perseverance in prayer, does not hold its rightful place—the first place.

Peter was able to speak and act as he did because he was filled with the Spirit. Let us not be satisfied with anything less than hearty surrender to and undivided appropriation of the Spirit, as leader and Lord of our lives. Nothing less will help us. Then, for the first time, we shall be able to say that God 'hath made us able ministers ... of his Spirit' (2 Cor. 3:6).

Carnal or Spiritual?

There is a great difference between those two states which is but little understood or pondered. The Christian who 'walks in the Spirit' and has 'crucified the flesh' (Gal. 5:24) is spiritual. The Christian who walks after the flesh and wishes to please the flesh is carnal (see Rom. 13:14). The Galatians, who had begun in the Spirit, were ending in the flesh. Yet there were among them some spiritual members who were able to restore the wandering with meekness.

What a difference between the carnal and the spiritual Christian (I Cor. 3:1-3)! With the carnal Christian there may be much religion and much zeal for God, and for the service of God. But it is for the most part in human power. With the spiritual, on the other hand, there is a complete subjection to the leading of the Spirit, a deep sense of weakness and entire dependence on the work of Christ—it is a life of abiding fellowship with Christ, wrought out by the Spirit.

How important for me it is to find out and plainly to acknowledge before God whether I am spiritual or carnal! A minister may be very faithful in his orthodoxy, and be most zealous in his service, and yet be so, chiefly, in the power of human wisdom and zeal. And one of the signs of this is that there is little pleasure or perseverance in fellowship with Christ through prayer. Love of prayer is one of the marks of the Spirit.

What a change is necessary for a Christian who is chiefly carnal to become truly spiritual! At first he cannot understand what must happen, or how it can come to pass. The more the truth dawns upon him, the more he is convinced that it is impossible, unless God does it. Yet to believe truly that God will do it requires earnest prayer. Quiet retirement and meditation are indispensable, along with the death of all confidence in ourselves. But along this road there ever comes the faith that God can, God is willing, God will do it. The soul which earnestly clings to the Lord Jesus will be led by the Spirit to this faith.

How will you be able to say to others: I, brethren, could not speak unto you as unto spiritual, but as unto carnal, even as unto babes in Christ'? (1 Cor. 3:1). It is impossible unless you yourself have the experience of having passed from the one state to the other. But God will teach you. Persevere in prayer and faith.

Chapter 13

Just as God gave the apostle Paul as an example in his prayer life for Christians of all time, so he has also given George Mueller in these latter days as a proof to his church how literally and wonderfully he still always hears prayer. It is not only that he gave him in his lifetime over a million pounds sterling to support his orphanages, but Mr Mueller also stated that he believed that the Lord had given him more than thirty thousand souls in answer to prayer. And that not only from among orphans, but also many others for whom he (in some cases for fifty years) had prayed faithfully every day, in the firm faith that they would be saved. When he was asked on what ground he so firmly believed this, his answer was: 'There are five conditions which I always endeavor to fulfil, in observing which I have the assurance of answer to my prayer:

1. I have not the least doubt because I am assured that it is the Lord's will to save them, for he willeth that all men should be saved and come to the knowledge of the truth (see 1 Tim. 2:4); and we have the assurance 'that, if we ask anything according to his will, he heareth us' (1 John 5:14).

2. I have never pleaded for their salvation in my own name, but in the blessed name of my precious Lord Jesus, and on his merits alone (see John 14:14).

3. I always firmly believed in the willingness of God to hear my prayers (see Mark 11:24).

4. I am not conscious of having yielded to any sin, for 'if I regard iniquity in my heart, the Lord will not hear me' when I call (Ps. 66:18).

5. I have persevered in believing prayer for more than fifty-two years for some, and shall continue till the answer comes: 'Shall not God avenge his own elect which cry day and night unto him?' (Luke 18:7).

Take these thoughts into your hearts and practice prayer according to these rules. Let prayer be not only the utterance of your desires, but a fellowship with God, till we know by faith that our prayer is heard. The way George Mueller walked is the new and living way to the throne of grace, which is open for us all.

Hudson Taylor

When Hudson Taylor, as a young man, had given himself over unreservedly to the Lord, there came to him a strong conviction that God would send him to China. He had read of George Mueller and how God had answered his prayers for his own support and that of his orphans, and he began to ask the Lord to teach him also so to trust him. He felt that if he would go to China with such faith, he must first begin to live by faith in England. He asked the Lord to enable him to do this. He had a position as a doctor's dispenser, and asked God to help him not to ask for his salary, but to leave it to God to move the heart of the doctor to pay him at the right time. The doctor was a good-hearted man, but very irregular in payment. This cost Taylor much trouble and struggle in prayer because he believed, as did George Mueller, that the word, 'Owe no man any thing' (Rom. 13:8), was to be taken literally, and that debt should not be incurred.

So he learned the great lesson to move men through God—a thought of deep meaning, which later on became an unspeakably great blessing to him in his work in China. He relied on that—in the conversion of the Chinese, in the awakening of Christians to give money for the support of the work, in the finding of suitable missionaries who would hold as faith's rule of conduct that we should make our desires known to God in prayer and then rely on God to move men to do what he would have done.

After he had been for some years in China, he prayed that God would give twenty-four missionaries, two for each of the eleven provinces and Mongolia, each with millions of souls and with no missionary. God did it. But there was no society to send them out. He had indeed learned to trust God for his own support, but he dared not take upon himself the responsibility of the twentyfour, if possibly they had not sufficient faith. This cost him severe conflict, and he became very ill under it, till at last he saw that God could as easily care for the twenty-four as for himself. He undertook it in a glad faith. And so God led him, through many severe trials of faith, to trust him fully. Now these twenty-four have increased, in course of time, to a thousand missionaries who rely wholly on God for support. Other missionary societies have acknowledged how much they have learned from Hudson Taylor, as a man who stated and obeyed this law. Faith may rely on God to move men to do what his children have asked of him in prayer.

Read the book, Hudson Taylor's Early Years by Dr and Mrs Howard Taylor. There will be found in it a treasure of spiritual thought and experience concerning a close walk with God in the inner chamber and in mission work.

Light from the Inner Chamber

'But thou, when thou prayest, enter into thy closet, and when thou hast shut thy door, pray to thy Father which is in secret; and thy Father which seeth in secret shall reward thee openly' (Matt. 6:6).

Our Lord had spoken of the prayer of the hypocrites who desire to be seen of men and also of the prayer of the heathen who trust in the multitude of their words. They do not understand that prayer has no value except it is addressed to a personal God who sees and hears. In the text our Lord teaches us a wonderful lesson concerning the inestimable blessing which the Christian may have in his inner chamber. If we would understand the lesson aright we must notice the light that the inner chamber sheds on

1. The wonderful love of God

Think of God, his greatness, his holiness, his unspeakable glory, and then on the inestimable privilege to which he invites his children, that each one of them, however sinful or feeble he may be, every hour of the day, may have access to him and hold converse with him as long as he wishes. If he enters his inner chamber, then God is ready to meet him, to have fellowship with him, to give him the joy and strength which he needs with the living assurance in his heart that he is with him and will undertake for him in everything. In addition he promises that he will enrich him in his outward life and work with those things which he has asked for in secret. Ought we not to cry out with joy? What an honour! What a salvation! What an overflowing supply for every need!

One may be in the greatest distress, or may have fallen into the deepest sin, or may in the ordinary course of life desire temporal or spiritual blessing; he may desire to pray for himself or for those belonging to him, or for his congregation or church; he may even become an intercessor for the whole world—the promise for the inner chamber covers all: 'Pray to thy Father which is in secret; he will reward thee openly.'

We might well suppose that there would be no place on earth so attractive to the child of God as the inner chamber with the presence of God promised, where he may have unhindered intercourse with the Father. The happiness of a child on earth if he enjoys the love of his father; the happiness of a friend as he meets a beloved benefactor; the happiness of a subject who has free access to his king and may stay with him as long as he wishes; these are as nothing compared with this heavenly promise. In the inner chamber you can converse with your God as long and as intimately as you desire; you can rely on his presence and fellowship.

Oh, the wonderful love of God in the gift of an inner chamber sanctified by such a promise! Let us thank God every day of our lives for it as the gift of his wonderful love. In this sinful world he could devise nothing more suitable for our needs than a fountain of unspeakable blessing.

2. The deep sinfulness of man

We might have thought that every child of God would have availed himself with joy of such an invitation. But, see! What is the response? There comes a cry from all lands that prayer in the inner chamber is, as a general rule, neglected by those who call themselves believers. Many make no use of it; they go to church, they confess Christ, but they know little of personal intercourse with God. Many make a little use of it, but in a spirit of haste, and more as a matter of custom, or for the easing of conscience, so that they cannot speak of any joy or blessing in it. And, what is more sad, many who know something of its blessedness confess that they know little about faithful, regular, and happy fellowship with the Father, all the day, as something which is as necessary as their daily bread.

Oh, what is it, then, that makes the inner chamber so powerless? Is it not the deep sinfulness of man, and the aversion of his fallen nature for God, which make the world with its fellowship more attractive than being alone with the heavenly Father?

Is it not that Christians do believe the word of God, where that word declares that 'the flesh' which is in them, 'is enmity against God', and that they walk too much after 'the flesh', so that the Spirit cannot strengthen them for prayer? Is it not that Christians allow themselves to be deprived by Satan of the use of the weapon of prayer, so that they are powerless to overcome him? Oh, the deep sinfulness of man! We have no greater proof of it than this despite that is done to the unspeakable love which has given us the inner chamber.

And what is still more sad is that even ministers of Christ acknowledge that they know they pray too little. The word tells them that their only power lies in prayer: through that only, but through that certainly, they can be clothed with power from on high for their work. But it seems as though the power of the world and the flesh has bewitched them. While they devote time to and manifest zeal in their work, that which is the most necessary of all is neglected, and there is not the desire or strength for prayer to obtain the indispensable gift of the Holy Spirit to make their work fruitful. God give us grace to understand in the light of the inner chamber the deep sinfulness of our nature.

3. The glorious grace of Christ Jesus

Is there, then, no hope of a change? Must it be always thus? Or is there a means of recovery? Thank God! There is.

The man through whom God has made known to us the message of the inner chamber is no other than our Lord Jesus Christ, who saves us from our sins. He is able and willing to deliver us from this sin, and will deliver. He has not undertaken to redeem us from all our other sins and left us to deal with the sin of prayerlessness in our own strength. No, in this also we may come to him and cry out, 'Lord, if thou wilt thou canst make me clean' (Matt. 8:2). 'Lord, I believe; help thou mine unbelief' (Mark 9:24).

Do you wish to know how you may experience this deliverance? By none other than the well-known way along which every sinner must come to Christ. Begin by acknowledging, by confessing before him, in a childlike and simple manner, the sin of neglecting and desecrating the inner chamber. Bow before him in deep shame and sorrow. Tell him that your heart has deceived you by the thought that you could pray as you ought. Tell him that through the weakness of 'the flesh', and the power of the world, and self-confidence, you have been led astray and that you have no strength to do better. Let this be done heartily. You cannot by your resolution and effort put things right.

Come in your sin and weakness to the inner chamber, and begin to thank God, as you have never thanked him, that the grace of the Lord Jesus will surely make it possible for you to converse with your Father as a child ought to do. Hand over afresh to the Lord Jesus all your sin and misery, as well as your whole life and will, that he may cleanse and take possession of you and rule over you as his very own.

Even though your heart be cold and dead, persevere in the exercise of faith that Christ is an almighty and faithful Savior. You may be sure that deliverance will come. Expect it, and you will begin to understand that the inner chamber is the revelation of the glorious grace of the Lord Jesus, which makes it possible for one to do what he could not do himself; that is, to hold fellowship with God, and to experience that the desire and power are received which fit a man for walking with God.

Chapter 14

We seek sometimes for the operation of the Spirit, with the object of obtaining more power for work, more love in the life, more holiness in the heart, more light on Scripture or on our path. And yet all these gifts are only subordinate to what is the great purpose of God. The Father has bestowed the Spirit on the Son, and the Son has given him to us, with the one great object of revealing and glorifying Christ Jesus himself in us.

The heavenly Christ must become for us a real living personality, always with us and in us. Our life on earth must be every day lived in the unbroken and holy fellowship of our Lord Jesus in heaven. This must be the first and the greatest work of the Holy Spirit in believers, that they should know and experience Christ as the life of their life. God desires that we should become strengthened with might by his Spirit in the inner man, that Christ may dwell in our hearts through faith, and that so we may be filled with his love unto all the fullness of God.

This was the secret of the joy of the first disciples. They had received the Lord Jesus, whom they feared they had lost, as the heavenly Christ into their hearts.

And this was their preparation for Pentecost: they were entirely taken up with him. He was literally their all. Their hearts were empty of everything, so that the Spirit might fill them with Christ. In the fullness of the Spirit they had power for a life and service such as the Lord desired. Is this, now, with us, the great object in our desires, in our prayers, in our experience? 'Me Lord teach us to know that the blessing for which we have so earnestly prayed can be preserved and increased in no other way than through intimate fellowship with Christ in the inner chamber, every day practiced and cultivated.

And yet it has seemed to me that there was a still deeper secret of Pentecost to be discovered. The thought came that perhaps our conception of the Lord Jesus in heaven was limited. We think of him in the splendor, the glory of God's throne. We also think of the unsearchable love which moved him to give himself for us. But we forgot too often that, above all, it is as the crucified one he was known here on earth; and that, above all, it is as the crucified one he has his place on the throne of God. 'And, lo, in the midst of the throne ... stood a Lamb as it had been slain' (Rev. 5:6).

Yes, it is as the crucified one that he is the object of the Father's eternal good pleasure and of the worship of the entire creation. And it is, therefore, of the first importance, that we here on earth should know and have experience of him as the crucified one, so that we may make men see what his disposition and ours is, and what the power is that can make them partakers of salvation.

I feel deeply that, as the cross is Christ's highest glory, and as the Holy Spirit neither has done nor can do anything greater or more glorious than he did when he 'through the eternal Spirit offered himself without spot to God' (Heb. 9:14); so it is evident that the Holy Spirit can do nothing greater or more glorious for us than to take us up into the fellowship of that cross, and to work out also in us the same spirit of the cross which was seen in our Lord Jesus. In a word, the question arose whether this was not the real reason why our prayers for the powerful operation of the Holy Spirit could not be answered, because we had sought too little to receive the Spirit, in order that we might know and become like the glorified Christ in the fellowship of his cross.

Have we not here the deepest secret of Pentecost? The Spirit comes to us from the cross, where he strengthened Christ to offer himself to God. He comes from the Father, who looked down with unspeakable good pleasure on the humiliation and obedience and self-sacrifice of Christ, as the highest proof of his surrender to him. He comes from Christ, who through the cross was prepared to receive from the Father the fullness of the Spirit, that he might share it with the world. He comes to reveal Christ to our hearts, as the Lamb slain, in the midst of the throne, so that we on earth may worship him as they do in heaven. He comes, chiefly,— to impart to us the life of the crucified Christ, so that we may be able to say truly, 'I am crucified with Christ: nevertheless I live; yet not I, but Christ liveth in me' (Gal. 2:20).

To understand this secret in any way, we must first meditate on what the meaning and what the worth of the cross is.

The mind that was in the crucified Christ

The cross must necessarily be viewed from two standpoints. First, the work it has accomplished—the pardon and conquest of sin. This is the first message with which the cross comes to the sinner. It proclaims to him free and full deliverance from the power of sin. And then the second, the spirit or disposition which was there manifested. We find this expressed in Philippians 2:8: 'He humbled himself, and became obedient unto death, even the death of the cross.' Here we see self-abasement to the lowest place which could be found under the burden of our sin and curse; obedience to the uttermost to all the will of God; self-sacrifice to the death of the cross these three words reveal to us the holy perfection of his person and work. Therefore God hath so greatly exalted him. It was the spirit of the cross which made him the object of his Father's good pleasure, of the worship of the angels, of the love and confidence of all the redeemed. The self-abasement of Christ, his obedience to the will of God even to death, his self-sacrifice even to the death of the cross—these made him to be 'the Lamb, as it had been slain, standing in the midst of the throne'.

The spirit of the cross in us

All that Christ was, he was for us and desires to become in us. The spirit of the cross was his blessedness and glory. It should be this even more for us. He desires to manifest his likeness in us and to give us a full share of all that is his. Thus Paul writes the words we have so often quoted: 'Let this mind be in you, which was also in Christ Jesus' (Phil. 2:5). Elsewhere he writes: 'We have the mind of Christ' (1 Cor. 2:16). The fellowship of the cross is not only a holy duty for us, but an unspeakably blessed privilege, which the Holy Spirit himself will make ours according to the promise: 'He shall take of mine, and shall shew it unto you' (John 16:15); 'He shall glorify me' (John 16:14). The Holy Spirit wrought this disposition in Christ and will also work it in us.

Chapter 15

When the Lord told his disciples that they must take up the cross to follow him, they could have little understanding of his meaning. He wished to rouse them to earnest thought and so prepare them for the time when they should see him carrying his cross. From the Jordan, where he had presented himself to be baptized and reckoned among sinners, onward, he carried the cross always in his heart. That is to say, he was always conscious that the sentence of death, because of sin, rested on him, and that he must bear it to the uttermost. As the disciples thought on this and wondered what he meant by it, one thing only helped them—it was the thought of a man who was sentenced to death, and carried his cross to the appointed place.

Christ had said at the same time: 'He that loseth his life for my sake shall find it' (Matt. 10:39). He taught them that they must hate their own life. Their nature was so sinful that nothing less than death could meet their need; it deserved nothing less than death. So the conviction gradually dawned upon them that the taking up of the cross meant: 'I am to feel that my life is under sentence of death, and that under the consciousness of this sentence I must constantly surrender my flesh, my sinful nature, to death.' So they were slowly prepared to see later on that the cross which Christ had carried was the one power to deliver truly from sin, and that they must first receive from him the true cross spirit. They must learn from him what self-humiliation in their weakness and unworthiness was to mean; what the obedience was which crucified their own will in all things, in the greatest as well as in the least; what the self-denial was which did not seek to please the flesh or the world. 'Take thy cross and follow me' (see Matt. 16:24; Mark 8:34; 10:21; Luke 9:23)—that was the word with which Jesus prepared his disciples for the great thought that his mind and disposition might become theirs, that his cross might in very deed become their own.

Crucified with Christ

The lesson which the Lord wished his disciples to learn from his statement concerning the taking up of the cross and the losing of their life finds its expression in the words of Paul, after Christ had died on the cross and had

been exalted on high, and the Spirit had been poured out. Paul says: 'I am
crucified with Christ'; 'God forbid that I should glory, save in the cross of our
Lord Jesus Christ, by whom the world is crucified unto me, and I unto the
world' (Gal. 2:20; 6:14). He wished every believer to live so as to prove that
he was crucified with Christ. He wished us to understand that the Christ who
comes to dwell in our hearts is the crucified Christ, who will himself, through
his life, impart to us the true mind of the cross. He tells us that 'our old man
is crucified with him' (Rom. 6:6). Yea, more, that 'they that are Christ's have
crucified the flesh' (Gal. 5:24). When they received by faith the crucified
Christ, they gave over the flesh to the death sentence which was executed to
the full on Calvary. Paul says 'we have been planted together in the likeness
of his death' (Rom. 6:5), and that therefore we must reckon that we are dead
to sin in Christ Jesus.

These words of the Holy Spirit, through Paul, teach us that we must abide
constantly in the fellowship of the cross, in fellowship with the crucified and
living Lord Jesus. It is the soul that lives ever under the cover and shelter and
deliverance of the cross that alone can expect constantly to glory in Christ
Jesus and in his abiding nearness.

The fellowship of the cross

There are many who place their hope for salvation in the redemption of the
cross who understand little about the fellowship of the cross. They rely on
what the cross has purchased for them, on forgiveness of sin and peace with
God; but they can often live for a length of time without fellowship with the
Lord himself. They do not know what it means to strive every day after heart
communion with the crucified Lord as he is seen in heaven—'A Lamb in the
midst of the throne'. Oh, that this vision might exercise its spiritual power
upon us, that we might really experience every day that as truly as the Lamb
is seen there on the throne, so we may have the power and experience of his
presence here!

Is it possible? Without doubt it is. Why did that great miracle happen, and
why was the Holy Spirit given from heaven, if it were not to make the
glorified Jesus—'the Lamb standing, as slain, in the midst of the throne'—
present with us here in our earthly surroundings? Let us endeavor to make
this more plain in our further meditations.

Chapter 16

The Holy Spirit ever leads us to the cross. It was so with Christ. The Spirit taught him and enabled him to offer himself without spot to God.

It was so with the disciples. The Spirit, with whom they were filled, led them to preach Christ as the crucified one. Late on he led them to glory in the fellowship of the cross when they were deemed worthy to suffer for Christ's sake.

And the cross directed them again to the Spirit. When Christ had borne the cross, he received the Spirit from the Father, that he might be poured out. When the three thousand bowed before the crucified one, they received the promise of the Holy Spirit. When the disciples rejoiced in their experience of the fellowship of the cross, they received the Holy Spirit afresh. The union between the Spirit and the cross is indissoluble; they belong inseparably to one another. We see this especially in the epistles of Paul. 'Jesus Christ hath been evidently set forth, crucified among you... Received ye the Spirit by the works of the law, or by the hearing of faith?' (Gal. 3:1,2).

'Christ hath redeemed us from the curse of the law ... that we might receive the promise of the Spirit through faith' (Gal. 3:13,14). 'God sent forth his Son ... To redeem them that were under the law ... and ... hath sent forth the Spirit of his Son into your hearts' (Gal. 4:4-6). 'And they that are Christ's have crucified the flesh ... If we live in the Spirit, let us also walk in the Spirit' (Gal. 5:24,25). 'Ye also are become dead to the law by the body of Christ ... that we should serve in newness of spirit' (Rom. 7:4-6). 'For the law of the Spirit of life in Christ Jesus hath made me free from the law of sin and death. For ... God ... condemned sin in the flesh: That the righteousness of the law might be fulfilled in us, who walk not after the flesh, but after the Spirit' (Rom. 8:24).

In everything and always the Spirit and the cross are inseparable. Yes, even in heaven. The Lamb, as it had been slain, standing in the midst of the throne had 'seven eyes, which are the seven Spirits of God sent forth into all the earth' (Rev. 5:6). Again: 'He showed me a pure river of water of life, clear as crystal [Is this other than the Holy Spirit?] proceeding out of the throne of God and of the Lamb' (Rev. 22:1). When Moses smote the rock, the water streamed out and Israel drank. When the Rock Christ was actually smitten and he had taken his place as the slain Lamb on the throne of God, there flowed out from under the throne the fullness of the Holy Spirit for the whole world.

How foolish it is to pray for the fullness of the Spirit if we have not first placed ourselves under the full power of the cross! Just think of the one hundred and twenty disciples. The crucifixion of Christ had touched, broken, and taken possession of their entire hearts. They could speak or think of nothing else, and when the crucified one had shown them his hands and his feet, he said unto them: 'Receive ye the Holy Ghost' (John 20:22). And so also, with their hearts full of the crucified Christ, now received up into heaven, they were prepared to be filled with the Spirit. They dared to proclaim to the people: 'Repent and believe in the crucified one'; and they also received the Holy Spirit.

Christ gave himself up entirely to the cross. The disciples also did the same. The cross demands this also from us; it would have our entire life. To comply with this demand requires nothing less than a powerful act of the will, for which we are unfit, and a powerful act of God of which he may be assured who casts himself, in helplessness, but unreservedly on God.

The Spirit and the Cross

Why are there not more men and women who can witness, in the joy of their hearts, that the Spirit of God has taken possession of them and given them new power to witness for him? Yet more urgently arises the heartsearching question to which an answer must be given: what is it that hinders? The Father in heaven is more willing than an earthly father to give bread to his child, and yet the cry arises: 'Is the Spirit straitened? Is this his work?'

Many will acknowledge that the hindrance undoubtedly lies in the fact that the Church is too much under the sway of the flesh and the world. They understand too little of the heartpiercing power of the cross of Christ. So it comes to pass that the Spirit has not the vessels into which he can pour his fullness.

Many complain that the subject is too high or too deep for them. This is a proof of how little we have appropriated and brought into practice the teaching of Paul and Christ about the cross. I bring you a message of joy. The Spirit who is in you, in however limited a measure, is prepared to take you under his teaching, to lead you to the cross, and by his heavenly instruction to make you now something of what the crucified Christ wills to do for you and in you.

But then he wants you to take time, so that he may reveal the heavenly mysteries to you. He wants to make you see how the neglect of the inner chamber has hindered fellowship with Christ, the knowledge of the cross, and the powerful operations of the Spirit. He will teach you what is meant by the denial of self, the taking up of your cross, the losing of your life, and following him.

In spite of all that you have felt of your ignorance, and lack of spiritual insight and fellowship with the cross, he is able and willing to take you under his teaching and to make known to you the secret of the spiritual life above all your expectations.

Begin at the beginning. Be faithful in the inner chamber. Thank him that you can reckon on him to meet you there. Although everything appears cold, and dark, and strained, bow in silence before the loving Lord Jesus, who so longs after you. Thank the Father that he has given you the Spirit. And be assured that all you do not yet know, and still must know—about 'the flesh', and 'the world', and the cross—the Spirit of Christ, who is in you, will surely make known to you. O soul, only believe that this blessing is for you! Christ belongs entirely to you. He longs to obtain full possession of you. He can and will possess you through the Holy Spirit. But for this, time is necessary. Oh, give him time in the inner chamber every day. You can rest assured that he will fulfil his promise in you. 'He that hath my commandments, and keepeth them, he it is that loveth me: and he that loveth me shall be loved of my Father, and I will love him, and will manifest myself to him' (John 14:21).

Persevere, in addition to all that you ask for yourself, in prayer for your congregation, your church, your minister; for all believers; for the whole Church of God, that God may strengthen them with power through his Spirit, so that Christ may dwell in their hearts by faith. Blessed time when the answer comes! Continue in prayer. The Spirit will reveal and glorify Christ and his love, Christ and his cross 'as the Lamb slain standing in the midst of the throne'.

The Cross and the Flesh

These two are deadly enemies. The cross desires to condemn and put to death 'the flesh'. 'The flesh' desires to cast aside and conquer the cross. Many, as they hear of the cross as the indispensable preparation for the fullness of the Holy Spirit, will find out what there is in them which must yet be crucified. We must understand that our entire nature is sentenced to death and must become dead by the cross, so that the new life in Christ may come to rule in us. We must obtain such an insight into the fallen condition of our nature and its enmity against God that we become willing, nay desirous, to be wholly freed from it.

We must learn to say with Paul: 'In me (that is, in my flesh,) dwelleth no good thing' (Rom. 7:18). 'The carnal mind is enmity against God: for it is not subject to the law of God, neither indeed can be' (Rom. 8:7). It is its very essence to hate God and his holy law. This is the wonder of redemption, that Christ has borne on the cross the judgment and curse of God on 'the flesh', and has forever nailed it to the cursed tree. If a man only believes God's word about this 'cursed mind of the flesh', and then longs to be delivered from it, he learns to love the cross as his deliverer from the power of the enemy.

'Our old man is crucified' with Christ, and our one hope is to receive this by faith and to hold it fast. 'They that are Christ's have crucified the flesh' (Gal. 5:24). They have willingly declared that they will daily regard 'the flesh' which is in them as the enemy of God, the enemy of Christ, the enemy of their soul's salvation, and will treat it as having received its deserved reward in being nailed to the cross.

This is one part of the eternal redemption which Christ has brought to us. It is not something which we can grasp with our understanding or accomplish with our strength. It is something which the Lord Jesus himself will give us if we are willing to abide in his fellowship day by day, and to receive everything from him. It is something which the Holy Spirit will teach us, and he will impart it to us as an experience, and will show how he can give victory in the power of the cross over all that is of the flesh.

The Cross and the World

What the flesh is in the smallest circle of my own person, that the world is in the larger circle of mankind. 'The flesh' and 'the world' are two manifestations of the same 'god of this world who is served by both. When the cross deals with 'the flesh' as accursed, we at once discover what the nature and power of the world are. 'They ... hated both me and my Father' (John 15:24). The proof of this was that they crucified Christ. But Christ obtained the victory on the cross and freed us from the power of 'the world'. And now we can say: 'God forbid that I should glory, save in the cross of our Lord Jesus Christ, by whom the world is crucified unto me, and I unto the world' (Gal. 4:14).

The cross was to Paul every day a holy reality, both in what he had to suffer from the world and in the victory which the cross constantly gave. John also writes: 'The whole world lieth in wickedness' (1 John 5:19). 'Who is he that overcometh the world, but he that believeth that Jesus is the Son of God?

This is he that came by water and blood, even Jesus Christ ... And it is the Spirit that beareth witness, because the Spirit is truth' (1 John 5:5,6). Against the two great powers of the god of this world, God has given us two great powers from heaven, namely, the cross and the Spirit.

Chapter 17

A Testimony

In the following quotations from Starlight, by G. Sterrenberg, the great truth about the cross is expressed in simple and powerful words. Let the chapters on 'The Fellowship of the Cross' and 'The Holy Spirit and the Cross' especially be read.

Our Head Christ took the lowest place on the cross, and so He has marked out for us His members the lowest place. The brightness of God's glory (Heb. 1:3) became the rejected of men (Isa. 53:3). Since that time the only right we have is to be the last and the lowest. When we claim anything more we have not yet rightly understood the cross.

We seek for a higher life; we shall find it if we sink deeper into the cross fellowship with our Lord. God has given the crucified One the highest place (Rev. 5). Shall we not do the same? We do this when from hour to hour we act as those who are crucified with him (Gal. 2:19,20). Thus we honor the crucified Lord.

We long for full victory. We find this as we more fully enter into the fellowship of His cross. The Lamb obtained His Almighty only so long as we abide under the shadow of the cross. The cross must be our home. There alone are we sheltered. We first understand our own cross when we have understood his. And we desire to get so close to it that we not only view it but touch it, yes, still more that we take up the cross, and so it becomes as someone has said, an inner cross. Then the cross asserts itself in us, and we experience His power which especially manifests itself in this, that we do not faint under it but carry it with joy.

What would Jesus be without His cross? His pierced feet have bruised the head of the enemy, and His pierced hands have despoiled him utterly (Matt. 12:29). What are we without the cross? Do not let the cross go, but hold it fast. Do we think that we can go by another road than that He trod? Many can make no progress because they will not take up the cross.

Epilogue

A single word to the reader concerning the disposition of mind to which this book appeals! It is not enough that one should understand and appropriate the thought of the writer, and then rejoice because of the new insight he has obtained and the pleasure which knowledge has brought. There is something else which is of great importance. I must surrender myself to the truth so that I shall be ready, with an undivided will, immediately to perform all that I shall learn to be God's will.

In a book such as this, dealing with the life of prayer and hidden fellowship with God, it is indispensable that we should be prepared to receive and obey all that we see to be according to the word and will of God. Where this disposition is lacking, knowledge only serves to make the heart less capable of receiving fuller life. Satan endeavors to become master of the Christian's inner chamber because he knows that if there has been unfaithfulness in prayer the testimony will bring but little loss to his kingdom. Spiritual power to lead the unsaved to the Lord, or to build up the children of God, will not be experienced under it. Persevering prayer, through which alone this power comes, has been lacking.

The great living question has been before many: shall we really set ourselves to win back again the weapon of believing prayer which Satan has, in a measure, taken away from us? Let us set before ourselves the serious importance of this conflict. As far as each minister is concerned, everything depends on whether or not he is a man of prayer-one who in the inner chamber must be clothed each day with power from on high. We, in common with the church throughout the whole world, have to complain that prayer has not the place in our service of God that it ought to have, according to the will and promise of God and according to the need of minister and congregation and church.

The public consecration which many a believer has been led to make of himself at conferences is not an easy thing. And even when the step is taken, old custom, and the power of the flesh, will tend to bring it to naught. The power of faith is not yet vigorous. It will cost strife and sacrifice to conquer the devil in the name of Christ. Our churches are the battlefield where Satan will bring forth all his power to prevent us from becoming men of prayer, powerful in the Lord to obtain the victory in heaven and on earth. How much depends on this for ourselves, for our congregations, and for the kingdom!

Do not be surprised if I say that it is with fear and trembling, and not without much prayer, that I have written what I trust will help to encourage the brethren in the conflict. It is with a feeling of deep unworthiness that I venture to offer myself as a guide to the inner chamber, which is the way to holiness and to fellowship with God.

Do not wonder that I have asked the Lord that he would give this book a place in some inner chambers, and that he may assist the reader, so that, as he sees what God's will is, he may immediately give himself up to the doing of it. In war, everything depends on each soldier being obedient to the word of command, even though it costs him his life. In our strife with Satan we shall not conquer unless each one of us holds himself ready even in the reading of this simple book, to say from the heart: 'What God says I will do; and if I see that anything is according to his will, I will immediately receive it and act upon it.'

Do not wonder that I have written this testimony to remind the brethren that everything depends on the spirit of surrender to immediate obedience, in which we read all that is said according to the word of God. God grant that, in his great grace, this book may prove a bond of fellowship by which we may think of and help one another, and strengthen each other for the conflict in prayer by which the enemy may be overcome and the life of God may be gloriously revealed!

www.ingramcontent.com/pod-product-compliance
Lightning Source LLC
Chambersburg PA
CBHW030922090426
42737CB00007B/290